It's Not Just Gym Anymore

Teaching Secondary School Students How to Be Active for Life

Bane McCracken

Human Kinetics

Library of Congress Cataloging-in-Publication Data

McCracken, Bane, 1944-
 It's not just gym anymore : teaching secondary school students how to be active for life / Bane McCracken.
  p. cm.
 Includes bibliographical references and index.
 ISBN 0-7360-0127-1
  1. Physical education and training--Study and teaching (Secondary) 2. Physical
education and training--Curricula. I. Title

GV363 .M33 2001
613.7'071'273--dc21
                                          00-053520

ISBN: 0-7360-0127-1

Copyright © 2001 by Bane McCracken

Acquisitions Editor: Scott Wikgren; **Developmental Editor:** Melissa Feld; **Assistant Editor:** Susan C. Hagan; **Copyeditor:** Patsy Fortney; **Proofreader:** Pamela S. Johnson; **Indexer:** Gerry Lynn Messner; **Permission Managers:** Dalene Reeder and Courtney Astle; **Graphic Designer:** Robert Reuther; **Graphic Artists:** Dawn Sills and Yvonne Griffith; **Photo Manager:** Clark Brooks; **Cover Designer:** Keith Blomberg; **Photographers (cover):** Clark Brooks and Tom Roberts; **Photographer (interior):** Johnson Photo (pp. 46 and 247), Leisure Sports Photography (p. 52), and Bane McCracken (all others); **Art Manager:** Craig Newsom; **Illustrator:** Roberto Sabas; **Printer:** United Graphics

Printed in the United States of America

10 9 8 7 6 5 4 3 2 1

Human Kinetics
Web site: www.humankinetics.com

United States: Human Kinetics
P.O. Box 5076
Champaign, IL 61825-5076
800-747-4457
e-mail: humank@hkusa.com

Canada: Human Kinetics
475 Devonshire Road Unit 100
Windsor, ON N8Y 2L5
800-465-7301 (in Canada only)
e-mail: hkcan@mnsi.net

Europe: Human Kinetics
Units C2/C3 Wira Business Park
West Park Ring Road
Leeds LS16 6EB, United Kingdom
+44 (0) 113 278 1708
e-mail: humank@hkeurope.com

Australia: Human Kinetics
57A Price Avenue
Lower Mitcham, South Australia 5062
08 8277 1555
e-mail: liahka@senet.com.au

New Zealand: Human Kinetics
P.O. Box 105-231, Auckland Central
09-523-3462
e-mail: hkp@ihug.co.nz

This book is dedicated to Doc and Lil, my mom and dad.
They taught me to love nature and encouraged me to be creative. Thanks.

Contents

Preface

The Surgeon General's Report of 1996 and the Centers for Disease Control and Prevention guidelines of 1998 told us something we already knew: physically active people are less likely to get sick. People that participate in regular physical activity are more likely to live healthy, productive, and enjoyable lives than are people who are sedentary——and physically active people are less likely to develop serious ailments ranging from heart attacks to cancer to depression. Therefore, the rationale for quality physical education has never been better, yet enrollment in physical education has dropped from 41 percent in 1991 to 25 percent in 1995. Why? Because many high school physical education programs have failed to prepare their students for lifelong physical activity and are therefore expendable. In order for physical education to be a vital part of the high school curriculum, we must improve the quality of our programs and meet the needs of our society. In this book I provide the theoretical basis and practical strategies for building a high school physical education program that promotes lifelong physical activity for all students and will be a valued part of any high school curriculum.

Part I provides the framework for developing a contemporary high school physical education program that promotes lifelong physical education. I show you how to examine what motivates people in your community to stay fit, how to determine what local and regional resources are available, and then how to de-

sign courses according to the needs of your students. I also provide strategies for developing cross-curricular activity plans that reinforce basic skills and concepts by using hands-on technology to enhance both students' learning and their motivation. I also show you how to use appropriate teaching styles to reach all students and how to make meaningful assessment part of your lessons by developing a critical-thinking portfolio system that enables the student to be more active. I also show you how physical education can take an aggressive leadership role within your school and your community.

Part II offers specific examples from the program I developed at Cabell Midland High School. This program was included as a success story in the book *Active Youth* (Sammann, 1998), which was written to provide examples of programs that meet the guidelines developed by the Centers for Disease Control and Prevention.

Physical education must change if it is to meet the needs of students and therefore survive as part of public education in the 21st century. After teaching a traditional curriculum for 18 years, I made the change to a curriculum that promotes lifelong activity, and it has made a tremendous difference to me, my students, my school, and my community. I hope this book will help you make the change as well, whether you're a veteran physical educator, a new teacher, an administrator, or a district director.

Acknowledgments

I would like to acknowledge some of the many people that have made significant contributions to my career and helped me develop as a professional. All my high school teachers and coaches, the physical education faculty at Marshall University, especially Doc "T", the many outstanding teachers at Milton, Barboursville, and Cabell Midland High Schools, for sharing their techniques and strategies, especially Bob Lambert and Larry Langdon. John Ray, Supervisor of Physical Education for West Virginia; Richard Jefferson, Cabell Schools Superintendent; my principal, Dick Jefferson; and my supervisor, Peggy Campbell for their support. Thanks to Jo Anne Potter and Brian Cordel for helping me learn to use technology with my students. A special thank-you to my "buddy" Drexena Dilley for sharing her wonderful ideas. Thanks to the members of the West Virginia AHPERD, the Midwest District of the AAHPERD, and the leadership of each organization, especially Past Presidents Eloise Elliott and Rosie Monroe. Most of all I want to thank my wife, Joyce, for sharing her life and career.

part I

Lifetime Fitness Approach

Theoretical Basis and Practical Strategies

When I began teaching in the '60s there were no student parking lots, no classroom TVs, and no computers. At the end of the day, many students walked home from our neighborhood school. Other students rode a bus and then walked from the bus stop. When the students got home they pushed lawnmowers, did other chores, or played. Physical education provided an escape from the rigors of the day. The objective was to teach games and sports. Today our schools have been consolidated, the student parking lot contains 500 cars, and students seldom walk as they did to the old neighborhood schools. Every classroom has a television and most students have a computer and a cell phone. The objectives of physical education need to change as well.

What does a modern physical education program look like, what does it do, what are the objectives, and how does a teacher make changes? Part I of this book answers those questions. Using the physical education program at Cabell Midland High School as an example, part I provides a framework for developing a

☞

comprehensive contemporary physical education program. **Chapter 1** provides the rationale and plans for developing more diversity, featuring fitness and lifetime skills. **Chapter 2** provides a framework for developing individual units of study that focus on fitness, teach skill recognition, use cross-curricular activities, make use of technology, and help promote lifetime physical activity. **Chapter 3** deals with alternative methods of assessment. The reader will learn to develop a portfolio system that is authentic, meaningful, and less threatening to the student. **Chapter 4** shows the reader how to select and use appropriate technology for physical education, and **chapter 5** provides plans for promoting physical activity throughout the school.

chapter 1

Join the Revolution

My younger brother and I were riding our mountain bikes on a narrow trail in northern Cabell County in West Virginia. Greg was visiting for a weekend from his home in Fredericksburg, Virginia. Although we were both over 40 years old, we were, as usual, being physically active. The trail we were riding was rather flat with a few tight turns, mud puddles, and an occasional obstacle. Once in a while the trail would cross a creek. We had been riding for more than an hour, and the pace was quickening as we neared the finish. The lead had changed several times. The one riding in the rear would wait for the leader to make a mistake, then sprint to the front. Greg had tried to take a turn with too much speed and had gone off the trail, so I had the lead and I was determined to keep it. The competition was fierce!

Up ahead I could see that the trail was crossing the creek. I knew that to cross the creek and maintain momentum I had to put out a burst of power as I approached the bank, make a high-speed entry into the shallow water, fight the resistance of the sandy bottom, and grind up the far side. I pedaled hard and roared into the water, but the water was deeper than expected; the sandy bottom softer. My front wheel sank in deep and stopped, the rear wheel spun high in the air, and I landed headfirst in the muddy water.

My brother, in spite of his desperate attempt to retake the lead, fared no better and came to rest close by, after turning a cartwheel across the water. We looked at each other and roared with laughter. We retrieved our bikes, rinsed off some of the mud, and scrambled up the bank to take a break and recount the adventure. We sat by the creek, told and retold the episode, and continued to laugh at ourselves. Our sides were aching. After a while we regained our composure and began leisurely to continue to the finish. My brother turned to me and said, "You know, when we get together, it's like being 12 years old again."

At that moment I realized what I was trying to accomplish as a physical education teacher. I needed to design a program that would allow my students to play like 12-year-olds for the rest of their lives.

Most physical education teachers were involved in sports during high school, many continued to participate in college, and a few continued to participate for a time after graduation. We have the necessary skills to become highly proficient in these sports and have experienced the thrill of victory more often than the agony of defeat. As we matured and our bodies were no longer able to perform as they did when we were younger, the sports we loved in high school and college no longer offered the opportunities they once did. We love sports, though, and we design our programs to teach what we love.

Some students, however, do not like sports. They may not enjoy competition, or perhaps they lack the natural talent necessary to develop sport skills. For such students, a competitive team sport approach to physical education is not at all appealing. These are the students who often get turned off to physical activity.

Today's physical education teacher must realize that competitive team sports are not lifetime in nature, that developing a high level of skill is not possible for all people, and that not all students are athletes. A healthy lifestyle that includes regular physical activity should be the objective of our programs. Our programs must emphasize fitness and physical activity, not just skill and competition. Our objectives are to teach our children to enjoy physical activity, and what it takes to stay fit, so they can continue to enjoy physical activity as much in adulthood as they did when they were 12 years old.

The Surgeon General's Report on Physical Activity and Health (USDHHS 1996) tells us that a lack of physical activity is a serious health risk. Heart attacks, heart disease, obesity, diabetes, osteoporosis, and many other ailments have been linked to a lack of physical activity. Many children today begin to develop poor activity habits during infancy, and these habits continue through adolescence and adulthood. It is a fact that today's children are less active than those of previous generations. In his book, *Teaching with the brain in mind,* Eric Jensen cites a study that compared the amount of time children spent riding in cars. According to Jensen, a two-year-old child in 1960 spent 200 hours riding in a car. A two-year-old child today is estimated to have spent 500 hours riding in a car seat! (Jensen 1998). Today's youth are spending more time sitting in front of televisions and computers and less time playing. This lack of physical activity is part of the reason childhood obesity rates have doubled in the last five years (Wechler 1999). Physical education programs need to be teaching our students the importance of being physically active, and how to develop and maintain a physically active lifestyle throughout their lives.

THE LIFETIME FITNESS APPROACH

If you were to tour Cabell Midland High School on an afternoon after school in the fall, you would come across a 70-member football team practicing on the field, girls' and boys' soccer teams doing drills on another set of fields, a girls' volleyball team in the gym, girls' and boys' cross country teams running a trail, and a golf team leaving to compete at a local course. These students are physically active; they are athletes. Unfortunately, student-athletes account for less than 25 percent of the student body. What of the other 75 percent? Most of them get in their cars, go home, and begin to develop a lifestyle that does not include regular physical activity. Perhaps many of this 75 percent have played sports in little leagues and middle school but stopped because they felt they'd never have the skill necessary to make the high school team.

High school physical education offers the last best chance to change the physical activity habits of our youth and help reduce the health risks associated with inactivity. However, most of today's physical education programs are not reaching America's inactive students. Sixty percent of Americans get no regular physical activity, and children between the ages of 14 and 21 have a drastic drop in their activity levels from earlier in their lives. Furthermore, many administrators view physical education as an organized recess and an educational frill. As a result, enrollment in physical education classes has dropped from 41 percent in 1991 to 25 percent in 1995 (USDHHS 1996). To continue to do what we have been doing for the last two decades will continue to get the same results: a further decline in physical activity, lower numbers in physical education, and a continued rise in health care costs. In order to develop a more active populace, prevent a further decline of physical education, and improve the health status of our nation, we must make some changes. Physical education must change from emphasizing sport skills to focusing on lifetime fitness. A lifetime fitness approach

- offers more diverse activities;
- emphasizes fitness and physical activity;
- teaches skill recognition;
- provides opportunities for physical activity in addition to athletics for students, staff, and members of the community; and
- becomes more involved in the educational process by taking a more prominent role in the high school curriculum.

More Diverse Activities

Physical education programs that offer a narrow range of activities are attractive to a narrow range of students. A lifetime fitness physical education program, on the other hand, offers diversity in activities so that students are provided more opportunities to find an activity they enjoy and will continue to enjoy as they get older. Often, some of the activities that people do to stay fit throughout their lives are not covered in traditional physical education

programs. A study by the CDC (1993) lists the following activities in order of popularity: walking, jogging, bicycling, aerobics, swimming, conditioning with weight machines, racket sports, golf, hunting, and fishing. These activities, in addition to some of the more traditional activities such as team sports, offer more diversity than a sport-only approach and appeal to a much wider range of students.

Since more people walk to stay fit than participate in all other activities combined, a unit based on walking could include hiking, backpacking, and orienteering. Excellent fitness activities that require little skill and minimal equipment, and that can be adapted to virtually any environment, can easily be added to our classes. Many states, such as West Virginia, offer a wealth of recreational opportunities: hiking, backpacking, camping, mountain biking, cycling, skiing, climbing, white-water rafting, canoeing, fishing, and hunting. Including activities used by fit people to maintain fitness and taking advantage of local recreational opportunities will allow physical education to expand its range of activities. A wider range of activities will attract a wider range of students and increase the possibility that a student not interested in traditional physical education will find an activity he or she can enjoy. Many students who have been turned off by traditional physical education may find a renewed interest in physical activity.

Focus on Fitness and Physical Activity

Students need to learn to appreciate a physically active lifestyle, identify the fitness benefits and requirements of each activity, and develop fitness plans that will allow them to continue to be active as they mature. Programs that teach only skills lead students to believe that a high level of skill is necessary for participation. As a result, many low-skill students don't participate, and it turns them off from other activities. A fitness approach teaches students that a weekend golfer receives the same fitness benefits from a round of golf as does a professional golfer. In fact, weekend golfers may receive more fitness benefits than professional golfers because they don't use a caddie, so they carry their own clubs, take a lot more swings, and walk farther chasing their errant shots (see figure 1.1)

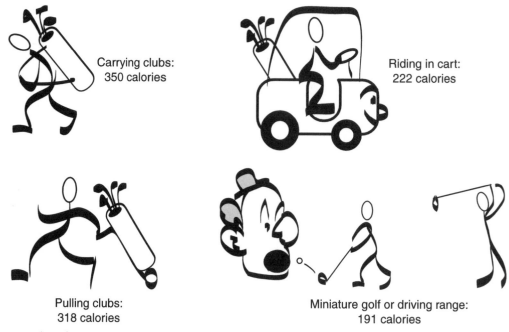

Figure 1.1 Varying the way you play golf can affect the number of calories burned per hour. (Calories burned is based on a body weight of 140 pounds.)

Caloric data derived by the Activity Profile of Nutristrategy Nutrition and Fitness on research from the Official Journal of the American College of Sports Medicine.

Skill Recognition Over Skill Development

While many traditional physical education programs emphasize skill development and mastery, few students are able to master the skills in the short amount of time available during physical education class. Moreover, physical education program goals are to encourage students to be physically active regardless of their skill level. A lifetime fitness approach teaches skill recognition and lifetime skills over skill mastery. Teaching students to recognize the elements of proper technique allows them to analyze their skill and to continue to develop it long after their classes are over. For instance, returning to our golf example, when golfers hit shots that spin widely to the left and hook out of bounds, they must know what adjustments to make in their technique.

Providing Opportunities Outside Athletics

Developing programs that promote physical activity involves more than just physical education classes. The CDC has developed guidelines for promoting physical activity among our youth.

These guidelines suggest that our schools offer physical activity opportunities in addition to athletics. Physical education programs must take a leadership role and develop schoolwide projects, such as walks; runs; fairs; field trips to local recreational outlets; and family nights that offer the opportunity to promote physical activity, connect with the community, and gain respect for physical education programs. When these events are promoted throughout the school and the community, much talk is generated, and physical education is seen as more important (see chapter 5 on organizing community events).

Crossing Curricula

The lifetime fitness approach is more comprehensive than traditional physical education. Teaching students to be physically active for a lifetime requires the use of cross-curricular strategies for learning. Students read, study history, do calculations, search the net, and learn anatomy in conjunction with learning about physical activity and lifetime fitness. Cross-curricular strategies not only help students learn the importance of developing a physically active lifestyle, but they also help students improve basic skills and raise test scores in academic areas.

Summary

The increased emphasis on fitness, health, and physical activity, and the findings of the surgeon general's report on physical activity and health, provide an outstanding rationale for quality physical education in our schools. Budget restrictions, however, are forcing educational administrators to make tough decisions about staffing. Physical education programs that are viewed as little more than recess will no longer survive. Physical education programs that can demonstrate their ability to help raise and maintain high test scores will have a much better chance for survival. Our field is in a fight for survival. To continue to survive, we must take a more prominent role in the high school curriculum and become involved in the various alignments. We must employ cross-curricular strategies to be more effective teachers, become more involved in the education process, and help raise test scores and improve learning. Finally, we must explore ways to provide physical activity opportunities for the students, staff, and members of the community.

MAKING THE CHANGE TO THE LIFETIME FITNESS APPROACH

Making the change from traditional physical education to a comprehensive program that promotes physical activity cannot be done quickly. Because the dramatic shift in focus can be disorienting to the students and overwhelming to the teacher, it's best to introduce changes gradually. One new activity may be added to a class during a grading period, another added during the next. Add a fitness station to a unit in the fall, another during the spring. Making the change may take years. Here's how I started making changes.

Spring

The year my brother and I went mountain biking had an early spring; the weather was warmer and dryer than usual, and the physical education classes had been able to get outside sooner and more often than normal. I took advantage of the good weather and began to teach a softball unit. The two fields next to the school were dry and ready for play. Although our school had coed physical education classes, my afternoon class was all boys. They were a good group of students with excellent skills. They could all play softball. There were four teams, two on each field; the class was going great. All I had to do was check roll, go to the field, settle an occasional dispute, and make sure the equipment was returned. This sounds like an ideal situation. The students were busy, active, and behaving. They were having fun. But what were they learning? What was I teaching? How was I helping them to be more physically active when they became adults?

One day I rode my mountain bike to school. When the afternoon class began, I took my bike outside with the class and rode from one field to the other. I was able to cover more ground, see more of my students, and be physically active myself. I stopped beside a line of students who were waiting for their turn to bat. One of the students asked if I would let him try my mountain bike. Mountain bikes were relatively new at the time, and he had never ridden one. I helped adjust the seat to his height, gave him my helmet, and he pedaled off. He toured the fields. All the students stopped their play and watched. When he had completed his circuit and returned, the other kids standing in line clamored for their turns. The next day I took my wife's bike as well. When the afternoon class went out to play softball, each at-bat team had a bike. The students became excited and asked numerous questions. How much does it cost? Where can you ride? What happens when they break? A visit from a local bike shop owner and racer answered their questions, and mountain biking became part of our physical education curriculum.

Later that spring a pro bass fisherman brought his boat and exotic equipment to our class for a demonstration. He showed the students casting techniques and the features of his boat and shared some of his secrets. The next day all the students brought their fishing poles; we walked the half-mile to a nearby river and went fishing. I borrowed a fly-fishing video and brought my fly rod for a demonstration on a rainy day. Fly-fishing and fly-tying became the next addition to the curriculum.

Students prepared for a single-track ride as part of the mountain biking unit.

Fall

The fall football schedule had an open date that allowed me to take advantage of the outstanding white-water rafting available on the Gauley and New Rivers in West Virginia. Upon returning, I played the video of my trip for my physical education classes. Their reaction prompted me to investigate the possibility of developing a white-water unit that would include a raft trip for the students. The initial attempts to get permission for the trip were met with strong resistance. I approached a local rafting outfitter for some help in developing a unit. The promotional and safety videos they provided along with some equipment and good advice allowed me to develop exciting lessons that taught our students about white-water rafting. The enthusiasm of the students and support of some parents convinced the board of education to support me in my efforts. The school board's lawyer helped write a permission form and advised me on legal techniques for protecting myself. That spring we took our first raft trip. It was awesome, and white-water rafting became a part of our physical education curriculum.

Winter

The next year I began to use the same procedure to develop a downhill ski unit. All was going well until I saw a report on our local news station. The reporter was interviewing a local orthopedic surgeon who was explaining the dangers of skiing without training. The doctor told the viewers that most injuries from skiing could be prevented by strengthening the muscles used and raising fitness levels to prevent fatigue. I needed to teach my students how to get ready to ski. Activities in the classes now had a meaning. My students ran, lifted weights, and did aerobics with more enthusiasm. They were exercising to get ready to go on a ski trip. The ski trip was a huge success. As usual, I took my video camera and recorded as much as possible of the students' actions. They enjoyed seeing themselves as much as they enjoyed the trip itself.

Offering new activities has added diversity to my program, and the ski unit showed me how to make traditional activities more lifetime in nature. During the ski unit, I taught my students how to get fit so they could ski without injury. The same strategy can be applied to any activity. For example, I was teaching a basketball unit in a small auxiliary gym with limited space. Only about half of the students could safely be on the floor at the same time. I used a small section of the remaining space to teach students to use dumbbells to strengthen basketball muscles. Another area was used for stretching. The strategy was then applied to all units. Fitness was no longer a unit by itself but an integral component of all units of study.

Summary

I continued to make small changes and acquire equipment for several years. When the school board decided to close Milton High School and open a new consolidated school, there were substantial funds available for new programs. A new course called Outdoor Recreation became an elective for the new Cabell Midland High School. The course includes mountain biking, white-water rafting, archery and bow hunting, fly-fishing and fly-tying, hiking, backpacking, camping, orienteering, wilderness survival, in-line skating, and downhill skiing. (Some of these units are covered in part II of this book.)

Making change is not always easy. Administrators are concerned about liability, and rightfully so. Colleagues find that it is much easier to continue to do what they feel comfortable doing rather than take the risks associated with change. Students are used to the traditional programs and can be skeptical of change as well. We can overcome these obstacles by addressing liability issues and making sure that our lessons are developmentally appropriate. Riding on our own enthusiasm, students accustomed to traditional programs can learn to adjust to the idea of reading and writing as a part of physical education class, and colleagues can begin to see the beauty in the lifetime fitness approach.

In addition, we must remember that not all we do will be successful. Sometimes our plans fail. When this occurs, we must reevaluate our procedure, make the necessary changes, and try again. The changes we make today will not always meet the needs of our students; changing our programs can never end.

CONCLUSION

Physical education can meet the needs of our students and help produce a more active populace by developing programs that emphasize fitness and physical activity. To change the scope and nature of physical education will be difficult. The process of changing from a sport-skill approach to a comprehensive approach is revolutionary, but necessary. When educational decision makers are forced to make decisions, and their view of physical education is one of a glorified recess, their choice is obvious. Members of the field of physical education have only one choice—join the revolution.

chapter 2

Elements of a Quality Physical Education Program

What does a physical education class that promotes a physically active lifestyle look like? An observer would see all members of the class actively involved in learning. Groups of students are arranged all about the gym; some are doing step aerobics, others are recording data from their pulse monitors. Some students are practicing a skill in front of a video camera alongside a group of students who have just finished and are now viewing and evaluating their techniques. A cluster of students in front of a computer is locating Web sites for equipment prices. Other students use dumbbells to strengthen muscles alongside a team of students quietly listening to classical music, relaxing, and stretching muscles used in the activity. The teacher continuously moves from station to station, offering encouragement and assistance, occasionally using a video camera to record students' actions. Student and teacher are learning partners as the film is replayed, observed, and critiqued by the student with help from the teacher. They share a laugh at an awkward moment, then share the thrill as the student recognizes an error and learns.

As you can see, there's a lot going on. In one class, I am able to cover fitness, skill recognition, and technology while helping to develop thinking skills. What do all of these components mean, and what are students specifically doing at each station? Let me show you. Developing lessons that promote lifelong physical activity requires careful, comprehensive planning. Each unit must develop the skills and knowledge necessary for students to participate in that activity now and as they mature. Units focus on fitness and lifelong physical activity. Students need to learn to assess their levels of fitness, recognize the fitness benefits and requirements of an activity, and develop fitness plans that will allow them to continue to participate as adults. Other elements of quality unit plans are

- skill development and recognition;
- cross-curricular activities to help students learn what they need to know to participate;
- improving basic skills, developing better thinking skills, and raising test scores;
- using technology to help students learn and provide hands-on experience; and
- exploring the relationship of a physically active lifestyle and employment opportunities.

I will discuss how you can fit all of these elements into a physical education class in part II of this book.

Physical education classes that focus on fitness may appear similar to traditional classes. Students still do warm-ups and cool-downs. There is still an introduction and a conclusion, drills, and skill practice. The difference is that in lifetime fitness classes fitness is a part of all activities. Some students may be practicing skills while others use pulse monitors to compare intensity levels while participating in a simulated game. Still others may be using dumbbells, stretch cords, and medicine balls to strengthen specific muscles and help improve their performance. In another area students may be using sport-specific stretching techniques to develop flexibility in muscles used during the activity to lessen the chances of injury. The objective of each physical education unit is to help students learn to identify the fitness benefits and requirements of each activity and what they need to do to continue to participate as adults.

EVALUATING FITNESS COMPONENTS

Classes that feature fitness should begin by teaching students how to evaluate their level of fitness. All components of fitness should be analyzed: muscular strength and endurance, cardiovascular fitness, body composition, and flexibility. Teaching students to evaluate their level of fitness places more of the responsibility on the student and makes assessment less intimidating for the low fit. Teachers must emphasize that fitness assessment serves as a reference and should not be viewed in a pass/ fail mode by either the students or the teacher. The objective of fitness assessment is to help students identify activities that are appropriate for their level of fitness, so they will find the activity more enjoyable and therefore receive maximum fitness benefits while participating. As the fitness of the students improves, they may find that they can enjoy other, more intense activities.

Assessing Cardiovascular Fitness

Most fitness tests are effort dependent and measure how hard the student tries rather than providing a valid measure of fitness. In a mile run, for example, the low-fit student who puts forth great effort may be assessed as having a better fitness level than the fit student who decides not to cooperate, slowly jogs, and puts forth little effort. Proper assessment of students' fitness should be done in a manner that ensures that all students are putting forth the same effort. This can be achieved with pulse monitors, which allow all students to be tested while working at the same pulse rate.

Exercise intensity recommendations for highly conditioned, competitive athletes call for 10 to 15 percent of the workout time to be spent at 95 to 100 percent of their maximum pulse rate, 20 to 30 percent of the time to be in the 85 to 95 percent range, and the remainder of the workout to be at the 70 to 80 percent level. Exercise pulse levels for nonathletes are less intense. The recommended rate is 60 to 80 percent. The objective of monitoring pulse levels is to prevent overexertion and help students identify activities that are appropriate for their levels of fitness. Exercise zones may be determined using the following formula:

How to Calculate Your Exercise Pulse Levels

Your maximum pulse is determined by subtracting your age from 220:

220 – (your age) = _____ (max. heart rate)
90% is _____ bpm
80% is _____ bpm
70% is _____ bpm
60% is _____ bpm
50% is _____ bpm

The pacing guide in figure 2.1 will help students determine their ideal pace for walking, jogging, or running. The pulse monitor regulates their effort and helps them find a pace that is not uncomfortable but will still provide maximum fitness benefits. Students are encouraged to reevaluate their cardiovascular fitness on a regular basis to help them learn to identify their comfort zone and record changes in fitness. Taking students to a measured track and recording their pulse and lap times while they circle the track at increasing speeds will teach them to recognize a pace that is within their zone. Completing form 6.1 helps students determine their proper pace. Students begin walking at a gentle pace (six minutes per lap) and record their time and pulse rate at the end of each lap. After every two laps, the pace is increased. This process continues until the student's pulse reaches 80 percent of the maximum. At this point students may stop or continue increasing their pace. All students are instructed to stop after reaching 90 percent of their maximum heart rate.

Completing this exercise helps students to realize how it feels to be in the proper exercise zone of 60 to 80 percent of their maximum pulse rate. As students participate in various activities, they can more easily identify those activities that have significant cardiovascular benefits and meet their fitness needs.

Pulse monitors will also identify students with low levels of fitness. Many students' level of fitness is so low that walking at a gentle pace

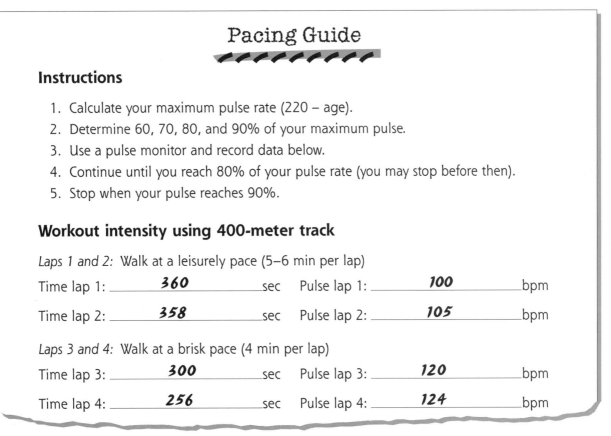

Pacing Guide

Instructions

1. Calculate your maximum pulse rate (220 – age).
2. Determine 60, 70, 80, and 90% of your maximum pulse.
3. Use a pulse monitor and record data below.
4. Continue until you reach 80% of your pulse rate (you may stop before then).
5. Stop when your pulse reaches 90%.

Workout intensity using 400-meter track

Laps 1 and 2: Walk at a leisurely pace (5–6 min per lap)

Time lap 1: _____ *360* _____ sec   Pulse lap 1: _____ *100* _____ bpm

Time lap 2: _____ *358* _____ sec   Pulse lap 2: _____ *105* _____ bpm

Laps 3 and 4: Walk at a brisk pace (4 min per lap)

Time lap 3: _____ *300* _____ sec   Pulse lap 3: _____ *120* _____ bpm

Time lap 4: _____ *256* _____ sec   Pulse lap 4: _____ *124* _____ bpm

Figure 2.1 Completed pacing guide. By walking a lap in 300 sec (5 min) the student has reached a pulse of + 120 bpm. See form 6.1 for the complete form you can reproduce.

will cause their pulse to rise into the 90-percent range. Participating in vigorous activities for these students may be impossible and is certainly unpleasant. For low-fit students, pulse monitors may be used to help them learn to regulate the intensity of an activity and make adaptations so they may participate longer and find the activity more enjoyable.

After using the pacing guide in my classes for several years, I have found that most of my students reach 80 percent of their maximum pulse by walking at a moderate pace of 20 minutes per mile. Very few students, less than 10 percent, must jog to reach the required 80 percent range. While these findings demonstrate that our students have very poor cardiovascular fitness, the results also serve as a means to help unfit students understand why intense activities are unpleasant and encourage participation in activities that will improve their fitness.

By wearing pulse monitors during physical education activities such as volleyball, students learn that their pulse rates seldom reach the desired 60 percent level and therefore that volleyball has little cardiovascular benefit. Other activities such as softball are even less beneficial. On the other hand, full-court basketball, which requires students to sprint up and down the floor, is too intense for many students. As their pulse levels escalate to the 90 to 95 per-

cent range, many quickly become exhausted and quit.

When students wear monitors during physical education, keep a log (figure 2.2), and record pulse levels for each activity, they can compare the pulse levels of each activity. This helps them identify activities that are appropriate for their level of fitness. Matching the fitness requirements of an activity with the fitness of the student makes the activity more enjoyable, and it is much more likely that they will participate in the activity as an adult. Because fitness, physical activity, and participation are emphasized (keeping pulse instead of keeping score), students with low skill are more likely to participate. In a volleyball game, for example, all students can wear pulse monitors. At the end of a volley, students can record and total their pulse rates. The team with the highest total pulse rate receives the point. Even students with low skill score, and in fact, low-fit students, usually score higher than highly fit, highly skilled students.

Assessing Muscular Strength and Endurance

The size of the student has a direct bearing on how well he or she may score on tests of muscular strength and muscular endurance. A large

Pulse Log

Name: _____

Date	Activity	Time	Pulse rate
10/13	Walking	20:00	135
10/14	Mountain biking	10:00	140
10/15	Full-court basketball	8:00	198
10/16	1-mile run	8:00	198

Figure 2.2 This student's pulse log shows pulse rates for a variety of activities. See form 13.3 for the complete form you can reproduce.

student with a high muscle mass may not be able to execute enough pull-ups to score as well in a strength test as a thinner student, even though the large student is obviously stronger. An obese student may not be able to do many push-ups and would score low on a strength test, not because he or she lacks strength, but because of obesity. A more valid measure of determining strength is needed.

To find a more equitable method, we begin by analyzing students' body composition and determining lean body weight for each. Strength tests are conducted on a flat bench with each student lifting a weight equal to a portion of his or her lean body weight. The number of repetitions a student can execute before failure is recorded and serves as a measure of muscular strength and endurance. The amount of weight used is kept low enough for all students to have some success. Boys use a larger percentage than girls; upper-class students use a higher percentage than those in lower grades.

More than one method of analyzing a fitness component also helps achieve validity. Exercise machines, such as rowers, treadmills, or exercise bikes, may be used to collect additional data and offer assessment alternatives for students. Some students may find a machine that is better suited to their talents and therefore produce better scores. Finding meaningful, valid methods for assessing student fitness helps students be successful and provides motivation. Nothing breeds success like success. Teachers should make use of all available equipment, keep records, and develop their own standards for a variety of situations and equipment.

Assessing Body Composition

High levels of body fat during the teen years lead to serious health problems as adults. Body composition is a component of fitness and should be part of the fitness assessment undertaken during physical education classes.

At least three methods are available for determining body composition. Each method has both good and bad features.

• Underwater weighing is considered to be the most accurate, but requires expensive equipment and therefore is not readily available.

• The impedance method, which uses a computer program to measure the rate at which electrical current flows through the body to analyze the relationship of lean tissue to fat, is very accurate. Most impedance programs provide a detailed printout for the subject with valuable information about body composition; ideal weight; rate of weight loss, if necessary; and exercise recommendations. (These machines are of particular value for obese students, for whom skinfold measures are inaccurate.) The impedance technology is very expensive and will not give a correct reading for subjects who are not well hydrated.

• The most common method for body fat analysis is to measure skinfolds using a caliper; the thicker the skinfold, the higher the percent body fat. See chapter 6, form 6.2, for a form that can be used to determine percent body fat. The more locations used on the body, the more accurate the test. A good set of calipers, costing over $300, is essential for accuracy. The most important factor for using the skinfold method is the skill and diligence of the test administrator.

No method of assessing body composition is completely accurate. All are estimates of the amount of body fat and therefore subject to error. While testing body composition, care must be taken not to embarrass obese students. Because these students are well aware of their condition, testing may not be necessary. The objective of analyzing body composition is to help students understand the relationship of body fat to fitness, physical activity, and diet. We should help students understand that body composition is not a matter of looks, but one of fitness and health. Body type and genetics determine how we look, and no amount of exercise will make us all look like Greek gods and goddesses. Students learn how to combine physical activity and proper diet to establish and maintain their ideal body weight. Efforts should be made to help obese students learn to identify activities that are of lower intensity and longer duration, require the use of many large-muscle groups, consume more calories, and provide maximum benefits for their needs.

Assessing Flexibility

Flexibility assessments are conducted on several areas of the body. Since a single sit-and-reach test only measures the hamstrings and relative length of the subject's arms, additional measurements are performed on the trunk and shoulders. To measure trunk flexibility, the student lies on the floor face down with both hands behind the head, fingers locked. On a signal the student attempts to raise the head as far off the floor as possible. The flexibility of the trunk is measured using a yardstick placed vertically on the floor and measuring the distance from the floor to the student's chin. Shoulder flexibility can be measured in much the same manner. The student lies on the floor with both arms extended, the thumb of one hand grasped in the other, and raises the hands as high as possible. The distance from the floor to the hands measures shoulder flexibility. All measurements (sit-and-reach, trunk, and shoulders) are combined to determine total flexibility.

Total flexibility in inches:
   30 in. = poor
   35 in. = fair
   40 in. = good
   45 in. and up = excellent

The Fitness Rubric

The fitness rubric in figure 2.3 will help students develop a better understanding of the fitness relationship of various activities. Each activity is introduced by using the fitness rubric to help students visualize the fitness benefits of the activity. The students continuously review the five components of fitness—muscular strength, muscular endurance, cardiovascular fitness, flexibility, and body composition—and how much each component can be improved by participating in that particular activity. Students wear pulse monitors and use the pulse log to record pulse levels during the activity. The records maintained by the students while participating in drills are used to determine the fitness requirements of each activity.

In the first section of the rubric, students rate the fitness benefits they would receive from participation in the activity on a scale of zero to five. Students place an X on the line below the number they feel best represents the benefits they would receive. A score of five indicates an activity that provides maximum benefits in that area of fitness. Weightlifting, for example, is rated a five for muscular strength benefits, but receives a lower number for cardiovascular benefits. Each activity is rated on a scale of zero to five for each component of fitness. No activity should receive a zero since all physical activity has some fitness benefit. A zero rating is reserved for watching television and being a couch potato.

The second section of the fitness rubric has students rate the fitness requirements of the activity once they've had the opportunity to participate in the activity. We should teach students that some activities require a higher level of fitness in some components than may be developed by participating in that activity alone. Basketball, for example, requires a high level of cardiovascular fitness. Playing in a league only twice a week may not be enough to maintain the level of cardiovascular fitness required of the sport, however, and alternative methods of developing and maintaining fitness are necessary to continue to play. Other activities may need additional strength development in order to improve performance and prevent injury. Few activities develop adequate flexibility, but most require participants to be flexible in order to perform skills and escape injury. This indicates to the student that stretching to develop flexibility should be a part of any activity. Students realize from completing this section of the rubric that no single activity will provide total fitness.

In the final section of the rubric, the students rate their readiness for participation in an activity and investigate what they may need to do in order to continue to participate as they mature. Teachers should help students use their fitness assessment data, pulse logs, and pacing guides to make comparisons and help make judgments in completing the final section of the rubric. Students who mark the rubric in area 4 or 5 are indicating sufficient fitness for that component. Marking the rubric in area 1 or 2 indicates a need for improvement. For example, students who recorded high pulse levels while participating in a particular activity should realize that their cardiovascular fitness is poor, mark their rubric in the proper location, and seek activities to help develop that component of fitness. Students with low levels of strength and muscular endurance mark the rubric in the proper location and seek activities that help develop strength.

Portions of class time need to be spent helping students compare rubrics from different ac-

Fitness Rubric for _Skiing_

Name: _Joe Smith_   Date: _10/14_

Fitness benefits	0	1	2	3	4	5
Muscular strength				X		
Muscular endurance					X	
Flexibility		X				
Caloric consumption					X	
Cardiovascular				X		

Fitness requirements	0	1	2	3	4	5
Muscular strength					X	
Muscular endurance					X	
Flexibility						X
Caloric consumption		X				
Cardiovascular			X			

Are you ready for _skiing_? Rate your fitness level for _skiing_

Personal rating	0	1	2	3	4	5
Muscular strength				X		
Muscular endurance				X		
Flexibility			X			
Body composition					X	
Cardiovascular			X			

Figure 2.3 In the above example of the fitness rubric, Joe Smith has completed the fitness rubric for skiing. See form 6.4 for the complete form you can reduce.

tivities to help select activities best suited for their individual needs. The rubric should be used by the student to identify methods of improving fitness in weak areas and learning training techniques necessary to maintain adequate fitness so students may continue to enjoy the activity as adults. Using fitness stations to accomplish this task will be discussed in chapter 6.

The Activity Pyramid

The activity pyramid (figure 2.4) provides additional understanding of the intensity levels of different activities. Students wearing pulse moni-

tors and keeping records in their pulse logs can identify the appropriate category on the activity pyramid. Students learn to identify activities that best meet their fitness needs by comparing the activity pyramids from several activities.

FOCUSING ON SKILL RECOGNITION

Developing sport skills has been the main element of traditional physical education, and skills should still be an element in a comprehensive,

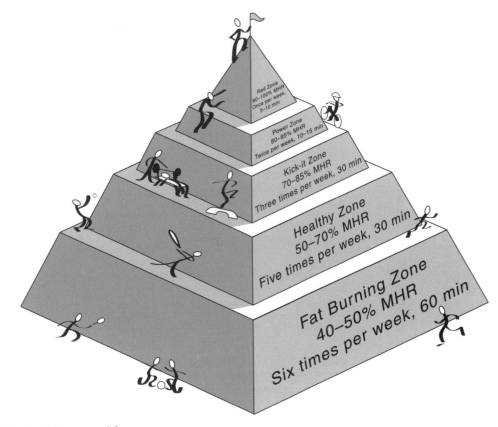

Figure 2.4 Activity pyramid.

lifetime approach. However, students should not be led to believe that it is always necessary to have a high level of skill. Overemphasis of skill development may lead students to believe that if they can't be highly skilled, they can't participate. Physically immature students with poor coordination, low strength, and low endurance have a greater need to develop good physical activity habits than do the gifted athletes.

Teaching students to learn to recognize proper skill is a much better strategy than teaching only skill development and testing performance. The objective of physical education is to teach students to recognize the benefits of, and lead, a physically active lifestyle. Testing students' ability to hit a target, make a goal, or score points does not necessarily reflect the proper objective. Many students with low skill levels who are unable to do well on skill tests become discouraged and may view their lack of success as a reason not to participate. A better approach is to teach students to recognize correct skill execution.

Teaching students to recognize skills may use many of the same techniques as teaching skill development. Lessons still begin with demonstrations, identifying learning cues and pin-

pointing specific actions. The difference is that students spend more time analyzing and learning how to develop proper technique and less time trying to hit a target, score points, or make the shot. Technology provides excellent tools for teaching students to analyze technique. Lessons may provide the opportunity for students to view videos of experts demonstrating near-perfect technique or to use video cameras to record and evaluate their own or others' actions. Checklists provided throughout this book will help students evaluate their actions.

An archery unit may use the 10 steps of shooting as an evaluation tool (figure 2.5 and form 12.4). Students evaluate their actions by placing the appropriate mark in the proper blank after taking their turn attempting to hit the target. The form used for archery has the students mark the blank with a plus sign when they feel they can successfully execute a skill. Students use an X to indicate improvement and a zero to indicate they are having trouble. The initial evaluations may be done from recall, but as student skills improve, additional methods are employed. A view cam can be used for instant feedback and assistance in evaluations, or a video can be made and used later in the class period or the next day. Providing a video of students' actions is a great teaching tool. Students can use slow motion and stop action to analyze their performance, which can provide more accurate evaluation and result in greater improvements in skill execution.

Evaluation forms may be very broad in nature and be concerned only with basic skills, such as that in figure 2.5. Other activities may need to be concerned with more than physical skills. The form used for mountain biking (form 11.6) includes an element for bike repair and safety. Complex activities, such as golf and tennis, require detailed evaluation and a more complex evaluation form. Figure 2.6 shows a highly detailed form used for golf.

Student Shooting Self-Evaluation

Name: __Joe Smith__

Place the appropriate symbol in the space provided.

O = not yet	**X** = getting better	**+** = proper technique

Date: __9/13__   __9/15__   __9/17__   __9/19__

1.	_0_	_X_	_+_	_+_	Stance
2.	_0_	_0_	_X_	_+_	Bow grip

Figure 2.5 Shooting self-evaluation that can be used in an archery unit. Student has completed archery self-evaluation on four dates. On the last two dates the student was videotaped. See form 12.4 for the complete form you can reproduce.

Stance Self-Evaluation

Name: __Joe Smith__

O = not yet	**X** = getting better	**+** = proper technique

Set up (front view)

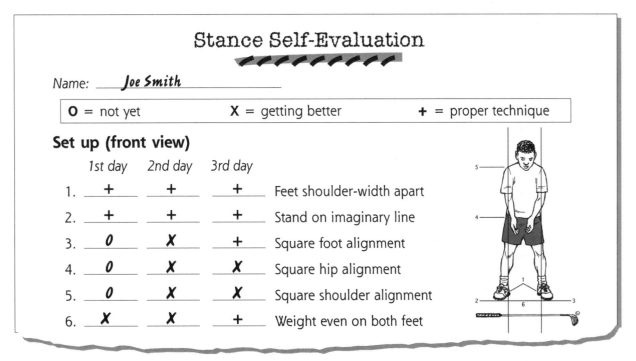

	1st day	2nd day	3rd day	
1.	+	+	+	Feet shoulder-width apart
2.	+	+	+	Stand on imaginary line
3.	0	X	+	Square foot alignment
4.	0	X	X	Square hip alignment
5.	0	X	X	Square shoulder alignment
6.	X	X	+	Weight even on both feet

Figure 2.6 In the above golf self-evaluation, the student indicates improvement in his golf stance. See form 8.9 for the complete form you can reproduce.

Teaching students to recognize skills through self-evaluation is much more effective and less threatening than traditional skill evaluation. Because students are less intimidated, evaluation is more positive. Most important, learning is lifetime in nature. After high school physical education classes are over, students who have learned to recognize skill will continue to learn. When we play golf, for example, and hit a bad shot, we can't expect our physical education teacher to come running down the fairway to help correct the flaws in our golf swing. Students who have learned to recognize skill will be able to analyze their mistakes and make the necessary corrections. Students who learn skill recognition are lifetime learners.

USING CROSS-CURRICULAR ACTIVITIES TO ENHANCE A PHYSICALLY ACTIVE LIFESTYLE

Motivating students to develop physically active lifestyles requires more than teaching sport and fitness skills. Students who wish to participate in the activities presented in physical education also need to know where to go, how much it will cost, the price and availability of equipment, what to wear, etiquette, and proper procedure. Students learn these lifetime skills best through cross-curricular activities.

City, county, state, national, and world maps are used to have students locate and document recreational and fitness sites as well as learn geography. A city map can be used to locate fitness centers and gyms; county maps to locate golf courses, swimming pools, and tennis courts; and state road maps can be used to locate parks that offer mountain biking, hiking trails, and camping areas. National and world maps can be used to locate ski resorts, wilderness areas, and forests. Students learn where to go to play golf while they are improving their knowledge of geography.

Reading an article about fly-casting techniques after holding a fly rod makes the reading more meaningful. More meaningful reading makes better readers, and better fly casters.

Students learn the cost of an activity and improve basic math skills by preparing a budget. Developing a budget for a ski trip, for example, helps students understand the cost of skiing, how to dress, and where to find the best value in equipment. Items to include in a budget are transportation, lodging, meals, fees, equipment rental, lessons, and special clothing. State and local travel agencies are more than happy to supply pamphlets and brochures for students to use with their assignments. Clothing and equipment catalogs from mail-order companies are a readily available resource for students to use in assignments designed to teach about the cost and the availability of equipment and clothing. Field trips at the conclusion of a unit allow the students to test the accuracy of their assignments before making entries in their portfolios.

Physical education offers an excellent opportunity to reinforce basic science skills as well. Students learn anatomy while deciding what muscles they need to develop in order to prepare for a backpacking trip. A fly-tying unit helps teach entomology, a hunting unit can teach plant identification by looking for animal food supplies, and ecology is reinforced with a "Leave No Trace" camping ethics unit.

Cross-curricular activities are a must for today's physical education programs. These activities help students become better at basic skills, raise standardized test scores, and make physical education a more valuable component of the school curriculum. Many of our students are kinesthetic learners; they learn best from hands-on experience and are intellectually stimulated by physical activity. For these students, physical education can do a better job of teaching basic skills than any other area of the curriculum because it provides the hands-on experience they need. Taking advantage of these opportunities helps us maintain and improve the status of our field. Educational decision makers are much more likely to support physical education when we demonstrate its ability to improve test scores, and when we are more involved in the overall education of our students.

DEVELOPING THINKING SKILLS

When first-grade students are asked if they are good dancers, a roomful of hands appears, and the students are eager to demonstrate their ability. Questions about any subject will receive a similar response. The same questions posed to high school students will find students reluctant to answer. Students at the secondary level have learned that many questions have only one right answer, that there are wrong answers, and that wrong answers are painful. Thinking and creativity have been extinguished. Physical education offers an excellent opportunity to help students develop thinking skills and rediscover their creativity. Physical education assignments should require students to analyze movement, compare and contrast actions, develop plans, and learn from what they do. Activities that only require students to recall data do not stimulate higher levels of thinking.

Robert Marzano's (1992) book, *A different kind of classroom,* is an excellent resource for developing lessons that promote thinking. Using the concepts of the book as a model, assignments can be developed that help students learn to think by following the dimensions of learning. An assignment following the dimensions of learning takes the students through five levels of thinking. At the first level, students make a prioritized list of what they need to know to execute the skill or to participate in the activity. The second level requires students to make a list of similar activities. At the third level, students choose one of the previously listed activities and compare that activity to the one they are attempting to learn. Level four requires the students to make a plan of action for actually participating in the activity or for how they would execute the skill. The final question asks the students what they have learned.

Marzano's "dimensions" technique can be used to teach a new skill or introduce a new activity. When teaching a backhand during a tennis unit, for example, students do the following:

1. List, in the order of importance, five things you need to know to hit a backhand (dimension 1).
2. List three ways a backhand is similar to a forehand (dimension 2).
3. Choose one of the above and tell how it is similar (dimension 3).
4. Make a plan for hitting your first backhand (dimension 4).

5. Now that you have hit your first backhand, write what you learned (dimension 5).

The same format can be used when teaching a new activity. An assignment for a mountain biking unit has students respond to the following:

1. What do you need to go mountain biking? List five items in the order of importance.
2. List five activities that are similar to mountain biking.
3. Choose one of the above and tell how it is similar.
4. Make a plan. Who will go with you, where will you go, when are you going, how long will you be gone, how far will you ride, what will you take along?
5. Now that you have gone mountain biking, what did you learn?

Samples of dimensions can be found in part II of this book. The "dimensions" model is an excellent tool for evaluating student progress and developing thinking skills. Students have difficulty the first time they are faced with such an assignment, and many need help. Progress becomes obvious each time students complete a "dimensions" assignment. I usually conclude my units with a dimensions assignment.

CONCLUSION

Physical education is not organized recess, and courses that teach only sport skills and competition are no longer acceptable. In order to change the activity habits of today's youth, physical education must take a more comprehensive approach. Our programs must focus on fitness and lifetime physical activity, use technology and cross-curricular strategies, and demonstrate how physical education can effectively contribute to the education of our youth. Our programs should adopt the theme: we don't stop playing because we get old; we get old because we stop playing.

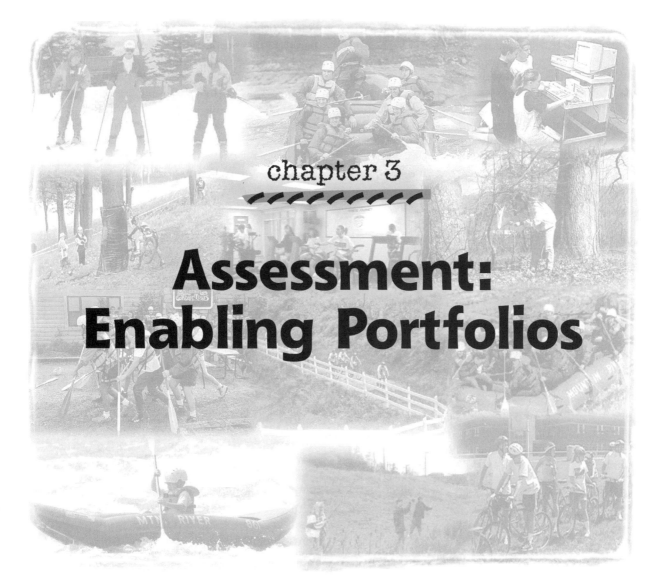

chapter 3

Assessment: Enabling Portfolios

Four freshman girls, part of the physical education class, occupy the tennis court nearest the school. Two of the girls are very thin and frail and have barely enough strength to lift the rackets. Another girl is overweight and huffs and puffs with the slightest effort. The fourth girl is poorly coordinated and awkward. Each of the girls has a tennis racket and a ball. They bounce the balls on the court and attempt a forehand. Most of their attempts produce a shot that hits the net or bounces short; sometimes they miss the ball completely. Occasionally a ball makes it over the net surprising the opponent who makes an attempt at a return, then runs to the back of the court to retrieve the ball. A successful shot by any of the girls produces squeals of delight, and all four run to the net and exchange high fives. They are laughing and having fun. They are playing tennis and being physically active. The activity continues until the teacher appears, clipboard in hand, and the girls are instructed to move to the base line for the TEST. There the girls are told to hit the balls diagonally to the opposite service court. The girls slowly retreat, dejectedly dragging their rackets. They stand with their heads down and wait their turn. Each attempt produces failure and a stern look of disapproval from the teacher as the scores are recorded. The fun and physical activity have stopped.

What is the teacher testing? What do the girls learn from the test? Each of the girls learns that tennis can only be played one way, that tennis must be done correctly, and that they can't play tennis. Is this what physical education tests should show our students—that they can't do something? Instead, we can use tests in physical education to help students learn what they can do. We can use tests to show students how to have fun, be physically active, and do it for the rest of their lives.

USING PORTFOLIOS TO TEACH

Students can learn from tests. Unfortunately, as in the previous scenario, our tests don't always teach our students what they need to learn. Physical education that teaches only skill can only use skill to evaluate. Thus, students who are low skilled fail and learn not to participate. The goal of physical education is to produce students who are physically active, and our methods of assessment should reflect this objective. We need to develop assessment tools that teach our students what they need to know in order to develop a physically active lifestyle. What we need is a portfolio assessment system that will enable our students to meet these goals!

My enabling assessment technique uses student-generated portfolios and cross-curricular strategies to collect information about the various activities. Information collected includes what students need to know to participate, tools for recognizing and improving skills, fitness data and training programs, equipment costs and availability, maps, Web sites, activity logs, reflections, and graphic organizers.

My first attempts at using portfolios were little more than notebooks. I began to research portfolio assessment and attended every conference session about portfolios in an effort to develop a satisfactory system. Connie Stokes of Minnesota had developed a wonderful portfolio system and made a presentation at the Midwest AAHPERD conference. I wanted to use her ideas and imitate her system, but she advised me that I needed to develop my own system and that it would take years. She was right. Although Connie's portfolio system was won-

derful, it would not work well for me. I needed to develop a system that would reflect my own unique goals and objectives.

Any discussion of assessment must first consider the local policy. Cabell County School's policy for physical education mandates that students' grades be based on 50 percent participation, 25 percent written, and 25 percent skill. This policy is similar to that of other schools I have visited. Second, we must consider what we are trying to assess. We should be assessing how well our students have met the objective of our physical education units of study. The objective of my units of study is to have the students participate in the activity during the class and learn what they need to know and do to participate in the activity for the rest of their lives.

The participation segment of assessment was the easiest to develop. To participate in class students must be present, come prepared for the activities (in proper attire), and document their participation in an activity log. The logs are included in their portfolios and may include pulse logs; exercise-equipment-use logs; or logs of weight, repetitions, and number of sets in the weight room. A student's participation is kept in both the grade book and in the student's portfolio. The grade book is used to keep attendance, and the portfolio is used to evaluate the actual participation in class activities. If a student is present, but for some reason refuses to participate in an activity, he or she will have no results to record and will lose a percentage of the possible grade.

PRINCIPLES OF ASSESSMENT

Over the years, I fine-tuned my philosophy of assessment to include five basic principles. In short, assessment must

1. be meaningful,
2. be authentic,
3. be positive,
4. have no wrong answers, and
5. assess students' abilities to participate in the activity for the rest of their lives.

Meaningful

Too many times I have seen written exams for physical education ask trivial questions, such as, How high is the volleyball net? The exams should ask questions that reflect the student's ability to participate in the activity and not be a training ground for Trivial Pursuit or *Who Wants to Be a Millionaire?* A better way to ask a question about the height of the volleyball net may be, If the net were lowered one foot, how would that change game strategy? A question of this nature requires knowledge rather than rote memorization. To answer such a question, students must analyze and compare and therefore demonstrate their knowledge of how the game is played.

Authentic

When I first began teaching, I conducted skill tests in the traditional manner. I soon began to experiment with alternative methods. Having our students stand and deliver by hitting a target or scoring a point on command is not the way the game is played, and hitting a target or scoring a point does not reflect a student's knowledge of how the skill should be performed. I no longer give my students skill tests. My students are tested for their skill recognition under authentic conditions.

To assess my students' abilities to recognize proper technique, I have each student conduct a self-evaluation, evaluate another student, be evaluated by another student, and participate in a video evaluation. Forms are provided in their portfolios that list skills, and students evaluate their own ability to execute the proper technique. When a skill is introduced, and students have made their first attempts, they then look at each skill listed and decide if they met the criteria or need improvement. Students are allowed to practice and improve on weak areas, then participate in partner evaluations in which a fellow student evaluates their technique and then is evaluated by the partner. Finally, students evaluate their techniques from a video taken in actual game situations. A tennis unit, for example, may have the students evaluate their techniques for the forehand, backhand, and serve. The final exam for the tennis unit may have students evaluate their techniques using a video of themselves during a volley.

Positive

In the scenario presented at the beginning of this chapter, the girls learn that they can't play tennis. We don't want to teach our children what they can't do; instead, we need to teach them what they can do. A more positive approach to assessment may be accomplished by using learning projects. Such a project may have students keep a record of their diet and exercise for a week, then calculate the calorie differential. Using digital images and computer presentation packages such as Microsoft® PowerPoint® to have students analyze technique is another example of learning projects that create a more positive assessment climate and enhance learning. In such an assignment, pictures are taken of students performing a skill, such as hitting a golf ball. The students use the computer to import the image into the PowerPoint® program, insert text and use arrows to critique their execution, then print out the image and place it in their portfolio, or turn in the project to the teacher.

No Wrong Answers

When we ask trivial questions on physical education tests, we are asking our students to use only lower-level thinking skills. These questions have only one right answer; all other answers are wrong. Student thinking, creativity, and ingenuity are suppressed, and so is learning. In order to help our students develop higher-order thinking skills and become better learners, we need to structure our evaluation tools so that our students must think. Such tools require students to express their opinions, compare and contrast, and find new ways of doing things. This type of assessment tool has many answers, most of which are correct. See figure 3.1 for how I evaluate a dimensions worksheet. Students learn that there's more than one way to do something, more than one way to be physically active, more than one way to hit a golf ball, and more than one way to play tennis.

Assessing the Likelihood of Lifelong Participation

The objective of physical education is to teach our students to be physically active for the rest

Dimensions of Skiing

Name: _____   Date: _____

1. What do you need to know to go skiing? List at least five items in their order of importance.

    1) Where to go
    2) How much it costs
    3) Where to get equipment
    4) How to put skis on
    5) How to get up

2. What other activities have you done that are similar to skiing? List five.

    1) In-line skating
    2) Ice skating
    3) Water skiing
    4) Sledding
    5) Nordic Track

3. Choose one of the activities you listed above and tell how it is similar to skiing.

    Water skiing: you use skis and you fall down a lot.

4. Let's go! Make a plan to go skiing (who, when, where, how).

    Me and my friends
    During Christmas break
    Timberline ski resort
    Mom will take us.

5. Now that you have finished the unit, what did you learn?

    You need to get fit to keep from getting hurt while skiing.

Figure 3.1   The Dimensions of Skiing form as completed by the student. The student is given credit for completing the assignment.

of their lives. They don't have to be highly skilled athletes. To be physically active, students need to understand fitness skills, develop lifetime skills, and recognize proper physical skill. Assessment should reflect these more appropriate objectives, not just the ability to execute a skill or hit a target.

To demonstrate their ability to analyze fitness, students complete the fitness rubric, use the fitness pyramid (see chapter 2), and participate in fitness activities. To show skill recognition, students evaluate their own techniques. To demonstrate lifetime skills, students complete budgets, compare equipment prices, and locate facilities on maps.

MAKING AND USING PORTFOLIOS

Technology has made it possible to create much more sophisticated documents to use in portfolios. Most of the documents I use have been made using Microsoft® Word. Some of the documents are simple text, while others have drawings or pictures inserted. I often scan drawings and maps so they can be saved in a computer file and not in a file cabinet. Order blanks from catalogs are imitations. Organizing and storing is much easier as well. I have created a file for each class that I teach, with a subfile for each unit. Each unit file contains entries for that unit's portfolio. When it comes time to start a new unit, I go to my file manager, open the file for that unit, select the documents I wish to use, print them, and use a copy machine to make enough copies for all of the students in the class. I make a few extras for the inevitable students that misplace their portfolios.

When developing a portfolio for a unit, I divide the entries into three categories: those that deal with fitness, those that deal with skill recognition and analysis, and those that deal with what I call lifetime skills. Fitness entries are designed to help students analyze their personal levels of fitness, understand the fitness benefits and requirements of the activity, and investigate techniques for maintaining fitness to allow for continued participation in the activity as adults. Fitness entries could include rubrics, logs, pacing guides, pulse tables, and calculations. This data is for the students to use as a

reference and is not to be used for determining students' grades.

Skill entries are designed to help students learn to recognize proper skill or technique. When making skill entries, I include descriptions of the skill I want the students to learn. Pictures and drawings may be included or inserted directly into the document. Students attempt to execute the skill and then evaluate their efforts. Students are evaluated on their ability to evaluate their technique.

The final group of entries deal with lifetime skills. These are assignments designed to help students learn what they need to know to participate in the activity after they have finished school. The assignments include maps for students to locate golf courses, tennis courts, or trout steams; sometimes they include equipment order forms and Web addresses. Lifetime-skill assignments are designed to help students learn where to go, how to dress, how much it costs, how to maintain and repair equipment, and what behavior is expected while participating in their activities of choice.

At the beginning of the semester students are given a file folder for their portfolios, which they label and decorate. Students document their assignments using form 3.1. I begin each new unit by distributing the portfolios to the students. Students place their portfolios in the folder to aid in identification. Folders are kept in a plastic box. While students are changing for class, I place the box containing the portfolios in an area designated for their assembly. After changing, the students go to the box, retrieve their portfolios, and begin working on assignments. The students keep their portfolios during class to record entries into activity logs, pulse logs, self-evaluation forms, or other assignments. At the end of each day, students put their portfolios in their folders and place them in the portable container I use for storage.

CONCLUSION

Equitable assessment is essential to quality physical education. Implementing a portfolio system that evaluates my students effectively, helps them become lifetime learners, and enables them to be physically active has been one of my most successful ventures as a teacher. The enabling portfolio system has been

Student Portfolio Documentation

Name: _____

Entry #	Date	Document	Teacher check	Points

an effective tool, and each year I make subtle changes that continue to refine and improve the unit.

The portfolio system is particularly effective because the students know from the first day what is expected of them. When a unit begins, the students receive all of their assignments. They know that if they complete the assignments in the portfolio, they will get a good grade. The portfolios are the students' responsibility, and completing the assignments is their responsibility as well.

It is especially rewarding to see student performance improve throughout the duration of the class. Many students have trouble with the assignments in the beginning. They are not used to questions that don't provide a choice of answers. Because they are accustomed to true-false or multiple-choice questions, their initial answers are often shallow and reflect their lack of thinking skills. But I have found that their performance usually improves quickly, and it is very satisfying to see the improvement.

chapter 4

Multimedia Applications for Physical Education

Technology is an integral part of our daily lives and should be used as a part of our physical education programs. Using technology in our classes allows us to enhance our teaching, provide hands-on experience for our students, and use resources to gather information that is otherwise not readily available. Technology provides nearly unlimited opportunities for the innovative teacher to greatly enhance student learning. Laptop computers with multimedia capacity, exciting presentation packages, large-screen LCD projectors, and digital cameras all have applications for physical education and can make programs come alive. The vast array of technology applications can be overwhelming, but you can use technology in your classes without becoming a technology expert. This chapter identifies applications that are particularly useful for physical education. Selection and use of pulse monitors, view cams, digital cameras, computers and software, scanners, and the Internet are explained and examples are provided.

PULSE MONITORS

The easiest and simplest application of technology in the physical education setting is the pulse monitor. Athletes can monitor their pulses during exercise to develop more efficient training programs. Resting pulse rates stabilize as fitness increases and drop as cardiovascular strength and endurance improve. Many highly conditioned athletes have resting pulse rates of 40 beats per minute or less, while 70 or more is considered normal.

Using pulse monitors during physical education helps students recognize the cardiovascular benefits and requirements of the activities. Pulse monitors also help students effectively evaluate their personal cardiovascular fitness, and can be used to help students identify activities appropriate for their fitness needs.

Pulse Stick Monitors

Two types of pulse monitors are recommended: the "pulse stick" and those with chest straps. The pulse stick is a one-inch diameter rod, nine inches long, with brass contact points on each end and a display window in the center. The cost is about $100 per unit. The user holds the stick in both hands and waits for the display to show the pulse. The accuracy of the pulse stick depends on the user. Changing hand pressure can cause variations in pulse reading and result in an inaccurate display. Be sure to instruct students to hold the brass contacts with firm, steady pressure and not squeeze. Improper use will result in obvious discrepancies that are easily identified by the wide variations in the display. Squeezing the contacts will cause the display to fluctuate wildly.

The pulse stick allows you to monitor a large number of students with just one piece of equipment. In a fitness center, for example, you can move from student to student and check the intensity of their exercise. Students compare the reading of the stick to a chart on the wall and adjust their efforts accordingly. Taking walks and passing the stick from student to student is an excellent way to demonstrate that gentle activities such as walking are excellent for fitness. Students are better able to understand the relationship of exercise intensity to pulse levels by using the stick while walking at different speeds, going up hills, and carrying extra weight. The pulse stick is the cheapest method to monitor pulse levels of large numbers of students because of the low price and the ability to change users quickly. The problems with the stick are the sometimes inaccurate reading when used without close supervision and the use of both hands. Using both hands is not practical when participating in such activities as riding a bicycle or playing a game that requires both hands.

Chest Strap Monitors

Pulse monitors that are strapped around the user's chest are more widely used than pulse sticks. The strap has two contact points that receive the signals from the heart and send the signal to a display monitor normally worn on the wrist. These monitors are available from most companies that specialize in fitness or physical education equipment.

Price varies according to the features. The simplest models only display pulse and can sometimes be purchased for less than $50. More expensive models display the time of day and have stopwatches with splits and recall and alarms that can be adjusted by the user to signal different pulse levels. The most expensive models, which can be interfaced with a computer, cost more than $400 each. Models found to be especially useful for physical education have a feature that displays average pulse rate and time spent below, in, and above the target zone. The setting can be changed, and the target zone raised or lowered according to the needs of the students. When a student's pulse level drops below the target zone, a sound is emitted to signal the student to go faster or work harder. When the student's pulse goes above the predetermined limit, a warning buzzer or beep is heard. This tells the student to slow down and control the pace.

In one of my classes, for example, a student wearing a pulse monitor during an activity such as tennis starts the watch on the pulse monitor at the beginning of the first set of drills and stops the watch at the end. The student is then able to recall the data recorded by the monitor and evaluate the activity. If the drills last for 30 minutes, the watch may tell the student that he spent 5 minutes below the exercise zone, 20 minutes in the zone, and 5 minutes above the zone, and that the average pulse rate for the entire 30 minutes was 140 beats per minute.

Students checking and recording pulse levels.

Using Pulse Monitors in Class

Students' first experience with pulse monitors requires the allocation of some class time. After students have changed and are ready for class to begin, explain the proper procedure. Although straps and monitors are interchangeable, they should be marked and number coded for identification. Assign students specifically numbered monitors and have them be responsible for their return. Place the straps around students' chests and adjust them so the contact points are located just below the pectoral muscles, one on each side. The contacts must then be moistened before the monitors can be activated. A container of water on a nearby table allows students to dip their fingers and wet the contacts. First-time users will take some time to learn how to adjust and activate the monitor. At the end of class have students remove straps and monitors, wipe them with a clean cloth, and place them on a table where they are sprayed with a disinfectant and allowed

to dry. Once students are familiar with this procedure, you can distribute pulse monitors to designated students before they change clothes for physical education. In this way, class pulse monitors are in place when students return to the gym, and class time is not lost.

VIEW CAMS

The first time I saw a view cam was at a cross country meet. One of our parents was recording members of our girls' team as they prepared to race. After recording the girls in action, she would review what she had been recording by looking at a small 3" × 3" screen on the back of the camera. I was in the market for a video camera, and this was what I wanted. After some hints and a promise to be good, there was a package under the Christmas tree with an "open me first" label. My new view cam was inside.

The view cam was for personal use, but I began using it as a coaching aid. Wrestlers in particular found video review useful while learning new techniques. The same applied to physical education. The view cam replaced the whistle hanging around my neck.

How to Select a View Cam

When selecting a view cam, take care to select features that are most useful with physical education students. The view cam I use is simple to operate and moderately priced. It is small, lightweight, and highly portable and has a rechargeable battery. A strap allows me to hang the camera around my neck and carry it wherever the class goes. Another model purchased by our school has an external battery, which allows for bigger, longer-lasting batteries, an eyepiece that helps find the subject in bright sun, and a tape that can be placed in an adapter and inserted into any VCR.

Viewing screens come in different sizes. Some screens are in the back of the camera in a stationary position, while others may be on a panel that opens and swings out and up from the body of the camera. If you plan to use the camera mainly outside in bright light, a panel may be difficult to see. An additional viewfinder, with a shaded eyepiece, may be a desirable feature. A rechargeable battery, a battery charger, and an auxiliary power supply should be supplied with the camera. Additional batteries with extended life and more power are also available.

Playback features and the tape cartridge may be the critical issue in the selection process. All view cams have a miniature VCR to allow playback through the LCD panel, and there should be connections available to allow for playback through a TV or separate VCR. Cameras that use small tapes work well for providing instant feedback; however, to view the recording on a TV, the camera must be used for playback or played through a VCR and re-recorded to a full-size tape. Cameras that use larger cartridges and come with an adapter allow the tape to be removed, placed in the adapter, and viewed through a VCR while the camera is used to make additional recordings. Features of the newest cameras have many improvements over earlier models. Research all styles and makes to find the features best suited for your intended use.

Using View Cams in Class

You can use the view cam through all phases of a unit. Students can be recorded in small groups performing lead-up drills. Recordings are reviewed and critiqued through a TV at the end of class as part of closure and to prepare for the next day's lesson. Students can also be recorded individually as they attempt to learn a skill, then review their attempts in the LCD screen and make corrections. Recordings of limited competition help students recognize strategy and evaluate their skills under authentic conditions. You will find many uses for the view cam, and students enjoy seeing themselves in action.

COMPUTERS

Advances in computer technology happen so fast it is almost impossible to keep up with the pace. Computers are now faster and have more capacity than anyone believed possible only a few years ago. When I purchased my last computer, I was advised to get the largest, most powerful, and fastest model I could afford. This is good advice.

Students using a view cam to check tennis technique.

A computer's capacity is determined by the size of its hard drive, the speed of its processor, and the amount of its random access memory (RAM). The computer hard drive can be compared to a large closet full of file cabinets where all files and programs are stored while not in use. More and larger programs and files require more hard drive space. Processor speed is expressed in megahertz. Higher operating speeds are responsible for making programs load and images appear at a reasonable rate. Presentation software that uses pictures requires a higher processor speed than simple word processor programs. RAM refers to the computer's ability to work with active programs. RAM can be compared to a workbench. Just as a large workbench can accommodate more projects, larger RAM capacity can accommodate more and larger active files.

Recommendations for specific capacities have increased with the growth of the technology industry. Computers with 100 megahertz processor speed, one gigabyte of hard drive space, and 8 megabytes of RAM were considered state of the art in 1995. In 1998 computers with 200 megahertz of processor speed, 4 gigabytes of hard drive space, and 32 megabytes of RAM were considered adequate. The new millennium has computers with 1,000-megahertz operating speeds, 20-gigabyte hard drives, and 100 megabytes of RAM. Purchasing a new computer with maximum capacities will not prevent the computer from becoming outdated. As technology grows, the need for newer and more powerful machines will mean that our physical education programs and teachers will need to continually update their technology equipment and skills.

While desktop computers placed on carts with wheels allow the computer to be moved out of the lab or office and into the gym, laptop computers may be more suitable for most physical education applications. Laptops are available with the same capacities as desktop models and may power the same hardware. These portable computers are more expensive than desktop models but are well worth the extra investment. Rechargeable batteries provide complete portability, allowing easy computer access in the field, on the track, or at home. Computers and software acquired for the physical education department should be compatible with those used in the school.

The purchase price of most computers includes software. The most popular software setup is the Microsoft® Windows® operating system used with Microsoft® Office. This combination will provide most of the essential programs. Basic software programs will help you develop and organize lessons, create handouts and worksheets, generate tests, and create a variety of forms such as those seen in part II of this book. You will find presentation software packages especially useful. There are several brands of presentation software available that allow you to make lessons more exciting, glamorous, and effective. Brightly colored slides with bullets that can be made to whistle and flash as they appear help students focus and enhance learning. Pictures can be imported to illustrate specific details of proper technique and provide a basis of comparison for students. Best known of the presentation software is Microsoft® PowerPoint®. All brands have products with similar features, however. Your choice of a soft-

ware package is most likely to reflect your previous experience.

Saving Your Work

Sometimes computers malfunction and "crash," which means that all programs stop working and all files are lost. When this happens, the computer must be "rebuilt" by reinstalling the software to the hard drive. The files, however, are lost forever. To avoid disaster, all computer users should develop a backup system for files. Small files such as those used in word processing may be backed up with a standard floppy disk. Larger files require a system with larger capacities. A zip drive or CD writer may be added and used to make backup files for the system.

Using Computers in Class

Presentations are viewed by the students through a computer using an LCD projector and a screen, on a lightly colored wall, or with a TV using a converter that changes the signals of the computer monitor to the RC signals of the TV. Presentations may also be played through a VCR and recorded. When displayed through a VCR, presentations and lessons may be recorded and combined with videos of students in action. Teaching cues and pinpointing may be accomplished with the tools provided by the software. Sequential learning steps may be displayed with bullets, arrows, and symbols in appropriate places to draw attention to specific details, and text boxes may be added to include special instructions.

DIGITAL CAMERAS

Digital cameras take pictures that may be imported directly into the computer and used in other programs. These cameras operate similarly to regular cameras: find a subject in a viewfinder, and push a button when ready. The images are stored in the camera's memory, then downloaded to the computer's memory using software provided by the manufacturer. Some models have an LCD panel in back to allow images to be viewed as they are taken. Undesirable images may be deleted to save space. Some models use removable floppy disks, each of which may hold up to 22 images. These can be removed from the camera and inserted into the computer's disk drive. Pictures can be viewed by any photo software program or may be imported directly to other applications. The Mavic is particularly suitable for physical education because of its removable-disk feature. Each student is given a disk. Students are photographed while in action, then the disk is removed and given to them. The students then use a computer to view their pictures and analyze their techniques.

SCANNERS

Scanners make copies for computers in the same manner as a photocopier. Text or images are placed in a viewing screen and scanned. The scanner's software converts the images to computer files. Small, portable models may only copy text from sheets of paper, while larger scanners may be able to copy large signs, posters, and pictures. Most scanners work well, but there seems to be some difficulty with some software applications. It may be necessary to remove and reinstall software repeatedly in order to receive satisfactory performance. Make sure when purchasing a scanner that the price includes desirable software that will be adequate for your intended use.

INTERNET

Many educators are finding that the Internet is a valuable educational resource. Schools have computer labs available with Internet capabilities. Teachers schedule class time to visit the lab and complete assignments. Other schools may be networked to allow computers throughout the school to be connected to a large central computer or server. Physical education departments should make sure that they are able to take advantage of these resources. Lab time should be available to physical education classes, and the gymnasium and other physical education facilities must be connected to the school's network.

Including the use of the Internet in unit plans will enhance student learning and stimulate interest. A visit to the computer lab to view re-

lated Web sites is an excellent way to introduce a new unit. Students visit designated Web sites and find answers to questions in order to complete assignments. You should find the sites in advance and record the addresses (URLs) so students can go directly to the proper location. Be sure the assignments are specific and well researched, and monitor students closely to make sure they visit only acceptable sites.

If a computer lab is not available and there is no access to the Internet in the gym, Web sites may be saved and viewed at a later time. Software programs used to search the Internet are called browsers. Browsers such as Netscape allow an entire site to be stored on the computer's hard drive. Web sites stored in this manner may be viewed in the same manner as those viewed directly from the Internet. Web sites may also be stored one page at a time on conventional disks using the commands on the browser. Saving Web sites has several advantages; no time is lost waiting for connections and downloads, disks still work when remote servers are down, and students can only view those sites saved on the disk.

E-MAIL AND LIST SERVES

E-mail (electronic mail) provides a convenient and efficient form of communication through the Internet. Many of us are not very good about writing letters, and a phone call is sometimes an intrusion. E-mail communications, however, can be dealt with at the convenience of the recipient—no stamps, no post office, and no charges. There is no better means of establishing and maintaining worldwide contact with fellow professionals. Contact made at district and national conventions can be maintained year round. Ideas shared with a colleague during an annual meeting may be mutually nourished across thousands of miles.

List serves are basically mailing lists organized by a central host. Subscribers register their e-mail addresses with the provider. Messages are sent to the host and distributed to all those on the list. One message is usually distributed to hundreds of readers. E-mail list serves and list serves such as the NASPE list serve of Virginia Tech and PE Talk of Sportime International are two examples of list serves for physical education teachers. You can find instructions for signing up for the NASPE list serve on the PE Central Web site: **pe.central.vt.edu**. Instructions for subscribing to PE Talk may be found at **www.sportime. com/discussion.shtml**.

PUTTING IT ALL TOGETHER

I have organized all my classes with computer programs. Each class has a file folder, and each unit has a subfile folder. The file for the outdoor adventure class has subfolders for mountain biking, rafting, archery/bow hunting, fly-fishing, downhill skiing, hiking/backpacking, orienteering, and wilderness survival. The conditioning and weight-training class has a file folder with subfolders for each of the three grading periods. The files contain a cover page for students' portfolios, a documentation page for records, all assignments, readings, reflections, forms, graphic organizers, evaluations, and daily lesson plans. Before starting a unit, I open, review, and update all files. I print student portfolios, copy and staple them, and then distribute them to students at the beginning of the unit.

I begin my units with videos of experts, and sometimes former students, performing the skill. Slow motion and stop action help demonstrate and analyze proper technique. I like to use PowerPoint® to show slides for each step of the skill on a screen. Each action is pinpointed, and text boxes contain special instructions with arrows pointing out highlights. Students attempt to imitate proper grip or stance while viewing the screen. I am free to move from student to student, making corrections and adjustments. A remote control mouse allows me to move through the class while changing the slides on the computer.

A video camera connected to a television allows the students to have a live view of their attempts. Students have a view of the correct skill on the PowerPoint® screen and a view of themselves on a TV at the same time. For a golf lesson, for example, I may show a golf professional demonstrating proper stance on a PowerPoint® slide displayed on a screen. Students stand in front of the video camera and attempt to imitate the stance of the professional. The television displaying the student's image is positioned so that both images can be seen simultaneously and corrections made. Students' actions are recorded and used for clo-

sure of daily lessons, to review previous lessons, to help them recognize proper skill, and for self-evaluation.

While some students are working on skill development, other students are at the computer. These students are either completing an assignment in which they view designated Web sites and respond to questions, or using an image from a digital camera to complete their own PowerPoint® slide in which they critique their actions. Still other students are participating in simulated competition while wearing pulse monitors. When the drills are completed, the students record their pulse levels in their activity logs.

When our school opened in 1994, many of our students had no computer skills. Five years later most of our students are highly proficient. Assignments that took several trips to the computer lab to complete in 1994 are finished in less than 30 minutes now. The continued growth of technology will mandate increased use of computers in education. Students will use disks instead of notebooks and electronic portfolios for evaluation and assessment. What seems like science fiction will be common practice. Initial attempts at using technology in our classes can be intimidating. While there is so much available and so much to learn, a little knowledge can go a long way. We don't have to be technology experts to be expert teachers using technology to help our students learn better and faster.

CONCLUSION

Physical education teachers must make sure that facilities are properly equipped and technology is available in the gym as in other parts of the school. We must identify technology applications that are especially appropriate for use in our field, acquire training in the proper use of equipment and software, and create situations for the use of technology in our classes. Computers may be blamed for a decrease in physical activity, since many children spend more time playing computer games and less time being physically active. However, we can use technology to help students develop better skills, identify opportunities for physical activity, locate facilities and equipment, communicate with people with similar interests, and promote lifelong physical activity.

chapter 5

Promoting Physical Activity in the School Community

The Centers for Disease Control and Prevention recommendations for creating a more active populace include offering physical activity opportunities for our youth in addition to competitive athletics. I specifically address the following recommendations in this chapter:

Recommendation 2: Environment. *Provide health promotion programs for school faculty and staff.*

Recommendation 5: Extracurricular Activities. *Provide extracurricular physical activity programs that offer diverse, developmentally appropriate activities, both noncompetitive and competitive, for all students.*

Recommendation 6: Family Involvement. *Encourage parents and guardians to support their children's participation in physical activity, to be physically active role models, and to include physical activity in family events.*

Recommendation 7: Training. *Provide training to enable teachers, coaches, recreation and health care staff, and other school and community personnel to promote enjoyable, lifelong physical activity among young people.*

While physical activity programs abound (little leagues, the Amateur Athletic Union, the YMCA, church groups, and other youth organizations offer an abundance of competitive sports), for those who don't excel or may not be competitive, few programs exist. Physical education programs should accept this challenge and develop programs that offer activities for the nonathlete. Field trips to ski resorts, after school hikes/walks, dances, bike rides, aerobics classes, and family nights are some examples. Using the recommendations as a guide, I have developed my own programs in my school. In this chapter, I explain the development and procedures of my program. Physical activity is center stage in my school. Taking a leadership role and promoting physical activity reinforces the messages you send in your physical education classes: kids see that physical activity is important and that it can take place outside of the gymnasium.

RUN/WALK

At Milton High School our cross country team began the season by participating in the Midsummer Night's Run. This event is held each year during the first week of August in Lexington, Kentucky. The coaches, parents, and students meet at the school early on Saturday morning to make the two-hour trip. The day is spent visiting area attractions before joining the 3,000 to 5,000 participants for the 8:00 P.M. start. The team members, coaches, and many of the parents complete the 5 K run, invade a local restaurant, and arrive home about midnight. It is a great way to start the season. Coaches and parents spend the day getting to know each other, team members are motivated to train for the season during the summer, and we have fun participating in a running event!

We decided to attempt to create the same atmosphere at Milton High School by conducting a run/walk for the students, staff, and members of the community. Students were required to preregister so they could be excused from classes on the afternoon of the event. Participants reported to the gym to pick up their numbers and get ready for the race. Two hundred and seventy-one students and several faculty members took part. The race started in the parking lot behind the school and followed a police escort along the route. Members of the cross country team served as officials, the sports medicine class provided a water aid station along the course, and the home economics classes had refreshments for the finishers. Two video cameras were used to record the action—one camera in a vehicle leading the race, and another along the course. Every runner was recorded crossing the finish line. The principal allowed the remainder of the students to go to the finish area and cheer the runners as they completed the run. After the last runner crossed the line, all students and staff went to the gym for the awards ceremony and to view the video of the race.

Our cross country and track teams had a large collection of trophies left over from many years of success. A local trophy supplier provided new nameplates at a nominal fee, and the leftover trophies were used as awards for the winners of the race. Awards categories were male and female overall winners, each grade level, and faculty. Local businesses contributed merchandise for door prizes. After all awards and door prizes were distributed, the video of the race was played. The event was a great success. The faculty who did not participate wanted to know if there was going to be a race the next year and how they could be involved. Planning for the second Milton High School Covered Bridge Run/Walk began at the next faculty meeting.

The race date for the next run/walk was set for the Friday afternoon of fitness week in May, and fitness became the academic theme for the week. I decided to attempt to involve the whole school and make the event more academically legitimate by using fitness as a theme for lessons. Each department chair made a list of lesson ideas for his or her subject area relating to running, walking, and fitness. A booklet for the staff included an invitation to the event, an entry form, lesson suggestions, a guest letter and entry, a four-week training program, a map of the course and other routes and distances in the area, race day instructions for students and staff (plan of operation), a list of awards, and a race day schedule (figure 5.1). The event was introduced and the booklet distributed at a faculty meeting six weeks before the week of the race.

Fellow Faculty Member:

The Physical Education Department, with the sponsorship of Project Wellfit, will present the annual Cabell Midland High School All Knight Run/Walk on May 15, 2001.

Enclosed please find:

Race entry form
Suggestions for lesson plans to coordinate your subject area with the event
Four-week training cycle
Plan of operations
Race day schedule
List of awards
Course map

We want to do everything possible to help you and your students participate. Please let us know if we can be of assistance.

Good luck,

The Physical Education Department

All Knight Run/Walk Official Entry

Date: Tuesday, May 15, 2001: 1st and 2nd blocks (awards, 4th period)

Course: 3000 meters (2 miles) through the campus of Cabell Midland High School and the surrounding area.

Registration: The entry fee is $1.00. Proceeds go to the Cabell Midland High School physical education program.

Awards: Awards will be given to the top runners in both the male and female divisions. Awards will also be given to the top five finishers in each class in both male and female divisions. In addition the top five male and female staff members will also receive awards.

Tear off the bottom of this form and return it to a member of the Physical Education Department.

All Knight Run/Walk entry form

Last name: _____   *First name:* _____

Please circle the appropriate identifiers.

Male   Female

Freshman   Sophomore   Junior   Senior   Staff/guest

Figure 5.1   Race booklet.

Some Suggested Activities to Coordinate With the All Knight Run/Walk

English, Reading, Language Arts

Study poems related to running, speed. Write and read poetry.

Foreign Language

Learn vocabulary related to Olympics/running, translate race packet, investigate running events in other countries on the Internet.

Math

Calculate speed and distance, convert metric to miles, etc., measure steps and calculate distance/time, study map and contours, calculate calories, total miles for Walk Across West Virginia.

Music

Relate rhythm to running and racing, compose or select music for running and walking (marching music).

Science

Aerodynamics of running clothing, shoes, etc., speed and acceleration (physics), genetics (biology)

Home Economics

Clothing for running, foul weather clothing for performance, food for running and performance

Social Studies

Olympic games—history of legality of drug testing, Berlin games, Jim Thorpe, Jesse Owens and race relations, map of the course

Business Education

Create database for race and sort numbers and times, reports related to fitness, report on businesses that encourage "fit" employees, keyboarding races related to fitness, make spreadsheets to determine average time of runners, create pages related to fitness and events leading to All Knight Run.

Art

Create posters, banners, photos, paintings of the event.

Cabell Midland High School All Knight Run/Walk

70 Awards (trophies/medals/ribbons, etc.)

Top 10 males/females (20 awards)
Top 5 senior males/females (10 awards)
Top 5 junior males/females (10 awards)
Top 5 sophomore males/females (10 awards)
Top 5 freshman males/females (10 awards)
Top 5 faculty males/females (10 awards)

Figure 5.1 Race booklet *(continued)*.

Cabell Midland High School All Knight Run/Walk
Plan of Operation

All participants must preregister.

All participants will have a race number assigned.

A list of student runners will be provided to teachers on race day morning.

After roll call in first block, students should place valuables in school lockers.

Students proceed to gym A to pick up race numbers.

Race numbers not picked up will indicate students skipping or absent.

Race numbers will be delivered to participating staff members prior to the race.

The men's race is first. All female faculty members please help escort nonparticipating students to the athletic field bleachers on the press box side or to the cafeteria.

The race will be recorded on video from several locations in order to verify winners.

Participants must follow the official course in order to receive prizes or awards.

All participants must exit through the runners' shoot to have numbers recorded.

All participants must have race number stamped to verify finish.

Refreshments will be provided at the finish line area. Only participants wearing race numbers with stamp will be allowed in the refreshment area.

The entrance to the refreshment area will be through the finish line only.

Third block will be regular class and lunch times.

Video of the race will be shown via library at the end of fourth block.

All Knight Run/Walk

Race Day Schedule

7:45 A.M. All students report to first block.

7:55 A.M. Those students who have registered for the run/walk report to the gym to pick up their race numbers.

8:00 to 9:00 A.M. Registration continues while warm-up activities take place.

9:00 to 9:15 A.M. Introduce special guests while all participants proceed to the starting line.

9:15 A.M. Boys' race begins.

9:45 A.M. Girls' race begins.

10:15 to 11:09 A.M. Refreshments are available during post-race cool-down and stretching.

11:09 A.M. to 1:20 P.M. Students go to lunch and third block.

1:28 P.M. Students report to fourth block.

2:30 to 3:00 P.M. Students view race video via library.

Figure 5.1 Race booklet *(continued)*. ☞

Four-Week Training Cycles for the Cabell Midland High School All Knight Run/Walk

Choose a training cycle for your current level of fitness. The first week should be a routine you can comfortably achieve. Proceed through two complete four-week cycles. Start date should be Monday, March 14. The CMHS All Knight Run/Walk will be held Wednesday, May 8. Your last training week should end the Saturday before the event. The Monday before the race should be the same as the first day of your first cycle. The Tuesday before the race should be a day of rest.

Level I			
Week	Days	Distance	Pace
1	Mon., Wed., Fri.	1 mile	Gentle walk
2	Mon., Tues., Fri., Sat.	1 mile	Gentle walk
3	Mon. through Sat.	1 mile	Gentle walk
4	Mon., Wed., Sat.	1 mile	Gentle walk
	Tues., Thurs.	1 mile	

Level II			
Week	Days	Distance	Pace
1	Mon. through Fri.	2 miles	Gentle walk
2	Mon., Wed., Fri.	2 miles	Gentle walk
	Tues., Thurs., Sat.	2 miles	Brisk walk
3	Mon., Wed.	2 miles	Brisk walk
	Sat.	3 miles	Gentle walk
4	Mon., Wed., Fri.	2 miles	Gentle walk
	Tues., Thurs.	2 miles	Brisk walk
	Sat.	3 miles	Brisk walk

Level III			
Week	Days	Distance	Pace
1	Mon., Wed., Fri.	3 miles	Gentle walk
	Tues., Thurs.	3 miles	Brisk walk
	Sat.	3 miles	Jog mile 2
2	Mon., Wed., Fri.	3 miles	Brisk walk
	Tues., Thurs.	3 miles	Jog mile 2
	Sat.	4 miles	Jog miles 2–3
3	Mon., Wed., Fri.	3 miles	Jog mile 2
	Tues., Thurs.	3 miles	Jog miles 2–3
	Sat.	3 miles	Easy jog

Figure 5.1 Race booklet *(continued)*.

Cabell Midland High School All Knight Run/Walk

Official Course Map

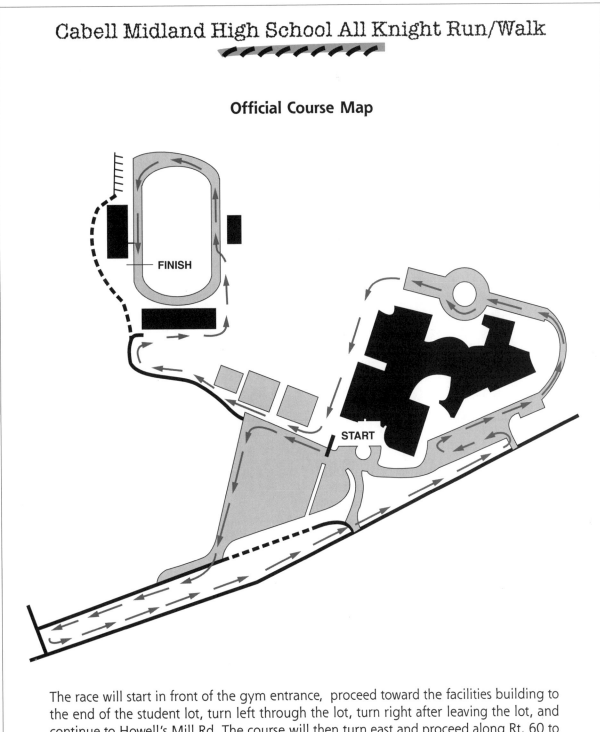

The race will start in front of the gym entrance, proceed toward the facilities building to the end of the student lot, turn left through the lot, turn right after leaving the lot, and continue to Howell's Mill Rd. The course will then turn east and proceed along Rt. 60 to the east entrance of the school. Next the course will enter and loop the guest lot in front of the main office, follow the bus route behind the school, and continue around the school following the "Bob Overmoyer Expressway." Turn right at tennis courts, continue past the facilities building, and enter the track from the visitor's side. The finish line will be in front of the main grandstands.

Figure 5.1 Race booklet *(continued).*

Fitness Week

Fitness week began with a five-minute introductory video of the previous year's event. The art classes had been making posters for a poster contest advertising the race, and the halls were decorated with the winning posters. English classes studied running and poetry, science classes studied anatomy and muscles, social studies classes investigated the history of the Olympics, and math classes measured stride length and calculated time and distance. Each day brought additional excitement and enthusiasm from the students and staff.

When I arrived at school on the morning of the event, it was obvious something special was happening. The students were filled with excitement. As I walked through the halls, all conversations were about the big event. I overheard the students talking among themselves: "What are you going to wear?" "How fast are you going to run?" "I can't run that far, so I'll just walk." The faculty was likewise excited. All conversations were about fitness, running or walking, and the event.

The Race

The race began with the mayor firing the starting gun and concluded in the parking lot behind the school. The same procedure was followed as that of the previous year. Of the 800 students and staff of Milton High School, 735 completed the course. The awards ceremony began with academic awards. Each department presented a prize to the student with the best project related to their lesson on fitness, running, or walking. Trophies were presented to the event winners, and then the door prizes were given out. The day concluded with a viewing of the race video. Many faculty members said that the run/walk was the best school project they had ever experienced.

Milton High School closed and was consolidated with Barboursville High School to produce Cabell Midland High School. Staff members of the other school were told of the run/walk and liked the idea, but because the new school had a population of over 2,000 students, some changes were necessary. First, we needed a new race name. The mascot for our new school was a medieval knight, and since all students were encouraged to participate, the

Participants in the first All Knight Run/Walk.

event was called the Cabell Midland High School All Knight Run/Walk. The large numbers expected made it necessary to conduct two races, one for the boys and another for the girls. We also decided that we needed to use technology to accommodate the huge numbers; the computer/keyboarding classes provided the manpower as part of a class project. Computers were also necessary at the finish line. We purchased race numbers that were barcoded so they could be scanned by computers at the finish. Our local track club volunteered to handle these duties with the help of the track team and coaches.

The first annual Cabell Midland High School All Knight Run/Walk had 1,586 finishers and was concluded without any major problems. Students received over $3,500 in prizes for their academic projects and trophies for their race performance. Our faculty had begun training programs to prepare for the event and vowed to continue so as to improve their performance next year. Most important, the physical education department had taken a leadership role in a schoolwide event and performed so well that other departments began to look to us for help and leadership in other projects.

FITNESS FAIR

A few years before the closing of Milton High School, some money became available to the physical education department for the purchase of exercise equipment. We purchased two rowers, two Airdynes, a NordicTrack, and an exercise bike. We also procured an impedance body fat computer. Step aerobics was just beginning to become popular, and our shop had made several boxes. Most of our students complete their physical education requirement as freshmen or sophomores and therefore juniors and seniors were not introduced to our new equipment. We wanted to give the upper class a demonstration of the latest in physical fitness equipment and techniques. It was decided that the best format would be a fair, in which students could come to the gym and move about to experience all the attractions. Since the juniors and seniors were the students we were targeting for the fair and all juniors and seniors were enrolled in English classes, we invited the English teachers to bring their classes to the fitness fair. Teachers readily accepted the chance to see what was new.

Plans were proceeding well, and those of us that were also teaching health realized that this would be an excellent opportunity to bring in guests. We went to the community to search for additional resources. Many members of the health fitness community eagerly accepted our invitation to participate. In addition to our in-house exhibits, our fair included exhibits from the American Red Cross, the American Heart Association, the Cabell County Public Health Department, the Prestera Mental Health Center, and a local hospital.

We arranged the new equipment along the wall on one side of the gym, provided tables for the guests' exhibits on the opposite wall, and saved the center for step aerobics. Members of our physical education classes were selected to demonstrate proper use of the equipment. Other physical education students were part of the step aerobics team.

At an information booth located at the entrance, students distributed a list of exhibits to each of our guests as they entered. Students and faculty were free to roam about the exhibits, try out the equipment, visit the displays, have their body fat calculated, or have their diet analyzed. Periodically the music would start and our students would do a brief step aerobics routine. Toward the end of each class period, the guests were invited to join some of our students for some step aerobics. The physical education classes would teach the guests a short, simple step pattern and help as they made their attempts.

Our first fair was very popular. The students and faculty saw that there were some exciting things happening in physical education, and the guest exhibitors were pleased with their exposure and were anxious to return for the next fair. Our only problem was space and time.

Over the years our fitness fair has continued to be successful. There have been only minor changes in format, but the list of exhibits and activities is never the same from one year to the next. The new Cabell Midland High School has two gyms, a fitness center with additional equipment, and a free exercise room. Our fair has a much larger area for activities, and the school system made the move to the block schedule, so our fair was able to expand our size and time.

Increased size requires more planning and organization. The fitness fair is our physical education department's fall project, usually taking place near Thanksgiving. Planning begins at the beginning of the school year in September. Members of the health and physical education departments submit ideas for activities and exhibits. Each department member has the responsibility for making arrangements for his or her assigned activities. Invitations are sent to prospective exhibitors. After receiving the returned invitations and confirming them all, we produce a final list of exhibits/activities. Space and time is allocated, responsibilities agreed to, students selected, signs printed, number of tables and chairs calculated, and a list of equipment requirements is made (see figure 5.2).

The week of the fair is devoted to gathering and storing equipment. The night before the fair, members of the physical education department return to school at the end of basketball practice. Members of the basketball

Station	Number of students needed	Equipment
Information	2	1 table
Body composition (skinfold, impedance, and Skyndex)	5	Forms, calipers, 2 tables, calculator, pencils, power
YMCA	0	1 table, 1 chair, power
Health Center (diet analysis)	0	3 tables, 4 chairs, power
American Cancer Society	1	1 table, 2 chairs
University Human Performance Lab (stength and fitness analysis)	0	2 tables
Hiking the Appalachian Trail: Bryan Butts	0	2 tables, space for a tent, TV, VCR, display or PowerPoint®, power
Mountain State Outfitters (fly-tying/fly-fishing)	0	1 table, 2 chairs, TV, VCR, power, space for casting demo and practice
Health South	0	1 table, 2 chairs
County Health Department (tobacco display)	0	1 table, 3 chairs
American Red Cross	0	1 table, 2 chairs
Mental Health Center	0	1 table
Hospital	0	1 table, 2 chairs
Martial arts	0	1 table, 2 wrestling mats
Three-point shooting contest	0	Basketballs, ball rack, stopwatch
Table tennis tournament	0	6 tables, paddles, and balls
Line dancing	2 to 13	CD player, CD, power
Steps and slides	2 to 9	Slides, steps, CD player, CD, power

Figure 5.2 Fitness fair exhibits and activities.

team help set up tables and place signs. Final preparations are made early in the morning before the start of school. Student helpers arrive early, greet guest exhibitors, and provide assistance. We are ready by the time school starts.

Our school is on block scheduling with four 90-minute sessions. On the day of the fair the last session is abbreviated to 60 minutes so we can begin to close for the end of school and have the gym ready for the basketball team. With the help of the students and a few members of the basketball team, we are finished in less than 45 minutes. The day of the fair is intense and exhausting, but worth the effort. The week following the fair is spent addressing thank-you letters to the exhibitors who made our program a success.

FIELD TRIPS

I began taking field trips to recreational areas informally, with the senior members of my wrestling teams, as a reward for their hard work and leadership. One year we camped on the banks of the Ohio River and fished all night. Other trips involved water skiing, white-water rafting, and skiing. The trips were informal: I knew all the parents well and I got permission, the numbers were small, and many times the parents came along. I was never concerned about liability, and there was never a problem. Each year the seniors looked forward to their trip. Most of the kids were being exposed to activities they had never had a chance to experience before. After their initial exposure, they continued to participate as adults. These trips were a wonderful and fun way to encourage physical activity, and I realized that they could be part of physical education programs.

Taking large numbers of students on trips to participate in what may be considered high-risk activities takes careful, detailed planning and preparation. Special care must be taken to protect the trip organizers and sponsoring organizations from liability, as well as to protect the students from harm.

Addressing Liability

Before taking large groups on trips, I made sure to get the support of our school system. Our administration was supportive and willing to help with the arrangements. A school administrator, a lawyer, and I met to develop proper procedure, a parent permission form, and a waiver of liability. These forms are distributed to interested students along with an introductory letter, an itinerary, trip information, and a list of rules. Signed forms are returned along with payment. See figure 5.3 for a sample letter to parents, a permission /liability form, and ski trip information form.

Procedures and Preparation

The field trips I have organized, in addition to the ones mentioned earlier, can be separated into two categories: trips taken as part of our physical education program and trips taken as part of a school club activity. Procedures for all trips are the same. The difference is in the preparation of the students. For trips involving physical education students, it must be assumed that the students have no experience and instruction is required. The students are prepared for the activity as part of their physical education classes. Instruction includes physical preparation, basic skills, cost, dress, equipment, safety, injury prevention, proper procedures, and any special requirements. Students not enrolled in physical education classes can participate in field trips organized by activity clubs, such as ski clubs or hiking clubs. Students are required to join the club and attend meetings to be allowed to participate in the field trip.

Preparations for trips begin by contacting the recreational organization and negotiating group rates. Most organizations, especially ski resorts, offer significant discounts for groups. Additional savings are possible by scheduling trips at slack times, and special arrangements may be possible for such services as lessons, rental equipment, and meals.

The next step is to arrange for transportation. *At no time should a student be allowed to drive!* Although there have been times when I have driven, and parents have volunteered, I strongly recommend that school transportation systems or commercial carriers be used. Spending the day on the ski slopes is fun, but also tiring. Falling asleep at the wheel after a day of fun is an unnecessary risk that must be avoided.

Grants are available to help defray the cost of some trips—through state agencies designed to promote physical activity, school health, or state tourism, for example. Contact your state's department of travel and tourism, the state or governor's council for physical activity, or the state department of education office for information. Most often, however, students pay all their own fees. Transportation costs are divided equally and included in the total cost of the package. Most organizations offer special rates for or subsidize group organizers. Larger groups have additional free positions so that additional chaperones can attend at no charge. There should be at least two chaperones on each bus. In the event of a serious injury that requires hospitalization, one chaperone goes with the victim while the other stays with the

Bane McCracken
Chairman Physical Education Dept.
Cabell Midland High School
Ona, WV 25545

Dear Parent:

On February 22, the Physical Education Department of Cabell Midland High School will be sponsoring a ski trip to Timberline Resort. Students and chaperones will meet at the school and will be transported to the resort via West Virginia Coach, Inc. Your son/daughter has been given a trip itinerary, parent permission form, and further information about the trip. I hope many of our students will be able to participate in the activity. If you have any questions, please feel free to call me at my office. The number there is 555-7415.

Sincerely,

Bane McCracken

Permission Form

I/We give our permission for our son/daughter _____ to travel to Timberline Ski Resort and go skiing, in the company of other students and the trip sponsor, Bane McCracken. The group will leave Sunday, February 22, at 6:00 A.M. and return Sunday, February 22, at about 10:00 P.M.

I/We hereby release and agree to the indemnity of the trip sponsor, Cabell Midland High School, the Cabell County Board of Education, and their employees from all claims and responsibility of my child during this trip and give my permission for said child to be treated at any hospital/emergency care facility in case of emergency illness or injury.

Dated this _____ day of _____, 200_____

Father's signature _____

Mother's signature _____

Legal guardian's signature _____

Insurance _____ # _____

Emergency phone # _____

Student Ski Rental Information Form

Name _____

Height _____ Weight _____ Shoe size _____ Sex _____ Ski experience _____

Age _____ Do you want a free ski lesson? _____

Figure 5.3   Parent letter, permission form, and ski trip information.

Ski Trip Information

Cost

Equipment rental (skis, boots, poles), breakage insurance on equipment, and a lift ticket: $35.00

Transportation $20.00

Total $55.00

Seats on the bus are limited and will be reserved by payment in full on a first-come, first-served basis. **There will be no refunds unless the trip is canceled!** Please make checks payable to Cabell Midland High School. Students will need to bring additional money for food during the day, and a change of clothes for the ride home, as ski clothes will most likely be wet. **In the event of bad weather, call 555-7415 for current information about trip status.**

Itinerary

5:30 A.M. Check in at Midland High School.

6:00 A.M. Bus leaves. **Don't be late, we will not wait one second!**

10:00 A.M. Arrive Timberline. Check in and ski.

4:30 P.M. Finish last run and return equipment.

4:30 to 5:00 P.M. Change clothes and board bus.

5:00 P.M. Bus leaves: **If you are not on the bus, we will leave without you!**

6:00 P.M. Dinner in Elkins.

10:00 P.M. Bus arrives at Cabell Midland (time is approximate).

Figure 5.3 *(continued)*

group. The recommended procedure is to collect all student fees in advance. The money is deposited in a club fund and one check is written for the group. Additional savings are possible by using the school's tax exempt status.

Seats are limited to the size of the vehicle. Arrangements for transportation must be made in advance, and students reserve their seats by payment in full. When all seats are taken, a waiting list is made in the event a student is not able to go. Those on the waiting list are used as replacements and fees are refunded. Most of the trips are full long before the day of the trip, and students on the waiting list meet the bus hoping someone has a last-minute change of plans.

Over the years hundreds of our students have taken part in our field trips. Many have gone white-water rafting, skiing, backpacking, or mountain biking for the first time as a result of the physical education program. Many have continued to participate in these activities as adults. It is not uncommon for me to encounter a former student on the ski slope who reminds me of his or her first ski trip with our school. The trips promote physical activity, and

Members of the CMHS physical education classes rafting the New River.

they are enjoyable for the students, other chaperones, and me, but there are additional benefits. Many of our students know very little about our area's geography, the economy, the transportation system, and recreation and employment opportunities. Physical education lessons include map identification, budgets, anatomy, proper diet, safety, first aid, survival, and training techniques. Other faculty members have realized the educational opportunities and have taken advantage of the students' excitement to make assignments related to the physical education–sponsored event.

AFTER-SCHOOL ACTIVITIES

In our physical education program, participation is 50 percent of a student's grade. When a student is absent, he or she has the opportunity to make up the missed time. In the past we gave students written assignments as a means of making up missed class time. But the students are missing physical activity. Why not give them the opportunity to be physically active to make up for missed class time? I started the policy of giving my students the option of staying after school and joining me in some form of physical activity. When the weather is nice, we go for a bike ride, jog, or walk. In bad weather we use the exercise machines in the wellness center or go to the weight room. I exercise at this time of day anyway, so I'm not doing anything different. The only requirement is a permission form similar to the one used for field trips, and that the students make appointments. Days are scheduled as needed; normally one day a week is all that is necessary. It has never been necessary to have more than two days in any week. The num-

Charlie was in his second year of high school, but had yet to pass one class. It was his third attempt at passing physical education. Charlie was not slow; he lacked interest and motivation. A white-water rafting trip was planned for the class in early October. Charlie expressed a desire to take part. He was told that in order to go on the trip, he must have a passing grade in physical education. He reluctantly began to participate, completed his assignments, and passed a white-water quiz in order to qualify.

I made sure Charlie was in my raft. He was sometimes a discipline problem, and I wanted to keep an eye on him. I also wanted to make sure he got a great ride, so I placed him in the front of the boat. The Lower Gaulley River offers a great white-water experience. Charlie's screams of excitement could be heard on every rapid. He had the ride of his life. After the trip we returned to the lodge to take a hot shower, put on dry clothes, and get a bite to eat before the trip home. I was talking to Paul, the owner of Mountain River Tours, when Charlie came by. I introduced Charlie to Paul, and Paul asked if he had a good time. Charlie was so excited he could hardly speak. "This is awesome, I had a blast, I want to do this again, how do you become a raft guide?" said Charlie in one breath. Paul smiled and told Charlie that in order to be a raft guide he needed to be a good student and graduate from high school. Paul then turned to me and in front of Charlie asked, "Is he a good student?" "He's getting better," I responded. At the end of the semester, Charlie's lowest grade was a "C".

ber of students participating varies but is always small. The smaller number allows me to develop a better relationship with my students, and they get to see their physical education teacher practicing what he preaches: exercise and stay fit.

STAFF AND COMMUNITY PHYSICAL ACTIVITY OPPORTUNITIES

I bring a mountain bike to school to go for a ride or work out at the end of classes. Biking is a great way to stay in shape, and occasionally I get in good enough shape to enter a local race. Several of our students have taken up mountain biking, and some are very good competitive riders. We began taking rides together. The students would show me new trails, and I would show them the ones I was familiar with. During the mountain bike unit of the outdoor recreation class, other students would ask to join. I would have them call their parents to be sure they had permission, and we would hit the trail. Sometimes there are only two or three of us; at other times there may be 20 or more. The bike rides have been such a positive activity that I

decided to expand them to include more students.

The after-school bike rides attracted the attention of some of our staff. Their fitness levels were not adequate to keep up with the kids, they didn't know how to shift gears or use the brakes, and they weren't sure they could still ride, but they wanted to try mountain biking. I spent a few days one week showing interested staff members some bike techniques. A few have purchased their own bikes, and the bikes that belong to the school are now available on request.

Opportunities From Grants

Organizations that provide funding through grants to promote physical activity for their staffs and members of the community exist throughout the country. In our area the West Virginia Department of Education through the Office of Healthy Schools provided some of the funds to purchase equipment in the wellness center and additional funds for staffing. The Public Employees Insurance Agency (PEIA) is a source of funds and promotional programs. These grants have allowed us to staff the wellness center at night for members of the community.

Our school's wellness center is always open for two hours after the end of school for staff members. The center contains two treadmills, two exercise bikes, two Airdynes, two NordicTracks, two StairMasters, three Concept Rowers, four step machines, one cross aerobic machine, and one combination Nautilus equipment for dips and pull-ups. However, few staff members take advantage of this facility.

The physical education department has tried a variety of programs to encourage the staff and community to use our facilities. Opening the wellness center and allowing people to exercise on their own was poorly attended even though over 40 people paid $40 to join. Some came once and never returned. Aerobics classes were more successful. Programs seem to be more successful with specific instructions and an adult leader. Our most successful program is a combination of step aerobics, dumbbells, stretch cords, abdominal exercises, and stretching. The program starts at the same time three days a week. Instructors are paid through grants obtained through the PEIA programs.

Opportunities From Outside Agencies

Physical activity promotions have also come from outside agencies. As chair of the physical education department, I serve as the on-site coordinator for these agencies.

One of our promotions, the Walk Across West Virginia, is promoted by the West Virginia Coalition for Physical Activity. Organizations participate in a walking program and keep track of their total miles. The objective is to accumulate 280 miles, the distance necessary to walk across the state.

Another promotion, March into May, is sponsored by the national Centers for Disease Control and Prevention and the American Alliance for Health, Physical Education, Recreation and Dance (AAHPERD). This program organizes teams among faculty members. The goal is to change the exercise habits of the faculty and staff. Team members complete an exercise evaluation and are rated according to the amount of daily exercise. The team leader keeps records and organizes the team to encourage team members to meet and exercise together on a regular basis. Each team member may receive small incentives provided by

the event organizer with the support of local businesses. The reward may be a T-shirt or flower. The team with the greatest change at the end of the program is awarded a dinner at a local restaurant.

How much effect our programs have had in encouraging changes in staff activity habits is difficult to determine. Some of those who exercise regularly may have started as a result of one of our programs, and many continue to exercise as a result of the convenience of having a fitness center at our school. Additional change in activity habits among staff as a result of any promotional program is likely to be small. After several years, our staff received enough incentives to be sufficiently motivated. Those who still refuse to be active may make changes only after drastic measures, such as a life-threatening illness.

Family Fun and Fitness Night

Family Fun and Fitness Night had been mentioned several times on the physical education list serve of Virginia Tech. One of my colleagues and I decided to try such a program at the high school level. The purpose was to meet the CDC's objective of promoting physical activity through family involvement. The plan was for students to bring one or both of their parents back to school in the evening for a night of fun and physical activity.

Family Fun Nights were every Tuesday for six weeks. The first night included introductions and explanations, health screenings, wellness center demonstrations, and a walking tour of the school. The evening concluded with a stretching demonstration, participation, and relaxation. The evenings for the following five weeks started with a short presentation by a guest speaker and an activity for the whole group. The participants could then choose from a variety of activities, such as line dancing, aerobics, roller blading, table tennis, yo-yos, volleyball, basketball, the wellness center, and much more. The choice of available activities changed each week, but the format stayed the same. Each night concluded with the entire group participating in a stretching and relaxation activity. The event went well and was well attended by members of the community. However, the goal was to bring parents and children together to be physically active, and student attendance was low. It seems that students at this age would rather not spend time with their parents, and would rather participate in activities with their peers. The family fun and fitness night is better suited for the middle and elementary age group.

CONCLUSION

Lack of physical activity is a national problem and getting worse. Promoting a more active populace is a challenge that physical education programs should readily accept. The program at Cabell Midland High School has received national recognition for its example.

Nevertheless, the respect of our fellow teachers at the school may be a more significant accomplishment. Students not enrolled in physical education classes are still taking part in physical education programs. Learning is stimulated when teachers coordinate their lessons with activities initiated by physical education and members of the community become more involved with the school. Physical education in our school is not viewed as glorified recess, but as a significant contributor to the educational community. The local photographer who records our school's special events summed it up best when he said, "I love to come to this school; there's always something going on, and the physical education department is at the center."

part II

Sample Units

Now that we have developed a framework for changes in secondary physical education, let's get down to the nuts and bolts: unit plans. In Part II theory is put into practice. **Chapter 6** provides forms you may use in all units and describes how you can organize your classes. **Chapters 7** through **14** provide unit plans for different activities; and each unit includes objectives, lesson plans, and reproducible forms for students' assignments that can be used to develop assessment portfolios.

chapter 6

Putting It All Together

West Virginia requires one credit of physical education for all students in grades 9 through 12. At Cabell Midland High School, the block schedule allows students to receive one credit per semester. Students take Introduction to Physical Education as freshmen or sophomores to meet this requirement. The objective of the intro course is to expose students to a wide variety of diverse competitive and noncompetitive activities and help them develop basic skills in each. The intro units include aerobics, personal fitness, weight training, archery, roller blading, orienteering, mountain biking, golf, tennis, softball, basketball, and volleyball. Students are encouraged to develop mastery-level skills by taking elective courses. Elective courses are available to upper-class students after they have completed the required introductory class. The elective courses are Conditioning and Weight Training, Team Sports, Outdoor Recreation, Individual and Dual Sports, Aerobics, and Personal Fitness.

Each semester brings a new group of students to the gym for their physical education classes, and each semester requires redistribution of lockers, inventory of equipment and supplies, assignment of teacher instructional areas, and explanations of procedures and expectations. Two days are required for administrative duties and opening procedures. Classes begin in earnest on day three.

Students need to understand that the objective of physical education classes is to help them identify activities that meet their individual fitness needs so they will be able to enjoy the activity now and understand what they need to do to continue to participate in the activity as adults. Therefore, the introduction to all classes involves fitness assessment. If students are unfamiliar with fitness concepts, a week may be required to learn about muscular strength, muscular endurance, cardiovascular fitness, flexibility, body composition, and the relationship of each to physical activity. If students are already familiar with fitness concepts, a one-day review of the components may be all that's necessary.

During the first week of class the students may complete the following:

1. Pacing guide (form 6.1 on p. 62)
2. Body composition analysis form (form 6.2 on p. 63)
3. Flexibility and muscular strength and endurance form (form 6.3 on p. 64)

Information gathered in the first week is used for the entire class. Students are provided a rubric (form 6.4) and an activity pyramid (form 6.5) for each activity, and the individual fitness data is compared and analyzed. Students use their personal fitness data to help them learn to identify activities that meet their fitness needs, to understand the fitness requirements of an activity, and to investigate methods of improving performance in an activity by improving their individual fitness. Once fitness assessment is completed, instruction of individual units of study begins.

When planning a unit with a lifetime fitness approach, you need to consider the elements discussed in chapter 2. In addition, you also need to address the following factors, which help to make any physical education class efficient and effective:

1. Provide an environment that is safe and nonthreatening.

2. Make efficient use of time. Encourage time on task.
3. Keep students actively engaged in learning. No students should wait for a turn to learn.
4. Use multiple instructional strategies to provide for individual students' learning styles, talents, and ability levels.
5. Provide physical activity opportunity.
6. Provide for review and reflection.

Few programs have the facilities, space, and equipment necessary to keep all students actively engaged in the same activity all the time. A combination of activities involving both large and small groups or teams and learning stations provides a format that helps make the best use of limited space and equipment. Table 6.1 shows the block format for scheduling a physical education class and can help in your planning. The rest of this chapter explains the activities and the rationales for each block of the schedule.

CHANGING FOR CLASS

Students arriving for class go directly to the dressing facility, change into appropriate attire, and report to a designated area. At their designated area, students go to a portable file box containing their portfolios. While waiting for others to finish dressing and class to begin, students may complete or review previous assignments in their portfolios or view and critique videos from the previous day. Roll call is not necessary since portfolios that remain in the file box indicate students who are absent.

GREETINGS AND THE EDUCATIONAL SET

Many of our students come into our classes under stress. Abusive parents, divorce, and other poor home situations are very serious deterrents to learning. Other students have less serious situations—girl- or boyfriend problems, poor test scores—but are under stress nonetheless. As teachers we can do very little to help improve many of these situations, but we can keep from making them worse. The number one

Table 6.1 Daily Schedule: Block Format

Time	Activity
	I. Change for class

5 min	II. Greetings and educational set (happy music—invite students to bring or compose music for the class)
	    A. Hand shake, high fives, low fives, cross fives, etc. (students may create their own special greetings)
	    B. Active review from last week

5 min	III. Warm-up (whole brain/cross brain activities with baroque music)
	    A. Neck rolls, owl
	    B. Lazy eights, elephants
	    C. Cross crawls: seated, simultaneously move one arm and opposite leg in varied directions; behind-body, opposite foot crawl; slow-motion crawl; skipping cross crawl, eyes closed; cross-crawl sit-ups
	    D. Foot flex, calf pump, grounder
	    E. Hook, Xs

10 min	IV. Instruction and demonstration A. Initial instructions and daily lesson

10 min	V. Whole group drills/activities (lively music)
	    A. Relays
	    B. Tag games
	    C. Whole group drills
	    D. 10-min review of section IV

	VI. Group learning stations (lively music) (Time for parts VI and VII depends on number of students and number of groups.)
	    A. Skills (individual)
	    B. Skills (team/partner)
	    C. Sport-specific fitness/strength
	    D. Technology
	    E. Self-evaluation
	    F. Portfolio
	    G. Limited competition
	    H. Video/video review

	VII. Group fitness (house-rocking music)
	    A. Dumbbells
	    B. Stretch cords
	    C. Aerobics/steps
	    D. Belly burners

10 min	VIII. Cool-down and closure (baroque music)
	    A. Flexibility
	    B. Daily review
	    C. Final review
	    D. Next day instructions

15 min	IX. Change for next class

Pacing Guide

Instructions

1. Calculate your maximum pulse rate (220 – age).
2. Determine 60, 70, 80, and 90% of your maximum pulse.
3. Use a pulse monitor and record data below.
4. Continue until your pulse level reaches 80% (you may stop before then).
5. Stop when your pulse reaches 90%.

Workout intensity using 400-meter track

Laps 1 and 2: Walk at a leisurely pace (5–6 min per lap)

Time lap 1: _____ sec   Pulse lap 1: _____ bpm

Time lap 2: _____ sec   Pulse lap 2: _____ bpm

Laps 3 and 4: Walk at a brisk pace (4 min per lap)

Time lap 3: _____ sec   Pulse lap 3: _____ bpm

Time lap 4: _____ sec   Pulse lap 4: _____ bpm

Laps 5 and 6: Slow jog (3:00–3:30 per lap)

Time lap 5: _____ sec   Pulse lap 5: _____ bpm

Time lap 6: _____ sec   Pulse lap 6: _____ bpm

Laps 7 and 8: Jog (2:30–2:45 per lap)

Time lap 7: _____ sec   Pulse lap 7: _____ bpm

Time lap 8: _____ sec   Pulse lap 8: _____ bpm

Laps 9 and 10: Easy run (2:00–2:15 min per lap)

Time lap 9: _____ sec   Pulse lap 9: _____ bpm

Time lap 10: _____ sec   Pulse lap 10: _____ bpm

Laps 11 and 12: Run (1:30–1:45 sec per lap)

Time lap 11: _____ sec   Pulse lap 11: _____ bpm

Time lap 12: _____ sec   Pulse lap 12: _____ bpm

Your ideal pace: _____ sec per lap

Your ideal pace per mile: _____ min _____ sec

From *It's Not Just Gym Anymore: Teaching Secondary School Students How to Be Active for Life* by Bane McCracken, 2001, Champaign, IL: Human Kinetics.

Body Composition Analysis

Name: _____   Date: _____

	First	**Second**	**Third**	**Average**
Triceps	_____	_____	_____	_____
Calf	_____	_____	_____	_____

Sum of skinfold measurements is _____ + _____ = _____
                                 Triceps   Calf
                                 average   average

Body Fat

Males

A. $\dfrac{\rule{3cm}{0.4pt}}{\text{sum of skinfolds}} \times 0.735 =$ _____

B. Write down 1.0   <u>1.0</u>

C. Percent body fat = A + B = _____

Females

A. $\dfrac{\rule{3cm}{0.4pt}}{\text{sum of skinfolds}} \times 0.610 =$ _____

B. Write down 5.1   <u>5.1</u>

C. Percent body fat = A + B = _____

From *It's Not Just Gym Anymore: Teaching Secondary School Students How to Be Active for Life* by Bane McCracken, 2001, Champaign, IL: Human Kinetics.
Equation from Slaughter, M.H., et. al, 1988, "Skinfold equations for estimations of body fatness in children and youth," *Human Biology* 60:709.

Flexibility and Muscular Strength and Endurance Statistics

Flexibility Measurements

Sit and reach: _____ in.

Trunk: _____ in.

Shoulders: _____ in.

Total: _____ in.

Total flexibility in inches:

30 in. = poor

35 in. = fair

40 in. = good

45 in. and up = excellent

Muscular Strength and Endurance Statistics

Male

Lean body weight _____

Number of flat bench reps _____

Female

75% of lean body weight _____

Number of flat bench reps _____

From *It's Not Just Gym Anymore: Teaching Secondary School Students How to Be Active for Life* by Bane McCracken, 2001, Champaign, IL: Human Kinetics.

Fitness Rubric for _____

Name: _____   Date: _____

Fitness benefits	0	1	2	3	4	5
Muscular strength						
Muscular endurance						
Flexibility						
Caloric consumption						
Cardiovascular						

Fitness requirements	0	1	2	3	4	5
Muscular strength						
Muscular endurance						
Flexibility						
Caloric consumption						
Cardiovascular						

Are you ready for _____? Rate your fitness level for _____

Personal rating	0	1	2	3	4	5
Muscular strength						
Muscular endurance						
Flexibility						
Body composition						
Cardiovascular						

From *It's Not Just Gym Anymore: Teaching Secondary School Students How to Be Active for Life* by Bane McCracken, 2001, Champaign, IL: Human Kinetics.

Activity Pyramid

Name: _____   Date: _____

In what activity pyramid zone does _____ belong?

Red Zone
90–100% MHR
Once per week,
5–10 min

Power Zone
80–95% MHR
Twice per week, 10–15 min

Kick-it Zone
70–85% MHR
Three times per week, 30 min

Healthy Zone
50–70% MHR
Five times per week, 30 min

Fat Burning Zone
40–50% MHR
Six times per week, 60 min

From *It's Not Just Gym Anymore: Teaching Secondary School Students How to Be Active for Life* by Bane McCracken, 2001, Champaign, IL: Human Kinetics.

priority of the brain is survival, and stress is a very real threat. When stressed, the brain goes into a survival mode called "fight or flight." In fight-or-flight mode learning becomes difficult if not impossible. Taking the time to greet students as they enter the facility or gym is well worth the time. Beginning class with a formal greeting is even more effective in establishing a good environment.

Conduct a formal greeting at the beginning of the first class. Instruct the students to stand on a line facing you. Light, cheerful music is playing. Begin at one end of the line. Have the first student tell you her name and then shake his or her hand, smile, and welcome him or her to class. As you proceed down the line, the students previously greeted follow and greet other students. In only a few minutes you have greeted all students, and all students have greeted each other. This activity is an excellent way to learn students' names at the beginning of a semester. A warm smile and a heartfelt welcome puts the students at ease and promotes a better atmosphere. Continue this procedure for the first week, then change the greeting; high fives, low fives, or special student-generated greetings can be used, a new greeting for each week. After the first four or five weeks it is no longer necessary to do the greeting each day. Greetings may be exchanged two or three days a week or upon request. Students' reactions are very favorable, and it is not unusual for a student to request that class begin with the greeting. Frequently, a student has approached me before class and said, "I'm having a bad day, can we do a greeting? That always makes me feel better." As soon as the greeting is concluded, students go to instructional lines, and a quick review of material from the previous week is conducted.

This is a good time to conduct an active review of the previous week's activity. Weekly reviews help keep students focused on the essential course material. Active review may consist of a kinesthetic vocabulary session in which students act out the meaning of words, or having students review the steps of shooting a foul shot or redefine the parts of fitness.

WARM-UP FOR THE BRAIN

Typically, physical education classes begin with a warm-up. When the muscles are warm, we

are ready for action. However, when classes are to begin with an instructional section, it is a good idea to warm up the brain. Cross-lateral actions involving the eyes, ears, arms, and legs awaken both sides of the brain and help the students get ready to learn. In his book *Brain Gym,* Paul Dennison provides a complete set of cross-lateral brain warm-ups that are an excellent way to begin class. These exercises include the elephant, lazy eights, the cross crawl, and other activities that require the use of both sides of the body in unison.

INSTRUCTION AND DEMONSTRATION

With the students ready, instruction begins. Introduce, demonstrate, refine, and evaluate new skills using a variety of multimedia tools. You can also use this time period to explain daily procedure. Instruct teams or groups where to report during each time period and what to do at each station. Identify daily team leaders at this time.

WHOLE GROUP DRILLS/ACTIVITIES

This time period is used as a warm-up for the entire class. The period may begin with a brisk walk or gentle jog, then progress to more intense activities such as relays or tag games. During a basketball unit, for example, students may participate in a dribble relay; during a tennis unit they may dribble with a tennis racket. A bicycle unit may have the students pedal slowly and try to come to a stop without touching their feet to the ground. When the drills are completed, conduct a short review of instruction for the day.

GROUP LEARNING STATIONS

Few physical education teaching situations allow all students to be actively engaged in the same activity at the same time. Large classes with 40 or more students require 10 or more tennis courts or several volleyball courts. However, placing some students in the bleachers to sit and watch is unacceptable. No student should have to wait for a turn to learn! Dividing classes into groups and using learning stations allows for the best use of limited space and equipment. Facility space should be divided and appropriate materials placed in all areas. Divide the class into cooperative teams that work together and move from station to station at intervals you have established. The size and number of teams should depend on class load, facilities, and available equipment.

Divide the space available appropriately, and have a different activity take place in each. The following is a list of stations and a brief description of the activity for each:

1. Individual skill development: Students work individually on such activities as free throw shooting, hitting a golf ball, or a tennis serve.

2. Skill development for teams or partner: Students work in pairs or groups on such activities as a volleyball pass, team plays for basketball, or tennis volley.

3. Sport-specific fitness: Students work on fitness activities designed to improve performance for a particular activity. The activities may include the use of dumbbells or stretch cords to develop strength, aerobics for cardiovascular fitness, or stretching. The fitness station should focus on developing fitness specific for that activity.

4. Technology: Students use technology to enhance learning or complete assignments. Computers may be used for students to record data or complete assignments related to Web sites.

5. Self/partner evaluation: Students take time to reflect on their skill execution and complete designated forms.

6. Portfolios: Students complete assignments in their portfolios.

7. Limited competition: Students may participate in competitive activities. However, competition should be limited. Participation, fitness, and fun are emphasized; keeping score is discouraged. Students may wear pulse monitors and record pulse levels upon completion of the activity. If declaring a winner is necessary, the team with the highest total pulse should be declared the winner. Traditional competition is seldom used during intro classes; instead it should be reserved for advanced classes during elective courses.

8. Video and video review: This station is split into two areas. At the first area students record their actions while performing a skill. At the second area they view and critique their actions.

The number of stations used each day may vary depending on the activity and the number of students. All stations are not used each day. Larger classes may need more stations than smaller classes, and more stations for skill development may be desirable at the beginning of a unit. At the end of a unit or before the end of a grading period, you may allot more time for students to complete work in their portfolios. Determine the time spent at each station by the number of stations. Have the groups rotate from station to station and complete assignments at each.

GROUP FITNESS

The group fitness period focuses on developing overall strength and cardiovascular fitness. Activities include dumbbells and stretch cords for strength development, and aerobics, step aerobics, walking, or jogging for cardiovascular fitness. The fitness activities at this time slot should work to complement the fitness activities undertaken at the group learning stations.

COOL-DOWN AND CLOSURE

This block in the schedule has four objectives. First is the physiological objective. Students have been participating in vigorous physical activity, and their muscles have built up large amounts of lactic acid. Continuing gentle physical activity such as walking or light aerobics helps the body eliminate lactic acid and speeds recovery.

The second objective of this block is psychological. A great way to end a good workout is by properly cooling down. Gently walking and visiting with other students is enjoyable, and listening to classical music from the Baroque period is soothing because it closely matches the body rhythms. Ending a workout on a good note makes it easier to work out the next time. Cooling down also helps students calm down and get ready for the next class period.

The third objective is pedagogical. Students have been physically active, and their brains are filled with oxygen. Because they have been using both sides of their bodies, both sides of their brains are stimulated. This is a great time to conduct a review and prepare students for the next day's instructions.

The final objective of the cool-down and closure block is flexibility. Developing and maintaining flexibility is critically important for injury prevention and continued physical activity as adults. Because warm muscles stretch best, stretching at the end of classes is the best way to develop flexibility. Upon completion of the stretches, excuse the class to the dressing rooms with a brief evaluation of their performance. The evaluation should be positive and include a comment about some specific action that the class performed well. "This was a great class today; you did a really good job during the fitness activities," is an example of a proper ending.

CHANGE FOR THE NEXT CLASS

The amount of time allotted for changing clothes at the end of class depends on the activity of the day. Fifteen minutes is generally enough time. However, during very hot weather or after vigorous activities, many students may want to shower. In that case, more time may be necessary. Encourage students to dress quickly and then report to their designated areas in the main gym to wait for the bell.

ADAPTING FOR NONBLOCK SCHEDULES

The class format described in this chapter is designed to take advantage of a block sched-

ule with class periods of 90 minutes. Allocating 20 minutes per day for students to change and 10 minutes total for warm-up and cool-down leaves 60 minutes of actual class time. The format may be applied to nonblock classes with some modifications. Students still need time to change clothes before and after class regardless of schedule alignment, and proper warm-ups and cool-downs are highly recommended. A 45-minute class that allows only 15 minutes for changing and takes 10 minutes to follow proper warm-up and cool-down procedures leaves only 20 minutes for actual class time. Therefore, it would take at least three 45-minute classes to equal one 90-minute class. A weekly schedule may be more appropriate (see table 6.2).

CONCLUSION

Providing a safe environment, keeping students actively engaged, using multiple strategies, providing physical activity, reviewing, and reflecting may be accomplished by using the format provided in tables 6.1 and 6.2. Students begin to work as soon as class starts by collecting their portfolios, and a nonthreatening environment is encouraged during the greeting. Making use of learning stations compensates for lack of equipment and is conducive to the use of multiple strategies. Physical activity is provided throughout much of the class period and may be regulated to meet the needs of each student by using pulse monitors. The cool-down period allows for the students to reflect on the day's activities and provides an opportunity for you to conduct a review and prepare the students for future activities.

The following chapters provide lesson plans and reproducible portfolio forms. My lesson plans provide the basic outline of what should be covered, but you will also combine the use of learning stations, warm-up activities, and the like, and table 6.1 shows you how much time to devote to each activity as well as how it all fits together. You can use my lesson plans as I've provided them, or you can adjust the lessons by using table 6.1 or table 6.2.

Table 6.2 Weekly Schedule: Adapting for a Nonblock Schedule

Monday	Tuesday	Wednesday and Thursday	Friday
I. Greetings and educational set (happy music) A. Handshake, high fives, low fives, cross fives, etc. (students may create their own special greetings) B. Active review from last week	I. Warm-up (whole brain/cross brain activities with baroque music) A. Neck rolls, owl B. Lazy eights, elephants C. Cross crawls: seated, simultaneously move one arm and opposite leg in varied directions; behind-body, opposite-foot crawl; slow-motion crawl; skipping cross crawl; eyes closed, cross crawl sit-ups D. Foot flex, calf pump, grounder E. Hook, X's	I. Warm-up (whole brain/cross brain activities with baroque music) A. Neck rolls, owl B. Lazy eights, elephants C. Cross crawls: seated, simultaneously move one arm and opposite leg in varied directions; behind-body, opposite-foot crawl; slow-motion crawl; skipping cross crawl; eyes closed; cross crawl sit-ups D. Foot flex, calf pump, grounder E. Hook, X's	The final day of the week could be used to review or to cover areas not yet given proper attention. I find it best to leave Fridays open or just penciled in. Changes in the schedule and other interruptions make Friday a good catch-up day to do what didn't get done earlier in the week.
II. Warm-up (whole brain/cross brain activities with baroque music) A. Neck rolls, owl B. Lazy eights, elephants C. Cross crawls: seated, simultaneously move one arm and the opposite leg in varied directions; behind-body, opposite-foot crawl; slow-motion crawl; skipping cross crawl; eyes closed; cross crawl sit-ups D. Foot flex, calf pump, grounder E. Hook, X's	II. Whole group drills/activities (lively music) A. Relays B. Tag games C. Whole group drills D. Review from previous day	II. Instruction and demonstration A. Student groups/teams are assigned stations for the day. Each group participates in only one or two stations each day. Stations remain the same and each team rotates on a daily basis until each group has visited and completed assignments at each station.	

III. Instruction and demonstration
  A. Initial instructions and daily lesson

III. Group fitness (house-rocking music)
  A. Dumbbells
  B. Stretch cords
  C. Aerobics/steps
  D. Belly burners

III. Group learning stations (lively music)
  A. Skills (individual)
  B. Skills (team/partner)
  C. Sport-specific fitness/strength
  D. Technology
  E. Self-evaluation
  F. Portfolio
  G. Limited competition
  H. Video/video review

IV. Whole group drills/activities (lively music)
  A. Relays
  B. Tag games
  C. Whole group drills
  D. 10-min review of section III

IV. Cool-down and closure (baroque music)
  A. Flexibility
  B. Daily review
  C. Final review
  D. At this time, students are assigned groups or teams and given assignments for the stations that they will be participating in the next day.

IV. Cool-down and closure (baroque music)
  A. Flexibility
  B. Daily review
  C. Final review

V. Cool-down and closure (baroque music)
  A. Flexibility
  B. Daily review
  C. Final review
  D. Next day instructions

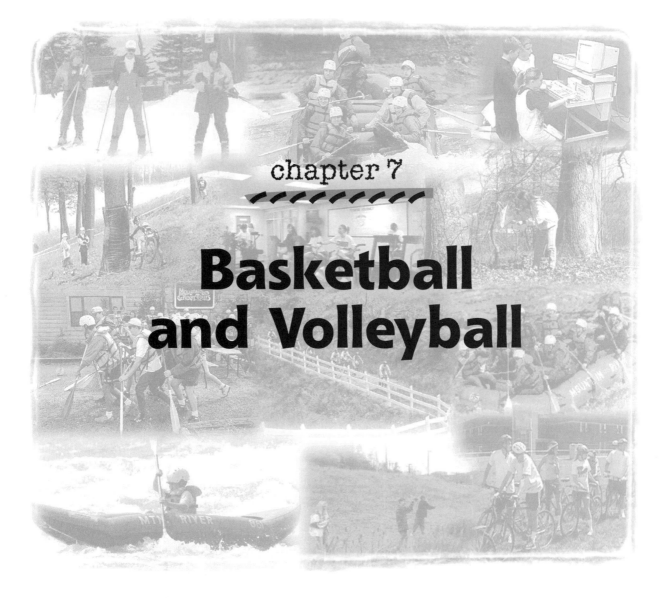

chapter 7

Basketball and Volleyball

Many of the traditional activities of secondary physical education, particularly team sports, are not the kinds of activities adults tend to engage in. This does not mean that team sports need to be eliminated from our programs; however, a change in approach is necessary. Adults often find it difficult to participate in team activities on a regular basis. Commitments to career and family place restrictions on their time and energy and make it difficult to find a group of adults available at the same time. Inactivity and poor fitness is the result. When an opportunity to participate is available, poor fitness makes the experience less enjoyable, and continued participation is unlikely. Adults who maintain a reasonable level of fitness can still enjoy many of the traditional competitive activities. Our lessons therefore must include sport-specific fitness activities that take a minimum amount of time and may be done on an individual basis. The objective is to teach students what they need to do to maintain a level of fitness as they mature that will allow them to continue to participate in the activities they enjoy.

The objectives of a basketball unit are to teach students to

- recognize the fitness benefits of basketball,
- analyze the fitness requirements of basketball,
- develop a personal fitness plan that will help them maintain a level of fitness necessary to continue to participate in basketball as an adult,
- recognize proper technique and methods of improving skill,
- adapt play for lesser skilled and lower fitness levels, and
- locate facilities available for adults.

BASKETBALL

Many of our students would be satisfied if physical education consisted of nothing more than going to the gym and playing basketball. It seems they could play for hours and never want to do anything else. Basketball goals are hung on garages and stationed in every playground. A basketball unit is always popular and eagerly anticipated by most of the students. Before you begin the unit, select teams of at least six students before the unit begins. Team captains are expected to keep teams on task and help other students.

Lesson 1

Introduction to Basketball

1. Pass out basketball portfolios, greet, review the parts of fitness, check roll.
2. Brain warm-up: lazy eights, elephant, cross crawl, walk with big arm swing, skip, calf pump, grounder (see Paul and Gayle Dennison's book, *Brain Gym*)
3. Introduce basketball: game history, basic rules, elements of the game, fitness benefits, and requirements (see form 7.1).
4. Demonstrate passing technique: chest, bounce, overhead. Have each team form a circle and practice after watching the demonstration.
5. Stations: Each team of five to six students goes to a station and rotates until all teams have completed the assignment at each station.
   a. Seven steps to great shooting (form 7.2)
   b. Star passing drill (two teams)
   c. Medicine-ball passing

d. Work on portfolios (form 7.3)
e. Defensive drills (form 7.4)

6. Stretch, review passing technique.

Lesson 2

Basic Skills, Part 1

1. Place portfolio box in designated area, check roll with the portfolios, greet, review passing.
2. Brain warm-up: owl, cross crawls, elephant
3. Dribble relays, run/pass relays (combine two teams)
4. Review passing technique: chest, bounce, overhead. Have each team form a circle and practice after the review.
5. Stations
   a. Seven steps to great shooting
   b. Star passing drill
   c. Medicine-ball shooting over a barrier: Set up volleyball standards and a rope. Students "shoot" a medicine ball over the rope using good technique to strengthen the muscles used for basketball.
   d. Fix up portfolio (enter name, date, and decorate).
   e. Defensive drills
6. Xertubes, or stretch cord, workout
7. Stretch, review passing technique.

Lesson 3

Basic Skills, Part 2

1. Place portfolio box in designated area, check roll with portfolios, greet, give shooting introduction.

2. Brain warm-up: lazy eights, elephant, cross crawl, walk with big arm swing, skip, calf pump, grounder

3. Dribble relays, run/pass relays (combine two teams). Teach figure-eight passing drill.

4. Foul shooting (form 7.5)

5. Stations

   a. Star drill (with a shot or jump shot)

   b. Foul shooting (video students) (form 7.5)

   c. Defensive drills

   d. Medicine-ball shooting

   e. Visit basketball Web site (**www. fitnesslink.com**) or work on portfolios.

6. Belly burners, push-ups, stretch, review passing and shooting

Lesson 4

Layups

1. Place portfolio box in designated area, check roll with portfolios, greet, review shooting. Have students review video of foul shooting from previous lesson.

2. Brain warm-up: lazy eights, elephant, cross crawl, walk with big arm swing, skip, calf pump, grounder

3. Teach how to shoot a layup and video students.

   a. Teams form two lines, go to the basket, shoot layups, rebound, and return to opposite line.

4. Dribble relays, run/pass relays, figure eights, with layup (combine two teams)

5. Stations

   a. Star drill with layup

   b. Free throws (video all students)

   c. Review video image and check evaluation.

   d. Jump plyometrics

   e. Web-site work

6. Dumbbell workout, stretch, review

Lesson 5

Jump Shot

1. Place portfolio box in designated area, check roll with portfolios, greet, review layup.

2. Brain warm-up: lazy eights, elephant, cross crawl, walk with big arm swing, skip, calf pump, grounder

3. Dribble relays, run/pass relays, figure eights, with layup (combine two teams)

4. Stations

   a. Web-site work: **www.fitnesslink.com**. Students use the Web site to view workout programs for basketball.

   b. Watch and evaluate your layup (use form 7.6).

   c. Work on the layup (right and left).

   d. Jump plyometrics

   e. Work on shooting.

5. Xertubes, review, stretch

Lesson 6

Shooting Skills

1. Place portfolio box in designated area, check roll with portfolios, review layup quickly. Tell students that portfolios are due in one week

2. Brain warm-up: lazy eights, elephant, cross crawl, walk with big arm swing, skip, calf pump, grounder

3. Dribble relays, run/pass relays, figure eights, with layup (combine two teams)

4. Stations

   a. Watch and evaluate your layup.

   b. Perform layups (in teams) for immediate feedback (video).

   c. Web-site work (**www.fitnesslink.com**) and portfolio work

   d. Shooting games: Basketball Golf or Beat the Clock (forms 7.7 and 7.8)

   e. Jump plyometrics

5. Push-ups, belly burners, stretch, review

Lesson 7

Team Defense

1. Place portfolio box in designated area, greet, take roll with portfolios, introduce defense.

2. Brain warm-up: lazy eights, elephant, cross crawl, walk with big arm swing, skip, calf pump, grounder

3. Pulse monitors, pulse levels, and pulse check competition. Explain team defensive concepts.

4. Dribble relays, run/pass relays, figure-eight drill

5. Stations

   a. Team defense: passing versus zone shift: One team is in a zone defense and the other on offense. The team on offense passes the ball from player to player to teach the defensive team proper shifting technique.

   b. Shooting games: Basketball Golf or Beat the Clock

   c. Medicine-ball passing and shooting

   d. Dribble and passing obstacle course

   e. Individual defense (one on one) and blocking out

6. Dumbbell workout, stretch, review (include pulse scoring)

Lesson 8

Offense and Defense Strategies

1. Place portfolio box in designated area, greet, review parts of fitness, check roll, collect portfolios.

2. Brain warm-up: lazy eights, elephant, cross crawl, walk with big arm swing, skip, calf pump, grounder

3. Pulse monitors, pulse levels, and pulse check competition

4. Defense review: position and types

5. Dribble relays, run/pass relays, figure-eight drill

6. Teach offense and defense strategies.

7. Stations

   a. Students set up an offense to run against a zone.

   b. Web-site work (**www.fitnesslink.com**)

   c. Defensive footwork with cones

   d. Shooting games (Horse, Gotcha)

   e. Medicine-ball shooting

8. Xertube workout, stretch, review (include pulse scoring)

Lesson 9

Basketball Fitness

1. Place portfolio box in designated area, greet, review parts of fitness, check roll, collect portfolios.

2. Brain warm-up: lazy eights, elephant, cross crawl, walk with big arm swing, skip, calf pump, grounder

3. Pulse monitors, pulse levels, and pulse check competition

4. Dribble relays, run/pass relays, figure-eight drill

5. Passing and layup drills

6. Stations

   a. Shooting games: Basketball Golf or Beat the Clock

   b. Five-on-five

   c. Work on portfolios

   d. Target passing and medicine-ball passing or shooting

7. Push-ups, belly burners, stretch, review (include pulse scoring)

Lesson 10

Completing Assignments

1. Place portfolio box in designated area, greet, review parts of fitness, check roll, collect portfolios.

2. Brain warm-up: lazy eights, elephant, cross crawl, walk with big arm swing, skip, calf pump, grounder

3. Pulse monitors, pulse levels, and pulse check competition

4. Dribble relays, run/pass relays, figure-eight drill

5. Passing and layup drills

6. Stations

   a. Five-on-five

   b. Shooting games

   c. Dribbling and defensive footwork

   d. Work on portfolios. Discuss and complete "Dimensions of Basketball" (form 7.9).

7. Xertube workout, stretch, review (include pulse scoring)

Basketball Study Sheet

Basketball was devised in 1891 by Dr. James A. Naismith, physical education director at the YMCA College in Springfield, Massachusetts, as an outgrowth of a project to create an interesting game to encourage young men to participate in indoor exercise and recreation programs during the winter. The first games were played with a soccer-type ball (some call this a football) using peach baskets as goals. There was no limit to the number of players on a team in these early games. This was soon changed, however, and within a few years the five-player game was accepted for men.

Naismith proposed 13 rules for basketball. The game and these rules were first publicized in 1892 in a YMCA magazine that circulated throughout the country. The game quickly caught on and spread to other YMCA playgrounds and schools. The first intercollegiate game was held in 1896 (Yale versus Connecticut Wesleyan).

In 1892 Senda Berenson of Smith College, recognizing the merits of basketball, modified the rules and introduced the game to Smith's women students. Under the leadership of Berenson, a group of women educators revised some of the original rules and published the *Basketball Guide*, the first such rule book for women, in 1901. These early rules required six players per team rather than five and restricted players' movements to only one division of the court. The court was divided into three parts until 1938, when it was changed to a two-part division. Players assigned to one division could not move into any other division.

In 1962 the roving player was added. This allowed two players to play on both the front and the back court so a team could develop a four-player offense and defense. Finally, in 1971, the rules were revised to reduce the number of players to five and to eliminate most of the differences between women's and men's rules. Nevertheless, some areas of the country still play the six-player divided-court game.

Men's intercollegiate rules were established to govern college play in 1904. Other groups, such as the YMCA and the Amateur Athletics Association, had their own variations. These groups standardized most of the rules for men in 1915, although some minor variations continued to be allowed. With the exception of the three-point play, the major rules for men have not changed much in recent years, although small revisions are made annually by national rules committees for high school and college play. Rules for high school basketball are published annually by the National Federation of State High School Associations. Rules for college men and women are published annually by the National Collegiate Athletic Association.

Basketball requires the development of cardiorespiratory endurance and the fundamental motor skills of balance, agility, and general forms of locomotion such as jumping and running. Arm and shoulder strength in addition to eye-hand coordination are enhanced by the throwing and basket-shooting activities. Leg strength is developed through running as well as jumping. The use of peripheral vision when dribbling or seeking pass outlets is essential and should be encouraged. Conditioning for this sport should begin before the actual games are played. If players have been involved in other vigorous activities such as soccer, speedball, or conditioning exercises, they will be able to participate more fully at the start of the unit. Otherwise, cardiovascular developmental activities should precede game situations.

Seven Steps to Great Shooting

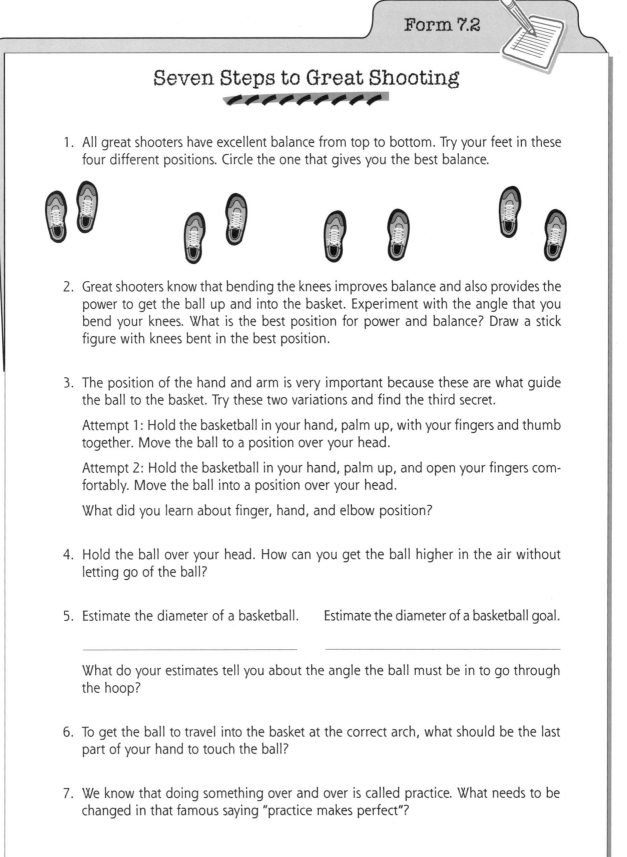

1. All great shooters have excellent balance from top to bottom. Try your feet in these four different positions. Circle the one that gives you the best balance.

2. Great shooters know that bending the knees improves balance and also provides the power to get the ball up and into the basket. Experiment with the angle that you bend your knees. What is the best position for power and balance? Draw a stick figure with knees bent in the best position.

3. The position of the hand and arm is very important because these are what guide the ball to the basket. Try these two variations and find the third secret.

   Attempt 1: Hold the basketball in your hand, palm up, with your fingers and thumb together. Move the ball to a position over your head.

   Attempt 2: Hold the basketball in your hand, palm up, and open your fingers comfortably. Move the ball into a position over your head.

   What did you learn about finger, hand, and elbow position?

4. Hold the ball over your head. How can you get the ball higher in the air without letting go of the ball?

5. Estimate the diameter of a basketball.   Estimate the diameter of a basketball goal.

   _____   _____

   What do your estimates tell you about the angle the ball must be in to go through the hoop?

6. To get the ball to travel into the basket at the correct arch, what should be the last part of your hand to touch the ball?

7. We know that doing something over and over is called practice. What needs to be changed in that famous saying "practice makes perfect"?

From *It's Not Just Gym Anymore: Teaching Secondary School Students How to Be Active for Life* by Bane McCracken, 2001, Champaign, IL: Human Kinetics.

Basketball Worksheet

Name: _____   Block: _____   Date: _____

Fill in the Blank

1. _____ created the game of basketball.

2. The original type of basket used for basketball was a _____ _____.

3. Basketball began in _____ and originated in the _____ _____.

4. Basketball was developed in what city? _____.

True or False

5. _____ When shooting a jump shot, balance and control are more important than gaining maximum height.

6. _____ When performing the bounce pass, you want to aim for a spot less than half the distance of the target.

7. _____ Confidence is the single most important part of free-throw shooting.

8. _____ Muscular endurance is an important part of rebounding.

9. _____ When executing the chest pass, you want to step slightly away from your target.

10. List the correct steps to shooting a free throw in proper order (1–5).

_____ Set shooting foot slightly outside mark.

_____ Think positively off the line.

_____ Take a deep breath and relax.

_____ Perform routine.

_____ Concentrate on target.

From *It's Not Just Gym Anymore: Teaching Secondary School Students How to Be Active for Life* by Bane McCracken, 2001, Champaign, IL: Human Kinetics.

Defensive Drills

1. Foot fire: Work with a partner and count the number of times the right foot hits the floor in 10 sec.

	Day 1	Day 2	Day 3	Day 4
Score 1	_____	_____	_____	_____
Score 2	_____	_____	_____	_____
Score 3	_____	_____	_____	_____

2. Lane slide: Work with a partner and start on the right side of the lane. Slide to the left side of the lane and back 15 times. Record your time.

	Day 1	Day 2	Day 3	Day 4
Score 1	_____	_____	_____	_____
Score 2	_____	_____	_____	_____

3. Two-foot vertical-jump test.

	Day 1	Day 2	Day 3	Day 4
Inches trial 1	_____	_____	_____	_____
Inches trial 2	_____	_____	_____	_____
Inches trial 3	_____	_____	_____	_____

4. One-on-one defense.

From *It's Not Just Gym Anymore: Teaching Secondary School Students How to Be Active for Life* by Bane McCracken, 2001, Champaign, IL: Human Kinetics.

Foul Shooting Self-Evaluation

Name: _____   Date: _____

| **O** = not yet | **X** = getting better | **+** = proper technique |

Preparation phase

	1st day	2nd day	3rd day	
1.	_____	_____	_____	See target
2.	_____	_____	_____	Feet shoulder-width apart
3.	_____	_____	_____	Toes straight
4.	_____	_____	_____	Knees flexed
5.	_____	_____	_____	Shoulders relaxed
6.	_____	_____	_____	Nonshooting hand under ball
7.	_____	_____	_____	Shooting hand behind ball
8.	_____	_____	_____	Thumb relaxed
9.	_____	_____	_____	Elbow in
10.	_____	_____	_____	Ball between ear and shoulder

Execution phase

	1st day	2nd day	3rd day	
1.	_____	_____	_____	See target
2.	_____	_____	_____	Extend knees, back, shoulders
3.	_____	_____	_____	Extend elbow
4.	_____	_____	_____	Flex wrist and fingers forward
5.	_____	_____	_____	Release off index finger
6.	_____	_____	_____	Balance hand on ball until release
7.	_____	_____	_____	Even rhythm

Follow-through phase

	1st day	2nd day	3rd day	
1.	_____	_____	_____	See target
2.	_____	_____	_____	Extend arm
3.	_____	_____	_____	Index finger points to target
4.	_____	_____	_____	Shooting hand palm down
5.	_____	_____	_____	Balancing hand palm up

From *It's Not Just Gym Anymore: Teaching Secondary School Students How to Be Active for Life* by Bane McCracken, 2001, Champaign, IL: Human Kinetics.

Layup Self-Evaluation

Name: _____   Date: _____

| O = not yet | X = getting better | + = proper technique |

Preparation phase

	1st day	2nd day	3rd day	
1.	_____	_____	_____	See target
2.	_____	_____	_____	Short step
3.	_____	_____	_____	Dip knee
4.	_____	_____	_____	Shoulders relaxed
5.	_____	_____	_____	Nonshooting hand under ball
6.	_____	_____	_____	Shooting hand behind ball
7.	_____	_____	_____	Elbow in
8.	_____	_____	_____	Ball between ear and shoulder

Execution phase

	1st day	2nd day	3rd day	
1.	_____	_____	_____	Lift shooting knee
2.	_____	_____	_____	Jump
3.	_____	_____	_____	Extend leg, back, shoulders
4.	_____	_____	_____	Extend elbow
5.	_____	_____	_____	Flex wrist and fingers forward
6.	_____	_____	_____	Release off index finger
7.	_____	_____	_____	Balance hand on ball until release
8.	_____	_____	_____	Even rhythm

From *It's Not Just Gym Anymore: Teaching Secondary School Students How to Be Active for Life* by Bane McCracken, 2001, Champaign, IL: Human Kinetics.

Basketball Golf

Name: _____   *Block:* _____   *Date:* _____

Rules Shoot from each spot until you make it. Record the number of shots it takes on the form.

Scoring:

Eagle = 2 under par

Birdy = 1 under par

Bogey = 1 over par

Double bogey = 2 over par

Shot record:

1 _____   6 _____

2 _____   7 _____

3 _____   8 _____

4 _____   9 _____

5 _____

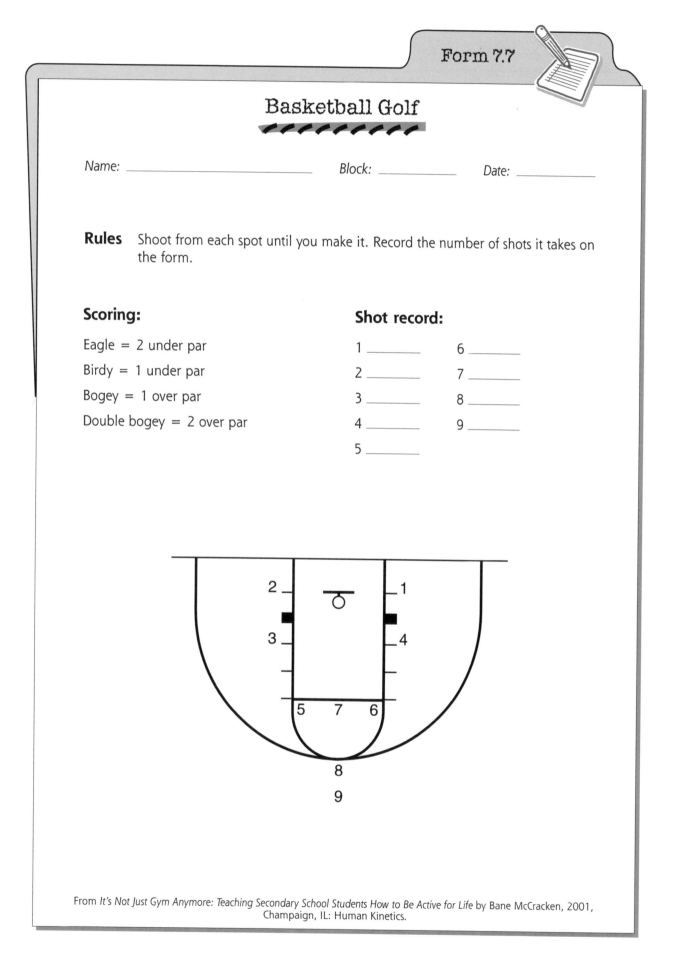

Beat the Clock: One-Minute Basketball Shooting Drills

Name: _____   Block: _____   Date: _____

Shooting Drills	Date	Score
1. Right-hand layup, stationary		
2. Left-hand layup, stationary		
3. Layup, run to foul line, return		
4. Alternating sides: layups from right side, then left		
5. Foul shots, rebound, repeat		
6. Side-to-side shots (alternate each shot from corner of foul line)		

From *It's Not Just Gym Anymore: Teaching Secondary School Students How to Be Active for Life* by Bane McCracken, 2001, Champaign, IL: Human Kinetics.

Dimensions of Basketball

Name: _____ Date: _____

1. What do you need to know to play basketball? List at least five items in their order of importance.

2. What other activities have you done that are similar to basketball? List five.

3. Choose one of the activities you listed above and tell how it is similar to basketball.

4. Let's play. Make a plan to play basketball (who, when, where, how).

5. Now that you have finished the unit, what did you learn?

From *It's Not Just Gym Anymore: Teaching Secondary School Students How to Be Active for Life* by Bane McCracken, 2001, Champaign, IL: Human Kinetics.

The objectives of a volleyball unit are to teach students to

- recognize the fitness benefits of volleyball,
- analyze the fitness requirements of volleyball,
- develop a personal fitness plan that will help them maintain a level of fitness necessary to continue to participate in volleyball as an adult,
- recognize proper technique and methods of improving skill,
- adapt play for lesser skilled and lower fitness levels, and
- locate facilities available for adults.

VOLLEYBALL

Although basketball is the most popular physical education activity, especially among boys, volleyball is a close second, and the popularity of the sport is growing. Many schools offer volleyball as an athletic event, and more nets are being erected in playgrounds, parks, and backyards. Providing students with the skills and knowledge to play volleyball will help make them lifelong participants.

Lesson 1

Introduction to Volleyball/ Forearm Pass

1. Greet students, hand out portfolios, and attend to administrative duties while students label their portfolios.
2. Brain warm-up: lazy eights, cross crawl, elephant, soccer kicks
3. Introduce volleyball: rules, number of players, elements of the game. Use fitness rubric to explain fitness benefits and requirements (see forms 6.4 and 6.5).
4. Demonstrate forearm pass (form 7.10).
5. Have students practice forearm-passing drills:
   a. Toss to partner on knees, progress to standing.
   b. In teams of six, keep it alive using forearm pass.
   c. Use a beach ball to help improve position and technique and bolster confidence.
6. Fitness: dumbbell workout, stretch, review

Lesson 2

Setting

1. Greet students and, as students collect portfolios, attend to administrative duties.
2. Brain warm-up: foot flex, calf pump, grounder, cross crawl, finger point
3. Review forearm pass and practice passing drills from previous lesson.
4. Introduce setting technique (form 7.11).
5. Have students practice setting drills:
   a. Pass to partner
   b. Set against the wall
   c. Use a beach ball to help improve position and technique and bolster confidence.
6. Combined setting and passing drills:
   a. In teams of six, keep it alive using forearm pass or setting technique.
   b. Video each team.
7. Fitness: eight-minute kick-boxing workout
8. Closure: stretch, review passing and setting, have students evaluate skill (forms 7.10 and 7.11).

Lesson 3

Serving

1. Greet students, have students collect portfolios and view video from the previous day, attend to administrative duties.
2. Brain warm-up: lazy eights, cross crawl, elephant, soccer kicks

3. Demonstrate underhand serving technique (form 7.12).

4. Have students practice serve across gym floor to partner.

5. Stations

   a. "Twenty-one": five players line up on the foul line. One player stands under a basketball goal and tosses to each player in turn. Each player attempts to pass the volleyball into the goal. Players score one point for hitting the backboard, two for hitting the rim, and three for scoring a goal. Teams attempt to reach 21. Tosser rotates with others after tossing to each player twice.

   b. Serving: One team on each back line serves to the other. Members of one team are videotaped to be evaluated tomorrow.

   c. Set against the wall

6. Fitness: belly burners

7. Closure: stretch, review, have students evaluate serving (form 7.12).

Lesson 4

Team Drills

1. Greet students. Attend to administrative duties while students collect portfolios and view the video from the previous day.

2. Brain warm-up: foot flex, calf pump, grounder, cross crawl, finger point

3. Explain ten-point volleyball: A team gets a point each time they pass the volleyball, with a limit of 10 passes per volley. Each team must successfully complete the volley to get their points. The objective is to teach players to pass and not just volley. Have two teams demonstrate.

4. Have all teams practice forearm pass, setting.

5. Stations

   a. "Twenty-one"

   b. Ten-point volleyball (two teams). Video one team in action.

   c. Review video from station b.

   d. Set against the wall

6. Fitness: stretch-cord workout

7. Closure: stretch, review.

Lesson 5

Review

1. Greet students and attend to administrative duties while students collect portfolios and view the video from the previous day.

2. Brain warm-up: lazy eights, cross crawl, elephant, soccer kicks

3. Review from the week: passing, setting, serving, fitness rubric. Explain use of the computer and the Web-site assignment (form 7.13).

4. Have teams review passing and setting.

5. Stations

   a. Ten-point volleyball

   b. Serving to a partner (video students)

   c. Video evaluation

   d. Volleyball Web-site assignment (form 7.13)

   e. "Twenty-one"

6. Fitness: eight-minute kick-boxing workout

7. Closure: stretch, review.

Lesson 6

Game Situations

1. Greet students, hand out pulse monitors, and attend to administrative duties while students collect portfolios.

2. Brain warm-up: foot flex, calf pump, grounder, cross crawl, finger point

3. Check that pulse monitors are working. Explain pulse levels (refer to fitness rubric and activity pyramid in forms 6.4 and 6.5). Instruct team captains to record pulse levels at the change of each station and total them at the end of class.

4. Have students walk or jog to get to their fitness zone.

5. Stations

   a. Six-on-six (two teams)

   b. "Twenty-one" (video students)

   c. Video review and self-evaluation (form 7.10)

d. Serving to other members of one's own team

e. Step aerobics

6. Fitness: dumbbell workout

7. Closure: check pulse "winners," stretch, review fitness rubric (form 6.4).

Lesson 7

Volleyball Fitness

1. Greet students, hand out pulse monitors, and attend to administrative duties while students collect portfolios.

2. Brain warm-up: lazy eights, cross crawl, elephant, soccer kicks

3. Review portfolio. Discuss "Dimensions of Volleyball" (form 7.14).

4. Jog to warm up to fitness zone on monitors

5. Stations

   a. Six-on-six

   b. Set against the wall (video students)

   c. Video self-evaluation of setting (form 7.11)

   d. Web assignment (form 7.13)

   e. Kick-boxing

6. Fitness: belly burners

7. Closure: check pulse "winners," review.

Lesson 8

Volleyball Fitness Continued

1. Greet students, hand out pulse monitors, attend to administrative duties while students collect portfolios. Remind students that portfolios are due in two days.

2. Brain warm-up: foot flex, calf pump, grounder, cross crawl, finger point

3. Review serving (form 7.12).

4. Stations

   a. Six-on-six

   b. Serving to partner (video students)

   c. Video self-evaluation (form 7.12)

   d. Work on portfolios

5. Fitness: dumbbell workout

6. Closure: check pulse "winners," stretch, collect portfolios to check for incomplete assignments.

Lesson 9

Game Video

1. Greet students, hand out pulse monitors, attend to administrative duties. Return portfolios with corrections. Students may check and correct mistakes for a second chance.

2. Brain warm-up: lazy eights, cross crawl, elephant, soccer kicks

3. Kick-boxing warm-up

4. Stations

   a. Six-on-six (video students while actually playing)

   b. Have students complete final self-evaluation by viewing the video in previous station.

   c. Ten-point volleyball

   d. Work on correcting portfolios.

5. Fitness: stretch-cord workout

6. Closure: review and stretch.

Lesson 10

Completing Assignments

1. Greet students, attend to administrative duties, pass out portfolios.

2. Brain warm-up: foot flex, calf pump, grounder, cross crawl, finger point

3. Use portfolios to review; check for understanding.

4. Stations

   a. Six-on-six (video students)

   b. Review video.

   c. Make any corrections in portfolios, and have students complete final self-evaluations.

5. Closure: review "Dimensions of Volleyball" (form 7.14), stretch.

Passing Self-Evaluation

Name: _____   Date: _____

O = not yet	**X** = getting better	**+** = proper technique

Preparation phase

	1st day	2nd day	3rd day	
1.	_____	_____	_____	Move feet to ball
2.	_____	_____	_____	Join hands
3.	_____	_____	_____	Feet shoulder-width apart
4.	_____	_____	_____	Knees bent, body low
5.	_____	_____	_____	Form a platform with arms
6.	_____	_____	_____	Thumbs parallel
7.	_____	_____	_____	Elbows locked
8.	_____	_____	_____	Arms parallel to thighs
9.	_____	_____	_____	Back straight
10.	_____	_____	_____	Eyes track ball

Execution phase

	1st day	2nd day	3rd day	
1.	_____	_____	_____	Receive ball in front of body
2.	_____	_____	_____	Slight extension of legs
3.	_____	_____	_____	No arm swing
4.	_____	_____	_____	Transfer weight forward
5.	_____	_____	_____	Contact ball away from body
6.	_____	_____	_____	Slant platform toward target
7.	_____	_____	_____	Hips move forward
8.	_____	_____	_____	Watch ball contact arms

Follow-through phase

	1st day	2nd day	3rd day	
1.	_____	_____	_____	Keep hands joined
2.	_____	_____	_____	Elbows remain locked
3.	_____	_____	_____	Platform follows ball to target
4.	_____	_____	_____	Keep arms below shoulder level
5.	_____	_____	_____	Transfer weight forward
6.	_____	_____	_____	Watch ball to target

From *It's Not Just Gym Anymore: Teaching Secondary School Students How to Be Active for Life* by Bane McCracken, 2001, Champaign, IL: Human Kinetics.

Volleyball Setting Self-Evaluation

Name: _____ Date: _____

O = not yet	**X** = getting better	**+** = proper technique

Preparation phase

1st day	2nd day	3rd day	
1. _____	_____	_____	Move to ball
2. _____	_____	_____	Establish position
3. _____	_____	_____	Square shoulders to target
4. _____	_____	_____	Feet in comfortable stride
5. _____	_____	_____	Bend arms, legs, and hips
6. _____	_____	_____	Hands above head
7. _____	_____	_____	Hands in front of forehead
8. _____	_____	_____	Look through hands
9. _____	_____	_____	Follow ball to target

Execution phase

1st day	2nd day	3rd day	
1. _____	_____	_____	Contact ball on bottom
2. _____	_____	_____	Contact ball on fingers
3. _____	_____	_____	Extend arms and legs toward target
4. _____	_____	_____	Transfer weight toward target
5. _____	_____	_____	Direct ball to desired height
6. _____	_____	_____	Direct ball to hitter's hand or toward sideline

Follow-through phase

1st day	2nd day	3rd day	
1. _____	_____	_____	Extend arms
2. _____	_____	_____	Point hand toward target
3. _____	_____	_____	Hips move toward target
4. _____	_____	_____	Transfer weight toward target
5. _____	_____	_____	Move in direction of set

From *It's Not Just Gym Anymore: Teaching Secondary School Students How to Be Active for Life* by Bane McCracken, 2001, Champaign, IL: Human Kinetics.

Volleyball Serve Self-Evaluation

Name: _____ Date: _____

O = not yet	**X** = getting better	**+** = proper technique

Preparation phase

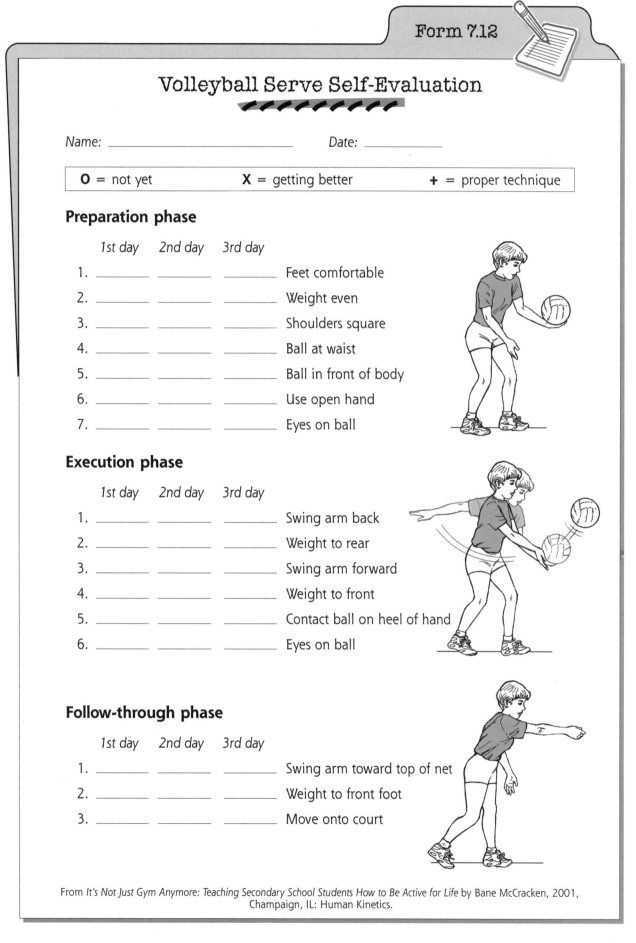

1st day	2nd day	3rd day	
1. _____	_____	_____	Feet comfortable
2. _____	_____	_____	Weight even
3. _____	_____	_____	Shoulders square
4. _____	_____	_____	Ball at waist
5. _____	_____	_____	Ball in front of body
6. _____	_____	_____	Use open hand
7. _____	_____	_____	Eyes on ball

Execution phase

1st day	2nd day	3rd day	
1. _____	_____	_____	Swing arm back
2. _____	_____	_____	Weight to rear
3. _____	_____	_____	Swing arm forward
4. _____	_____	_____	Weight to front
5. _____	_____	_____	Contact ball on heel of hand
6. _____	_____	_____	Eyes on ball

Follow-through phase

1st day	2nd day	3rd day	
1. _____	_____	_____	Swing arm toward top of net
2. _____	_____	_____	Weight to front foot
3. _____	_____	_____	Move onto court

From *It's Not Just Gym Anymore: Teaching Secondary School Students How to Be Active for Life* by Bane McCracken, 2001, Champaign, IL: Human Kinetics.

Cyber Spike

Name: _____   Date: _____

Go to **www.volleyball.org/general/index.html**.

1. List the four most important moves in volleyball.

2. How old is volleyball?

3. In what year was volleyball introduced at the Olympics?

4. What was the prize for the first two-man beach volleyball tournament?

5. Find a game at **www.volleyball.org/playing/index.html**.

From *It's Not Just Gym Anymore: Teaching Secondary School Students How to Be Active for Life* by Bane McCracken, 2001, Champaign, IL: Human Kinetics.

Dimensions of Volleyball

Name: _____   Date: _____

1. What do you need to know to play volleyball? List at least five items in their order of importance.

2. What other activities have you done that are similar to volleyball? List five.

3. Choose one of the activities you listed above and tell how it is similar to volleyball.

4. Let's play. Make a plan to play volleyball (who, when, where, how).

5. Now that you have finished the unit, what did you learn?

From *It's Not Just Gym Anymore: Teaching Secondary School Students How to Be Active for Life* by Bane McCracken, 2001, Champaign, IL: Human Kinetics.

chapter 8

Tennis and Golf

Tennis and golf are prime examples of activities that can provide physical activity opportunities for a lifetime. Each sport has excellent fitness benefits. Tennis is great for developing and maintaining cardiovascular fitness; the stop-and-go action and swinging of the racket improve muscular strength and endurance. Golf has similar benefits, especially when walking instead of riding a cart. Walking 18 holes is great for the heart, carrying a golf bag is good for muscular strength, and the golf swing is a wonderful way to maintain flexibility. A good way to help students understand the benefits of these activities is to let them see for themselves. Local octogenarian Campbell Neel is an avid tennis player who regularly visits my class during the tennis unit to demonstrate the benefits of a physically active lifestyle and his remarkable skill with a racket.

Tennis and golf are especially good for lifetime fitness because, unlike team sports, they don't require as many people to play. The busy schedule of adults makes it difficult to find enough team members to play volleyball or softball on a regular basis. Tennis, on the other hand, requires just two people and golf can be played alone. Both games may be played virtually every day.

The objectives of a tennis unit are to teach students to

- recognize the fitness benefits of tennis,
- analyze the fitness requirements of tennis,
- develop a personal fitness plan that will help them maintain a level of fitness necessary to continue to participate in tennis as adults,
- recognize proper technique and methods of improving skill,
- adapt play for lower skill and fitness levels, and
- locate facilities available for adults.

TENNIS

While some tennis lessons are better taught indoors, such as hitting balls against a wall or curtain, tennis is basically an outdoor sport. Rainy days will require some adaptation of lessons. Even on sunny days, however, there are not enough courts to accommodate all students. A variety of activities performed on a rotating basis is essential to keep all students actively engaged in learning.

Lesson 1

Introduction to Tennis/Forehand

1. Pass out portfolios, greet students, attend to administrative duties.
2. Brain warm-up: lazy eights, elephant, cross crawl, cross skip, finger point
3. Introduce tennis; use the fitness rubric (see form 6.4) to demonstrate fitness benefits.
4. Demonstrate and have students practice the grip.
5. Racket drills: check for proper grip while doing drills.
   a. Bounce ball on racket, palm up, 10 times.
   b. Bounce ball on racket, palm down, 10 times.
   c. Bounce ball on racket, alternating palm up and palm down, 10 times
   d. Dribble ball with racket following the lines on the court or gym floor.

6. Demonstrate the forehand. Have one student practice the forehand against a wall or net while a partner critiques technique using form 8.1.
7. Fitness: dumbbells for tennis (form 8.2)
8. Closure: stretch, and review grip and forehand.

Lesson 2

Forehand Rally

1. Pass out portfolios, greet students, attend to administrative duties.
2. Brain warm-up: soccer kicks, grounder, walk with big arm swings, cross crawl
3. Review grip and forehand with form 8.1.
4. Explain court markings (form 8.3). Have students run to the designated court lines while bouncing a tennis ball with their racket.
5. Racket drills
6. Toss to forehand: have one student stand at the net and toss the ball to a partner's forehand (partner stands at the service line).
7. Forehand rally: have students stand in pairs facing each other across the net no more than a racket length from the net. Students attempt to complete 10 very easy ralleys using only their forehand.
8. Closure: stretch, review.

Lesson 3

Backhand

1. Pass out portfolios, greet students, attend to administrative duties.
2. Brain warm-up: lazy eights, elephant, cross crawl, cross skip, finger point
3. Active review of court markings
4. Demonstrate two-handed backhand and have students practice (form 8.4). Have one student practice the backhand against a wall or net while a partner critiques technique using form 8.4.
5. Racket drills
6. Toss to backhand: have one student stand at the net and toss the ball to a partner's backhand (partner stands at the service line).
7. Backhand rally: Have students stand in pairs facing each other across the net no more than a racket length from the net. Students attempt to complete 10 very easy volleys using only their backhand.
8. Fitness: dumbbells for tennis (form 8.2)
9. Closure: stretch and review.

Lesson 4

Cat and Mouse

1. Pass out portfolios, greet students, attend to administrative duties.
2. Brain warm-up: soccer kicks, grounder, walk with big arm swings, cross crawl
3. Racket drills
4. Review: grip, forehand, backhand
5. Forehand toss, backhand toss
6. Cat and mouse: one student stands at net and tosses to a partner standing at the service line. Toss may be to either forehand or backhand.
7. Cat-and-mouse rally: students stand in pairs facing each other across the net no more than a racket length from the net. Students attempt to complete 10 very easy volleys using either the forehand or backhand.

8. Closure: stretch and review.

Lesson 5

Progressive Rally

1. Pass out portfolios, greet students, attend to administrative duties.
2. Brain warm-up: lazy eights, elephant, cross crawl, cross skip, finger point
3. Active review of court markings
4. Demonstrate punch serve and have students practice (form 8.5).
5. Cat and mouse
6. Progressive rally: have students stand in pairs facing each other across the net no more than a racket length from the net. Students attempt to complete 10 very easy volleys using either the forehand or backhand. After completing 10 rallies successfully, students move to the service line. After successfully completing 10 volleys at the service line, students move to the baseline.
7. Videotape students' forehands. Select students two at a time and have one toss while the other is being recorded. While this is happening, have other students practice the progressive volley.
8. Closure: stretch and review.

Lesson 6

Video Evaluations

1. Pass out portfolios, greet students, and have students watch and evaluate the forehand video (form 8.1) while you attend to administrative duties.
2. Brain warm-up: soccer kicks, grounder, walk with big arm swings, cross crawl
3. Explain scoring and doubles rotation.
4. Racket drills, court dimension active review
5. Active review of doubles rotation and scoring
6. Progressive volley
7. Doubles play

8. Videotape students' forehands. Select students two at a time and have one toss while the other is being recorded. While this is happening, have other students practice the progressive rally

9. Closure: stretch and review.

Lesson 7

Scoring

1. Pass out portfolios, greet students, and have students watch and evaluate the backhand video (form 8.4) while you attend to administrative duties.

2. Brain warm-up: lazy eights, elephant, cross crawl, cross skip, finger point

3. Active review scoring and doubles rotation

4. Progressive volley

5. Doubles play

6. Videotape students' serves. Select students two at a time and have one serve while the other retrieves the balls. While this is happening, have other students practice the progressive volley.

7. Closure: stretch and review.

Lesson 8

Video During Rallies

1. Pass out portfolios, greet students, and have students watch and evaluate the serve video (form 8.5) while you attend to administrative duties.

2. Brain warm-up: soccer kicks, grounder, walk with big arm swings, cross crawl

3. Assign partners for doubles competition and explain procedure.

4. Progressive volley for warm-up

5. Doubles competition, three games

6. Videotape each doubles partner during play for authentic evaluation (examining technique under game conditions).

7. Have students waiting their turn work on assignments in their portfolios.

8. Closure: stretch and review.

Lesson 9

Tennis Fitness

1. Pass out portfolios, pass out pulse monitors, greet students, and have students watch and evaluate play from the videos (forms 8.1, 8.4, and 8.5) while you attend to administrative duties.

2. Brain warm-up: lazy eights, elephant, cross crawl, cross skip, finger point

3. Racket drills warm-up

4. Doubles competition; students compare pulse levels at the end of each game.

5. Have students waiting their turn to play do dumbbells for tennis (form 8.2) and work on portfolios by reading "Strength Training for Tennis Players" (form 8.6) and completing "Reflections on Strength Training for Tennis Players" (form 8.7).

6. Closure: stretch and review. Discuss pulse levels during play and compare to other activities.

Lesson 10

Final Evaluation

1. Pass out portfolios, pass out pulse monitors, greet students, and have students watch and evaluate play from videos (forms 8.1, 8.4, and 8.5) while you attend to administrative duties.

2. Brain warm-up: soccer kicks, grounder, walk with big arm swings, cross crawl

3. Progressive volley for warm-up

4. Doubles competition (record pulse levels)

5. Have students complete portfolios.

6. Closure: discuss and have students complete "Dimensions of Tennis" (form 8.8). Collect portfolios, stretch, review.

Forehand Self-Evaluation

Name: _____ Date: _____

| **O** = not yet | **X** = getting better | **+** = proper technique |

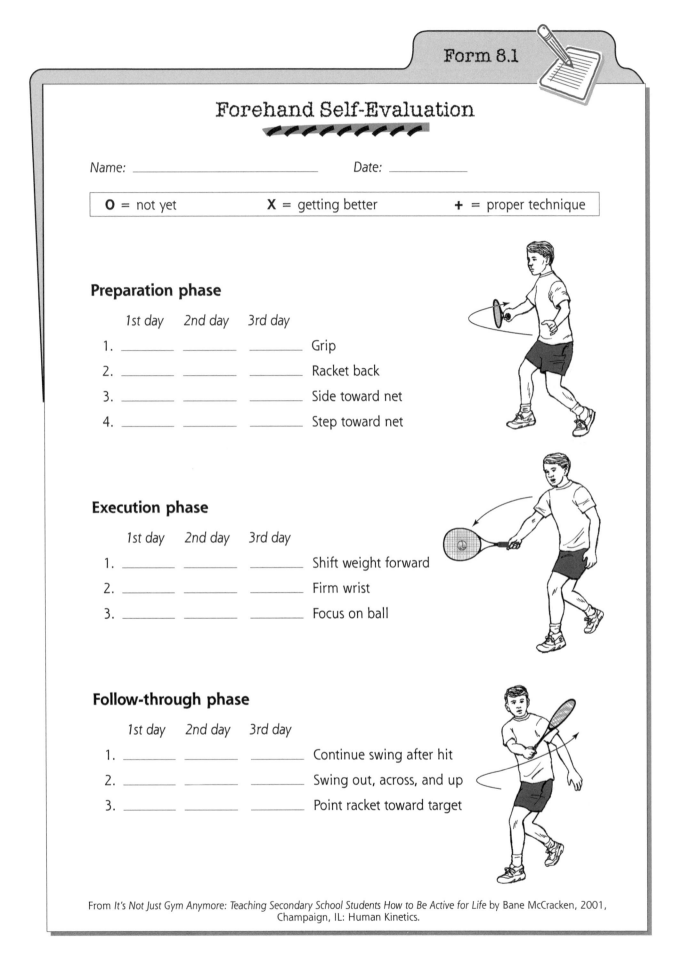

Preparation phase

	1st day	2nd day	3rd day	
1.	_____	_____	_____	Grip
2.	_____	_____	_____	Racket back
3.	_____	_____	_____	Side toward net
4.	_____	_____	_____	Step toward net

Execution phase

	1st day	2nd day	3rd day	
1.	_____	_____	_____	Shift weight forward
2.	_____	_____	_____	Firm wrist
3.	_____	_____	_____	Focus on ball

Follow-through phase

	1st day	2nd day	3rd day	
1.	_____	_____	_____	Continue swing after hit
2.	_____	_____	_____	Swing out, across, and up
3.	_____	_____	_____	Point racket toward target

From *It's Not Just Gym Anymore: Teaching Secondary School Students How to Be Active for Life* by Bane McCracken, 2001, Champaign, IL: Human Kinetics.

Dumbbells for Tennis

1. Alternate-arm overhead press, 10–15 reps

2. Fist rotation, 20 reps

3. Lunge, 8–10 reps

4. Standing fly, 8–10 reps

5. Forearm curl, 20 reps

6. Half squat, 10–15 reps

7. Alternate front raise, 8–10 reps

8. Reverse forearm curl, 20 reps

9. Toe raise, 20 reps

10. Behind-neck triceps press, 8–10 reps

From *It's Not Just Gym Anymore: Teaching Secondary School Students How to Be Active for Life* by Bane McCracken, 2001, Champaign, IL: Human Kinetics.

Court Markings

Name: _____ Date: _____

Matching

Place numbers in the proper location.

1. center service line
2. baseline
3. right service court
4. back court
5. net
6. alley
7. single sideline
8. left service court
9. service line
10. doubles sideline
11. center mark

Backhand Self-Evaluation

Name: _____   Date: _____

O = not yet	**X** = getting better	**+** = proper technique

Preparation phase

	1st day	2nd day	3rd day	
1.	_____	_____	_____	Grip
2.	_____	_____	_____	Racket back
3.	_____	_____	_____	Side toward net
4.	_____	_____	_____	Step toward target

Execution phase

	1st day	2nd day	3rd day	
1.	_____	_____	_____	Shift weight forward
2.	_____	_____	_____	Focus on ball
3.	_____	_____	_____	Make contact early

Follow-through phase

	1st day	2nd day	3rd day	
1.	_____	_____	_____	Continue swing after hit
2.	_____	_____	_____	Swing out, across, and up
3.	_____	_____	_____	Point racket toward target

From *It's Not Just Gym Anymore: Teaching Secondary School Students How to Be Active for Life* by Bane McCracken, 2001, Champaign, IL: Human Kinetics.

Punch Serve Self-Evaluation

Name: _____ *Date:* _____

| **O** = not yet | **X** = getting better | **+** = proper technique |

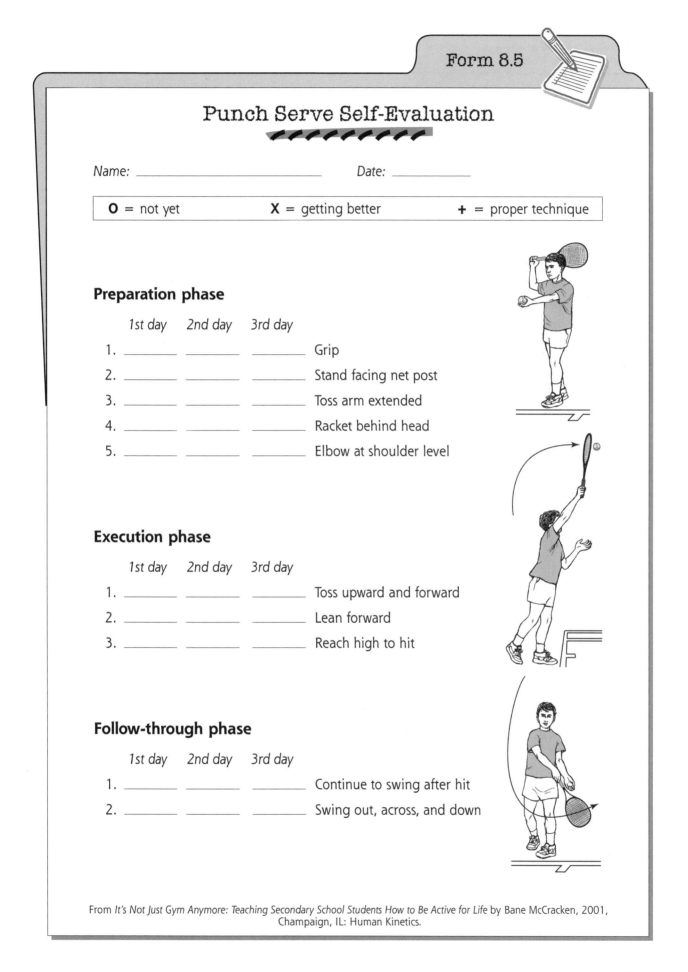

Preparation phase

	1st day	2nd day	3rd day	
1.	_____	_____	_____	Grip
2.	_____	_____	_____	Stand facing net post
3.	_____	_____	_____	Toss arm extended
4.	_____	_____	_____	Racket behind head
5.	_____	_____	_____	Elbow at shoulder level

Execution phase

	1st day	2nd day	3rd day	
1.	_____	_____	_____	Toss upward and forward
2.	_____	_____	_____	Lean forward
3.	_____	_____	_____	Reach high to hit

Follow-through phase

	1st day	2nd day	3rd day	
1.	_____	_____	_____	Continue to swing after hit
2.	_____	_____	_____	Swing out, across, and down

From *It's Not Just Gym Anymore: Teaching Secondary School Students How to Be Active for Life* by Bane McCracken, 2001, Champaign, IL: Human Kinetics.

Strength Training for Tennis Players

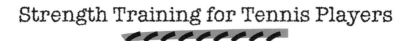

No matter what your sport, strength training can improve performance and prevent injuries. Distance runners, football players, and tennis enthusiasts should include resistance training as a regular part of their regimes. For the distance runner, strength training helps maintain stride length at the end of long runs. Football players need explosive power for short periods of time. Weightlifters need maximum strength for a few seconds. In the game of tennis, athletes need to be fit after hours of playing, but they also need to be able to deliver a maximum amount of work for a few seconds. The tennis player, therefore, needs an all-around and varied program.

Muscles become stronger when they are put under stress. When we lift weights, our muscles adapt to the increased resistance. During strength-training sessions muscle fibers wear out; they break down. Although this sounds bad, it is not. With rest and proper nutrition the muscles rebuild themselves and become stronger than before. What muscles need to be trained, how much weight we should lift, how many times, and how often are determined by our training goals and the activity for which we are training. Tennis calls many muscles into action from all areas of the body. Training for tennis should involve muscle groups from each body part but should focus more on those muscles of the forearm, shoulders, and legs that are particularly important to tennis.

A single exercise repeated nonstop is called a repetition (rep). Performing a group of reps is called a set. Studies indicate that two to three sets of an exercise with four to six reps is best for developing explosive strength. For developing power, 12 to 15 reps are best, and 15 to 25 reps are best for muscular endurance. Weight (resistance) should be adjusted so that proper repetitions can be successfully performed. Because tennis requires strength, power, and endurance, a varied program is necessary. An ideal program for tennis would require at least three days per week: one day for strength, one for power, and one for endurance.

A training session should always begin with a good warm-up. Get the blood circulating with the help of jogging, cycling, or using a machine for three to five minutes. After warming up, start strength training by working one muscle group at a time. Perform at least two sets of 8 to 12 reps. Try to focus on the muscle that is being trained. End the training session by cooling down on a bike, jogging slowly, or walking. Make sure to finish any workout by stretching to maintain flexibility and prevent injury.

From *It's Not Just Gym Anymore: Teaching Secondary School Students How to Be Active for Life* by Bane McCracken, 2001, Champaign, IL: Human Kinetics.

Reflections on Strength Training for Tennis

Name: _____   Date: _____

1. What were the key ideas?

2. What questions do you have? List three.

3. What should you do? Make a tennis strength-training plan.

4. How does tennis relate to any other subject you now have in school?

From *It's Not Just Gym Anymore: Teaching Secondary School Students How to Be Active for Life* by Bane McCracken, 2001, Champaign, IL: Human Kinetics.

Dimensions of Tennis

Name: _____   Date: _____

1. What do you need to know to play tennis? List at least five items in their order of importance.

2. What other activities have you done that are similar to tennis? List five.

3. Choose one of the activities you listed above and tell how it is similar to tennis.

4. Let's play. Make a plan to play tennis (who, when, where, how).

5. Now that you have finished the unit, what did you learn? List three things.

From *It's Not Just Gym Anymore: Teaching Secondary School Students How to Be Active for Life* by Bane McCracken, 2001, Champaign, IL: Human Kinetics.

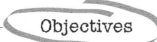

The objectives of a golf unit are to teach students to

- recognize the fitness benefits of golf,
- analyze the fitness requirements of golf,
- develop a personal fitness plan that will help them maintain a level of fitness necessary to continue to participate in golf as an adult,
- recognize proper technique and methods of improving skill,
- locate and compare local facilities to those in other locations, and
- identify sources of equipment and supplies.

GOLF

The focus of the golf unit is to teach students more than just how to hit a golf ball. Golf is a game rich in tradition and can be intimidating. To encourage nonaggressive students to actually play golf, we must take steps to give them confidence by answering many of their procedural questions. Take a video camera while playing a round of golf. Show students what a clubhouse and pro shop look like, how to sign up, where play begins, and the unique qualities of each hole. You can set up a Frisbee golf course at school, complete with tees and greens, hazards, and out of bounds. There students can experience the fitness benefits and requirements of golf, learn playing procedures, and practice etiquette.

Multimedia technology is especially helpful in teaching golf. Display a Microsoft® PowerPoint® presentation of a proper golf stance on a screen, then have students try to imitate the stance while standing in front of a video camera. By displaying the video through a TV, the students can see what a proper stance looks like and how they compare, receive instant feedback, and make corrections.

Like tennis, golf is an outside sport, and so the weather may interrupt lesson plans. I always included some rainy day alternative lesson plans.

Lesson 1

Introduction to Golf

1. Hand out portfolios while greeting students. Attend to administrative duties while students look over unit plans.

2. Discuss the lifetime nature of golf. Use the fitness rubric (form 6.4) as an example.

3. Show a video of a round of golf or of a pro tour from a TV program.

4. Show a video of a golf swing (either from previous classes, professional videos, or both). Use Microsoft® PowerPoint® to show the elements of the swing: stance, grip, backswing, downswing, impact, finishes.

5. Build the swing from the ground up: stance, grip, backswing, downswing, impact, and finish.

   a. Stance: show PowerPoint® slides of the stance and grip. Use a video camera connected to a TV so students can compare their stance as seen in the TV to the correct stance.

   b. Have students work in pairs and use the stance self-evaluation (form 8.9) to help them make corrections.

6. Swing warm-up drills

   a. Hold the club behind the back with the elbows. Point each end of the club to an imaginary ball.

   b. Hold the club head in the target hand and the grip in the other hand. Take a backswing with both hands on the club. Begin downswing by releasing the grip hand. Concentrate on a high finish with the grip of the club pointing toward the ground and the belt buckle toward the target.

   c. Videotape students.

7. Students begin with a quarter swing (chip shots) and work up to a three-quarter swing without using balls.

8. Closure: stretch, review.

Lesson 2

Terms and Basic Skills

1. Pass out portfolios, greet students, attend to administrative duties, and have students view videos from the previous day and evaluate their stances (form 8.9).

2. Brain warm-up: lazy eights, elephant, cross crawl, cross skip, finger point

3. Explain golf terms then administer quiz (form 8.10). Answers are provided on p. 239.

4. Demonstrate "good medicine for golf" (form 8.11).

5. Review the golf swing using a video and/or Microsoft® PowerPoint®.

6. Swing warm-up drills

7. Outside drills (in large, football-sized field). Separate the class into three groups and set up the following stations, rotating all students through all three:

   a. Hitting plastic golf balls (if space permits, real balls may be used in later lessons after students have developed some skill at hitting the ball). Videotape the students with a view cam and show them the results.

   b. Chipping to the target in the opposite direction using real balls

   c. Good Medicine for Golf (form 8.11)

8. Closure: stretch, review, and view video.

Lesson 3

Basic Skills

1. Pass out portfolios, greet students, attend to administrative duties, and have students view videos from the previous day and evaluate their swings (form 8.12).

2. Brain warm-up: soccer kicks, grounder, walk with big arm swings, cross crawl

3. Demonstrate putting technique and have students practice (use carpet of synthetic turf).

4. Swing warm-up drills

5. Outside drills (in large, football-sized field). Separate the class into three groups and set up the following stations, rotating all students through all three:

   a. Hitting plastic golf balls. Videotape students using a view cam and show them the results.

   b. Chipping to the target in the opposite direction

   c. Practicing putting

6. Closure: stretch, review, and view video.

Lesson 4

Frisbee Golf and Etiquette

1. Pass out portfolios, greet students, attend to administrative duties, and have students view videos from the previous day and evaluate their swings (form 8.12).

2. Brain warm-up: lazy eights, elephant, cross crawl, cross skip, finger point

3. Demonstrate and explain golf etiquette (form 8.13).

   a. Demonstrate and explain the procedure for playing Frisbee golf.

   b. Review and use Frisbee golf as an example of good golf etiquette.

4. Swing warm-up drills

5. Outside drills (in large, football-sized field). Separate the class into four groups and set up the following stations, rotating all students through all four.

   a. Hitting plastic golf balls. Videotape students using a view cam.

   b. Chipping to the target in the opposite direction

   c. Practicing putting

   d. Playing Frisbee golf

6. Closure: stretch, review, and view video.

Lesson 5

Indoor Lesson for a Rainy Day

1. Pass out portfolios, greet students, attend to administrative duties, and have students view videos from the previous day and evaluate their swings (form 8.12).

2. Brain warm-up: soccer kicks, grounder, walk with big arm swings, cross crawl

3. Demonstrate putting technique.

4. Divide the class into five groups and rotate them enough times so that each group gets to each of the following stations that you've set up:

   a. Practicing putting

   b. Hitting plastic balls into a divider curtain (videotape students)

   c. Reviewing video using form 8.12

   d. Good Medicine for Golf (form 8.11)

   e. Visiting, locating, and comparing state and local golf courses on the Web using form 8.14 (sites may be saved to a disk if the Internet is not available)

5. Closure: stretch, review.

Lesson 6
Digital Pictures

1. Pass out portfolios, greet students, attend to administrative duties, and have students view videos from the previous day and evaluate their swings (form 8.12).

2. Brain warm-up: lazy eights, elephant, cross crawl, cross skip, finger point

3. Review etiquette and Frisbee golf (form 8.13).

4. Swing warm-up drills

5. Divide the class into four groups and rotate them enough times so that each group gets to each of the following stations that you've set up outside in a large, football-sized field:

   a. Hitting plastic golf balls. Take digital photos of students at impact. Viewing their swing in stop action allows students to better evaluate their swing at impact.

   b. Chipping to a target in the opposite direction

   c. Practicing putting

   d. Playing Frisbee golf

6. Closure: stretch, review.

Lesson 7
In the Computer Lab

Have students make a PowerPoint® presentation by inserting their golf pictures and us-

ing arrows and text boxes to critique their swings.

Lesson 8
Equipment

1. Pass out portfolios, greet students, attend to administrative duties, and have students view videos from the previous day and evaluate their swings (form 8.12).

2. Brain warm-up: soccer kicks, grounder, walk with big arm swings, cross crawl

3. Show golf equipment and explain its use: woods, irons (2-, 3-, 4-, 5-, 6-, 7-, 8-, 9-, wedge), etc. Use PowerPoint® slides of golf holes to demonstrate the use of different clubs and strategy.

4. Divide the class into five groups and rotate them enough times so that each group gets to each of the following stations that you've set up in the gym:

   a. Practicing putting

   b. Hitting plastic balls into a divider curtain using different clubs (videotape students)

   c. Reviewing videos using form 8.12

   d. Good Medicine for Golf (form 8.11)

   e. Investigating equipment prices and availability on the Web using form 8.14 (sites may be saved to a disk if the Internet is not available)

5. Closure: stretch, review.

Lesson 9
Stations

1. Pass out portfolios, greet students, attend to administrative duties, and have students view videos from the previous day and evaluate their swings (form 8.12).

2. Brain warm-up: lazy eights, elephant, cross crawl, cross skip, finger point

3. Review strategy and rules using a Frisbee golf course to demonstrate parallel hazards, lateral hazards, out of bounds, and water hazards and the penalties and procedures for each.

4. Swing warm-up drills

5. Divide the class into four groups and set up the following stations outside in a large, football-sized field:

   a. Hitting plastic golf balls

   b. Chipping to a target in the opposite direction

   c. Practicing putting

   d. Playing Frisbee golf

6. Closure: stretch, review.

Lesson 10
Review and Improve Skills

1. Pass out portfolios, greet students, attend to administrative duties, and have students put on pulse monitors.

2. Brain warm-up: soccer kicks, grounder, walk with big arm swings, cross crawl

3. Discuss the fitness benefits of golf using the fitness rubric in form 6.4.

4. Divide the class into four groups and set up the following stations outside in a large, football-sized field. Students record their pulse levels before changing stations.

   a. Hitting plastic golf ball for a final self-evaluation (videotape students)

   b. Chipping to a target in the opposite direction

   c. Practicing putting

   d. Playing Frisbee golf

5. Closure: stretch, review, discuss pulse, and compare to other activities.

Lesson 11
Final Evaluation

1. Pass out portfolios, greet students, and attend to administrative duties.

2. Brain warm-up: lazy eights, elephant, cross crawl, cross skip, finger point

3. Conduct Frisbee golf tournament using medal play (i.e., total number of strokes [throws]).

4. Have students review their swing videos and complete final self-evaluations while waiting their turn to play in the tournament.

5. Closure: Discuss and have students complete PMI graph (form 8.15), in which they tell what they think is positive, negative, and interesting about golf. Collect portfolios, stretch, and conduct a final review.

Stance Self-Evaluation

Name: _____   Date: _____

| **O** = not yet | **X** = getting better | **+** = proper technique |

Set up (front view)

	1st day	2nd day	3rd day	
1.	_____	_____	_____	Feet shoulder-width apart
2.	_____	_____	_____	Stand on imaginary line
3.	_____	_____	_____	Square foot alignment
4.	_____	_____	_____	Square hip alignment
5.	_____	_____	_____	Square shoulder alignment
6.	_____	_____	_____	Weight even on both feet

Set up (side view)

	1st day	2nd day	3rd day	
1.	_____	_____	_____	Bend from top of hips
2.	_____	_____	_____	Flat back
3.	_____	_____	_____	Arms hang relaxed
4.	_____	_____	_____	Palms face each other

From *It's Not Just Gym Anymore: Teaching Secondary School Students How to Be Active for Life* by Bane McCracken, 2001, Champaign, IL: Human Kinetics.

Golf Terms

Name: _____   Date: _____

_____ 1. Par

_____ 2. Birdie

_____ 3. Eagle

_____ 4. Ace

_____ 5. Slice

_____ 6. Fore

_____ 7. Hook

_____ 8. Bogey

_____ 9. Etiquette

_____ 10. Tee

_____ 11. Greens

_____ 12. Rough

_____ 13. Sand trap

_____ 14. Clubhouse

_____ 15. Pro shop

a. The number of strokes in which a hole is designed to be played

b. The place in the clubhouse where professional grade equipment may be purchased

c. One stroke less than par

d. A hole in one stroke

e. A pit with sand in it

f. An area outside the fairway with higher grass

g. The target area, with smoother, shorter grass

h. Taking two strokes less than par on a single hole

i. Large building that houses the administration services associated with the golf course

j. A warning call

k. Hitting a ball that curves left to right for a right-handed golfer

l. Hitting a ball that curves left to right for a left-handed golfer

m. Manner of conduct expected of anyone while on a golf course

n. Area where play begins for each hole

o. Taking one stroke over par on a single hole

From *It's Not Just Gym Anymore: Teaching Secondary School Students How to Be Active for Life* by Bane McCracken, 2001, Champaign, IL: Human Kinetics.

Good Medicine for Golf

Equipment: four medicine balls, four tennis balls, four stretch cords

Eight people form a circle, facing inward.

1. Medicine-ball pick to waist 10 times then turn to left and hold arms out in passing position for 10 sec.

2. Tennis ball squeeze

3. Toe raises holding medicine ball 10 times then turn to left and hold arms out in passing position for 10 sec.

4. Back-to-back medicine-ball pass 25 times

5. Pass medicine ball around circle while standing in a good golf stance.

6. Stretch cord at impact (hold cord in left hand, partner holds other end while standing to the right. Perform practice swing. At impact area partner gives resistance to stretch cord.)

7. Medicine-ball push-ups

8. Overhead lateral bend

9. Seated twist

10. Side throw

11. Oblique crunches (stronger students hold medicine ball on chest)

From *It's Not Just Gym Anymore: Teaching Secondary School Students How to Be Active for Life* by Bane McCracken, 2001, Champaign, IL: Human Kinetics.

Swing Self-Evaluation

Name: _____

| **O** = not yet | **X** = getting better | **+** = proper technique |

Top of backswing

	1st day	2nd day	3rd day	
1.	_____	_____	_____	Hips turn to rear
2.	_____	_____	_____	Back to target
3.	_____	_____	_____	Club parallel to ground
4.	_____	_____	_____	Hands over rear shoulder

Impact view

	1st day	2nd day	3rd day	
1.	_____	_____	_____	Arms, hands, and club extend at impact
2.	_____	_____	_____	Target knee toward target
3.	_____	_____	_____	Rear knee toward target knee

Finish

	1st day	2nd day	3rd day	
1.	_____	_____	_____	Hips face target
2.	_____	_____	_____	Chest to target
3.	_____	_____	_____	Rear shoulder closer to target than target shoulder
4.	_____	_____	_____	Balanced ending

From *It's Not Just Gym Anymore: Teaching Secondary School Students How to Be Active for Life* by Bane McCracken, 2001, Champaign, IL: Human Kinetics.

Golf Etiquette

- Don't move, talk, or stand close to or directly behind a player making a stroke.

- Don't play until the group in front is out of the way.

- Always play without delay. Leave the putting green as soon as your group has holed out.

- Invite faster players to play through.

- Replace divots; smooth footprints in bunkers.

- Don't step on line of another's putt.

- Don't drop clubs on the putting green.

- Replace the flag carefully and in an upright position.

- Leave the course in the condition you would like to find it.

From *It's Not Just Gym Anymore: Teaching Secondary School Students How to Be Active for Life* by Bane McCracken, 2001, Champaign, IL: Human Kinetics.

Cyber Golf

Name: _____   Date: _____

Go to the home page of a golf course and answer the following questions about that course.

1. What is the course's location?

2. How much does it cost to play 9 holes?

3. What are the course conditions?

4. How many holes does the course have?

5. What is the phone number?

6. What are the names of some area accommodations (hotels)?

7. What are some special attractions?

8. How tough is the course (distance, water)?

From *It's Not Just Gym Anymore: Teaching Secondary School Students How to Be Active for Life* by Bane McCracken, 2001, Champaign, IL: Human Kinetics.

PMI Graph

Name: _____   Date: _____

1. Write one paragraph telling what you liked about golf (Plus).

2. Write one paragraph telling what you did not like about golf (Minus).

3. Write one paragraph telling what you found interesting about golf (Interesting).

Note: A paragraph consists of not less than three sentences with a common theme.

From *It's Not Just Gym Anymore: Teaching Secondary School Students How to Be Active for Life* by Bane McCracken, 2001, Champaign, IL: Human Kinetics.

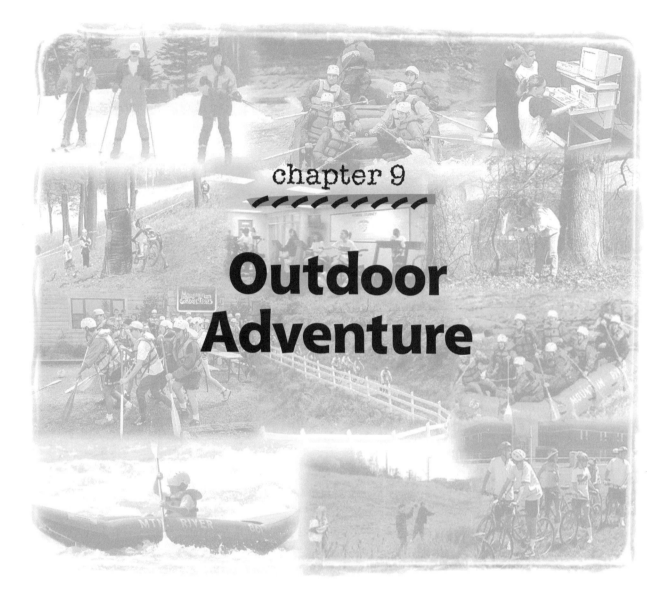

chapter 9

Outdoor Adventure

The outdoor adventure unit taught at Cabell Midland High School is designed to teach students what they need to know to hike the Appalachian Trail (AT). Few students will ever attempt to actually hike the AT, but there are ample opportunities to take advantage of the skills developed during this unit.

This unit was developed to do the following:

- *Align what we teach with what most people do to stay fit.* More people walk to stay fit than all other activities combined. Physical education classes should include units based on walking, and hiking is walking.

- *Provide a physical activity opportunity for low-fit, low-skilled students.* Many of our students and even more adults are not fit enough to participate in physically intense activities. Walking is more appropriate for their needs. Furthermore, many students don't have the talent necessary to feel comfortable participating in activities that require higher skill levels. Hiking provides opportunities for students with less skill.

- *Encourage participation at the base of the activity pyramid.* Activities at the base of the pyramid are of lower intensity and result in lower pulse levels. Lower levels of intensity allow people to participate longer and are most efficient for burning calories and helping control obesity.

- *Take advantage of available resources.* Many rural areas don't have the fitness/recreational resources available in the more urban areas, but many students can walk out their back doors and be in the woods. Several national trails exist in addition to the AT—the Continental Divide Trail, the Pacific Rim Trail, and the American Discovery Trail are just three. Our state and national parks and forests also provide abundant hiking resources.

- *Instill a love of and respect for nature.*

Student Objectives

The objectives of the outdoor adventure unit are to teach students to

- recognize the fitness benefits of hiking/walking,
- recognize the fitness requirements of hiking/walking,
- develop personal fitness to prepare for hiking the Appalachian Trail,
- develop map-reading and orienteering skills,
- develop outdoor cooking skills,
- develop proper wilderness ethics,
- develop proper planning skills, and
- survive wilderness disasters.

Lesson 1

Benefits of Hiking

1. Distribute and discuss briefly "The Health Benefits of Hiking" (form 9.1).

2. Take a 30-minute hike/walk around the school area.

3. Use the fitness rubric (form 6.4) to help discuss the fitness benefits of hiking.

4. Assign "Reflections on Hiking" (form 9.2).

Lesson 2

Pulse Levels and Hiking

1. Distribute pulse monitors to students.
2. Take a 30-minute hike/walk while students wear pulse monitors.
3. Discuss pulse levels and hiking. Use the fitness rubric and activity pyramid to aid illustration (see forms 6.4 and 6.5).

Lesson 3

Hiking Resources

1. Hand out information about local and state hiking resources. Contact state and national parks for information.
2. Have students locate hiking areas and trails from form 9.3 (National Scenic and Historic Trails) on state road maps.
3. Discuss the economic impact of recreational trails on the local economy.

Lesson 4

Cyber Hike

1. Take students to the computer lab and complete an Appalachian Trail cyber hike (form 9.4). In areas not close to the AT, another national trail could be used instead. The seven national and scenic historic trails, in addition to the AT, are
   - the Florida National Scenic Trail,
   - the Potomac Heritage National Scenic Trail,
   - the North Country National Scenic Trail,
   - the Natchez Trace National Scenic Trail,
   - the Ice Age National Scenic Trail,
   - the Continental Divide National Scenic Trail, and
   - the Pacific Crest National Scenic Trail.

Lesson 5

Time and Distance

1. Show part 1 of the video "How to Hike the Appalachian Trail" (Introduction). (The video "How to Hike the Appalachian Trail" is a highly recommended resource that is referred to and used repeatedly during this unit. To obtain a copy contact Lynne Whelden at 1025 Shaw Place, Williamsport, PA 17701.)
2. "How Far to Mount Katahdin: Part I" (form 9.5)

Lesson 6

Pulse Levels and Pace

1. "How Far to Mount Katahdin: Part II (form 9.6)

Lesson 7

Pulse Levels While Carrying a Load

"How Far to Mount Katahdin: Part III" (form 9.7)

Lesson 8

Preparation

1. Show part II of the video "How to Hike the Appalachian Trail" (Preparation).
2. "How Far to Mount Katahdin: Part IV" (form 9.8) is another cyber hike specific to hiking the Appalachian Trail. This activity is good for a bad weather day.

Lesson 9

Food

1. "How Far to Mount Katahdin: Part V" (form 9.9). Have students calculate the number of calories they will use while hiking and carrying a backpack and

view a Web site that features one-burner recipes.

2. Show part V of the video "How to Hike the Appalachian Trail" (Food).

3. Divide students into cooking teams of five or six each. Take a walk to a local grocery store and have the students take note of available foods.

Lesson 10
Gear (a good rainy day lesson)

1. Show part VI of the video "How to Hike the Appalachian Trail" (Gear).

2. Show students equipment: tents, sleeping bags, cooking equipment, stoves, clothing, and supplies. If you do not have this equipment available, local outfitters or individuals with equipment may visit as guest speakers. The Appalachian Trail home page has a list of people who have hiked the trail and their addresses. Many would be glad to visit the class, show their equipment, and share their experiences.

3. Have student cooking groups plan their one-burner meals, decide the cost, and collect money.

Lesson 11
Let's Eat

1. Have students cook one-burner meals. You may provide some equipment, and other equipment may be borrowed from or provided by the students. Hike to a secluded place that is as close to the wilderness as possible and cook. Because students always enjoy eating, this is a popular lesson.

Lesson 12
Leave No Trace

1. Discuss "Leave No Trace" ethics.
2. Take a "Leave No Trace" trash pickup walk.

Lesson 13
Take Only Pictures, Leave Only Footprints

1. Review "Leave No Trace" ethics.

2. Lead the students on a leisurely walk around the campus to a nearby campsite (selected in advance) that is not a good example of camping ethics. Have students continue walking in teams and ask each team to select a better site and tell why it is better, based on "Leave No Trace" ethics.

3. Have students pick up trash on the way back.

Lesson 14
Orienteering

1. Tape topographical maps of the school area and surrounding areas on the floor. Arrange the maps so the map containing the school is in the center, the map of the area to the north of the school is above or north of the center map, and the area south of the school is below or south of the center map. Place area maps for east and west likewise. Use a compass to orient each map to true north by placing the top of the map in a northerly direction. Topographical maps are highly detailed. Special lines indicate change in elevation and most structures are appropriately represented.

2. Begin the class by having students attempt to find their homes on the appropriate map and identify other structures of interest. You may attend to administrative duties and then help students with their assignments. Most students will eagerly explore the maps, identify their homes, and continue to locate points of interest.

3. Explain map features: elevation change, rivers, rails, roads, grids, structures, orientation, etc. (see form 9.10).

4. Distribute state road maps, orient them to north, and compare them to topographical maps.

5. Distribute a map of the school and orient it using features such as walls, hallways, and doors.
6. Take a walk around the school, stopping periodically to reorient maps using features.
7. Define and describe orienteering.

Lesson 15
Handrails

Handrails are defined as easily distinguished map features—such as rivers, roads, and rails—that may be used to help orient the map and serve as guides.

1. Make copies of a topographical map of the school area and distribute it to students.
2. Take a handrail walk. Have students use handrails to guide a walk to a point on the map such as the intersection of a road and a creek.
3. Back at the school, distribute copies of orienteering symbols (form 9.10). Define and discuss the use of each symbol.

Lesson 16
Group Orienteering

1. Distribute copies of a school orienteering map to each student. Have students select a control (a point on the map to find) and use their maps to proceed to that point.
2. Return and explain procedures for the next day's orienteering.

Lesson 17
Let's Go Orienteering!

If you are unfamiliar with orienteering, the following Web page will introduce you to the sport: **www2.aos.Princeton.EDU/rdslater/ orienteering**.

1. Your school orienteering map should have 20 controls. Controls are divided into quadrants and placed into four groups of

five controls each, then color-coded red, blue, green, and black. Each color-coded group should have all quadrants equally represented.
2. Divide the class into groups of four and give each group a color-coded control card. Give the first group one minute to identify their controls, make a plan, and begin. After recording the time for the first group, identify the second group and give them their color-coded control cards. Repeat this procedure until all students are on the course.
3. Students find their controls, mark their controls appropriately, and return to the starting area. Upon the return of each student, check their control cards for accuracy and record their finish times.

Lesson 18
Reading a Compass

1. Demonstrate how to use a compass.
2. Divide the class into groups of three and give each group a topographical map of the school. Groups read compasses, locate a landmark, walk to the landmark, then take another compass reading.

Lesson 19
Compass Challenge (forms 9.11–9.14)

1. Have students work in pairs. Each pair has one compass, a pencil, and a numbered compass challenge course. Each team has a designated starting location that corresponds to the numbered cones of the course. Students begin by recording the first cone number in the blank marked "Point _____" in part II of form 9.11. Students then take the first reading with their compass, proceed to the cone pointed to by the compass, and record the proper number. At the second cone students take the second reading and proceed to the cone indicated. All challenge courses end at cone 1. Upon completing the course, students may check their route using the answer sheet in form 9.15.

Lesson 20

Survival

1. Have students take "Survival Quiz" (form 9.16).
2. Discuss survival priorities.
3. "Take a Walk on the Wild Side" (form 9.17)

Lessons 21 and 22

Fire Building

1. Discuss and demonstrate fire-building techniques.
2. Take a walk, look for materials, and find fire locations. Be sure to follow "Leave No Trace" ethics for fire building and gathering wood. On the second day, establish survival teams. Each team gathers materials to build a fire.
3. Each team takes "the test": light a fire with one match!

Lesson 23

Survival Scenarios

1. Discuss survival priorities: positive mental attitude, first aid, shelter, signal, fire, water, food.
2. Give each team of five to six students a wilderness disaster scenario such as snake bite, being lost, serious injury, canoe flips, or a bike wreck.
3. Instruct each team to develop its assigned disaster scenario so that at least four of the survival priorities are used to save the team. Teams determine how they can illustrate each priority.

Lesson 24

Survival Disasters

1. Have each team of five to six students recreate a disaster and demonstrate survival techniques. Use a digital camera to capture the students being positive, administering first aid, building a fire, and so forth.

Lesson 25

Cyber Survival

1. In the computer lab have each student make an individual Microsoft® PowerPoint® survival scenario. Student presentations begin by describing the disaster. This should include a picture taken in previous class periods. The presentation then proceeds to show how the student would use the seven steps to survival to "escape" from the disaster. The students must use at least five of the steps and use the pictures to illustrate their actions.

Lesson 26

PowerPoint® Presentations

1. Have selected students make their PowerPoint® presentations to the class.

Lesson 27

Conclusion

1. Check and help students complete remaining assignments in their portfolios.
2. "Dimensions of Hiking" (form 9.18)

The Health Benefits of Hiking

- Reduces risk of heart disease

- Decreases hypertension (high blood pressure)

- Decreases cholesterol levels

- Helps in shedding excess pounds

- Slows the aging process

- Reduces risk of osteoporosis

- Improves and maintains mental health

- Improves the quality of the air we breathe

- Reduces risk of and controls diabetes

- Reduces incidence of the common cold and flu

- Improves arthritis

- Relieves back pain

- Establishes healthy habits for a healthy life

From *It's Not Just Gym Anymore: Teaching Secondary School Students How to Be Active for Life* by Bane McCracken, 2001, Champaign, IL: Human Kinetics.

Reflections on Hiking

Name: _____ Date: _____

1. What were the key ideas of this unit?

2. What questions do you still have about hiking? List three.

3. What should you do? Make a plan to start hiking.

4. How does hiking relate to any other subject you now have in school?

From *It's Not Just Gym Anymore: Teaching Secondary School Students How to Be Active for Life* by Bane McCracken, 2001, Champaign, IL: Human Kinetics.

National Scenic and Historic Trails

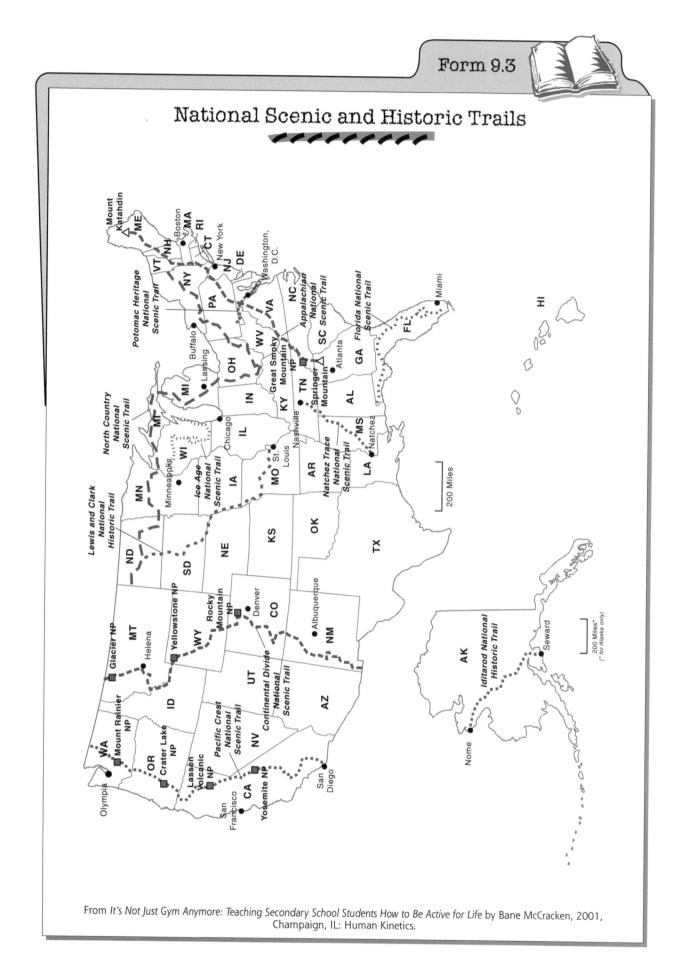

From *It's Not Just Gym Anymore: Teaching Secondary School Students How to Be Active for Life* by Bane McCracken, 2001, Champaign, IL: Human Kinetics.

Cyber Hike on the Appalachian Trail

Name: _____   Date: _____

Note: The Web addresses used in this form were accurate at the time of publication. If the site is no longer active, search **www.yahoo.com** or a similar search engine to find the answers.

1. Go to the National Park Services's Web site (**www.nps.gov**) to find information about the Appalachian Trail.

a. When will you be required to have a permit to camp on the AT?

b. Where can you find shelter?

c. Which states does the trail go through?

2. Go to this site for help in planning a hike on the AT: **www.appalachiantrail.org**

a. List three things you'll need to do before you hike.

b. How can you volunteer for the trail? What does a volunteer do?

3. This site offers help for people who want to hike the AT: **www.trailplace.com**

a. What is "Wingfoot's" real name?

b. What is a thru-hiker?

c. Read some of the thru-hikers' journals.

d. Would you want to become a thru-hiker?

From *It's Not Just Gym Anymore: Teaching Secondary School Students How to Be Active for Life* by Bane McCracken, 2001, Champaign, IL: Human Kinetics.

How Far to Mount Katahdin: Part I

Name: _____   Date: _____

The Appalachian Trail stretches more than 2,000 miles through 14 states, from Maine's mighty Katahdin to Georgia's forested Springer Mountain. Nearly two-thirds of the U.S. population lives within a day's drive of this continuously marked footpath. Each year about 2,000 hikers attempt to thru-hike the trail, but only 200 succeed. Can you step up to the challenge?

How Many Steps Would It Take?

A. Half-step measurement

Walk one lap around a quarter-mile track. Count every left footstep, and keep track of the amount of time it takes. Mark in space provided.

Repeat three times.

Half-step _____   Time _____

_____   _____

_____   _____

*Average _____   _____

*Add all 3 scores, divide by 3 to get average.

B. How many half-steps per quarter mile? _____

C. How many half-steps per mile? _____

D. How many total steps in mile? _____

E. How many steps for the entire trail? _____

It would take me _____ steps to hike the entire Appalachian Trail!

How Many Hiking Hours Would It Take to Complete the Trail?

A. How long does it take to hike a quarter-mile? _____

B. How long for one mile? _____

C. How many miles can you hike in one hour? _____

D. How many hiking hours would it take to do the entire 2,000 miles? _____

If I hiked _____ MPH for _____ hours, I could hike the Appalachian Trail!

From *It's Not Just Gym Anymore: Teaching Secondary School Students How to Be Active for Life* by Bane McCracken, 2001, Champaign, IL: Human Kinetics.

How Far to Mount Katahdin: Part II

Name: _____   Date: _____

How Fast Can You Hike?

Hiking all day with a loaded backpack is difficult. Monitor your pulse to determine how fast you should hike. In order to conserve energy and to be able to continue hiking for long periods, you should keep your pulse levels at 50 to 60% of maximum.

Calculate Your Pulse

A. 220

   − _____ your age

This is your maximum pulse rate

B. 50% of your maximum pulse rate = _____

C. 60% of your maximum pulse rate = _____

D. 70% of your maximum pulse rate = _____

E. 80% of your maximum pulse rate = _____

F. 90% of your maximum pulse rate = _____

How Fast Should You Hike?

On a measured quarter-mile track, walk at a comfortable pace. Record your pulse rate and time for each lap. Do not let your pulse rise above the 60% level!

A. Lap 1   Time: _____   Pulse: _____

B. Lap 2   Time: _____   Pulse: _____

C. Lap 3   Time: _____   Pulse: _____

At this pace, how long would it take to hike 10 miles?

From *It's Not Just Gym Anymore: Teaching Secondary School Students How to Be Active for Life* by Bane McCracken, 2001, Champaign, IL: Human Kinetics.

How Far to Mount Katahdin: Part III

Name: _____ Date: _____

How Fast Can You Hike With a Load?

On a measured quarter-mile track, walk at a comfortable pace while carrying a 40-pound load. Record your pulse rate and time for each lap. Do not let your pulse rise above the 60% level!

A. Lap 1   Time: _____ Pulse: _____

B. Lap 2   Time: _____ Pulse: _____

C. Lap 3   Time: _____ Pulse: _____

At this pace, how long would it take to hike 20 miles? _____

How Fast Can You Hike Uphill?

As you hike uphill, you must go at a slower pace. On a measured quarter-mile grade of 8% record your pulse and time. Do not let your pulse rise above the 60% level!

A. Climb 1   Time: _____ Pulse: _____

B. Climb 2   Time: _____ Pulse: _____

C. Climb 3   Time: _____ Pulse: _____

How long will it take to climb to the top of Mt. Katahdin? _____

From *It's Not Just Gym Anymore: Teaching Secondary School Students How to Be Active for Life* by Bane McCracken, 2001, Champaign, IL: Human Kinetics.

How Far to Mount Katahdin? Part IV

Name: _____   Date: _____

Let's take a hike in cyberspace with a visit to the following Web sites. (Note: The Web addresses used in this form were accurate at the time of publication. If the site is no longer active, search **www.yahoo.com** or a similar search engine to find the answers.)

1. Visit **www.gorp.com** and answer the following questions:
a. What source on this page gives you details on trails?

b. List three trails on this list that do not go through your state.

c. List and describe three trails you'd like to hike.

2. Surf the Internet and find three hiking sites. Describe the sites below.

3. Now that you've found three hiking sites answer the following questions.
a. What did you like about the site? What didn't you like?

b. What kind of information would you like hiking Web sites to provide? What information was helpful to you?

How Far to Mount Katahdin? Part V

Name: _____   Date: _____

Hiking really burns a lot of calories. Carrying a 20-pound pack while hiking burns 3.5 calories per pound of body weight per hour. Use the following formula to find out how many calories you will need to hike a day on the trail.

3.5 × your body weight × hours of hiking (8) = hiking calories

3.5 × _____ × 8 hours of hiking = _____ hiking calories

body weight × 10 = _____ regular calorie intake

Total calories needed per day: _____ (hiking calories + regular calorie intake)

What's for dinner? Use **www.yahoo.com** to find four different Web sites that provide backpacker recipes. List the addresses below:

1.

2.

3.

4.

Copy and paste one recipe for each meal of the day: breakfast, lunch, and dinner.

Use Microsoft® Word® and print out a copy for your portfolio.

From *It's Not Just Gym Anymore: Teaching Secondary School Students How to Be Active for Life* by Bane McCracken, 2001, Champaign, IL: Human Kinetics.

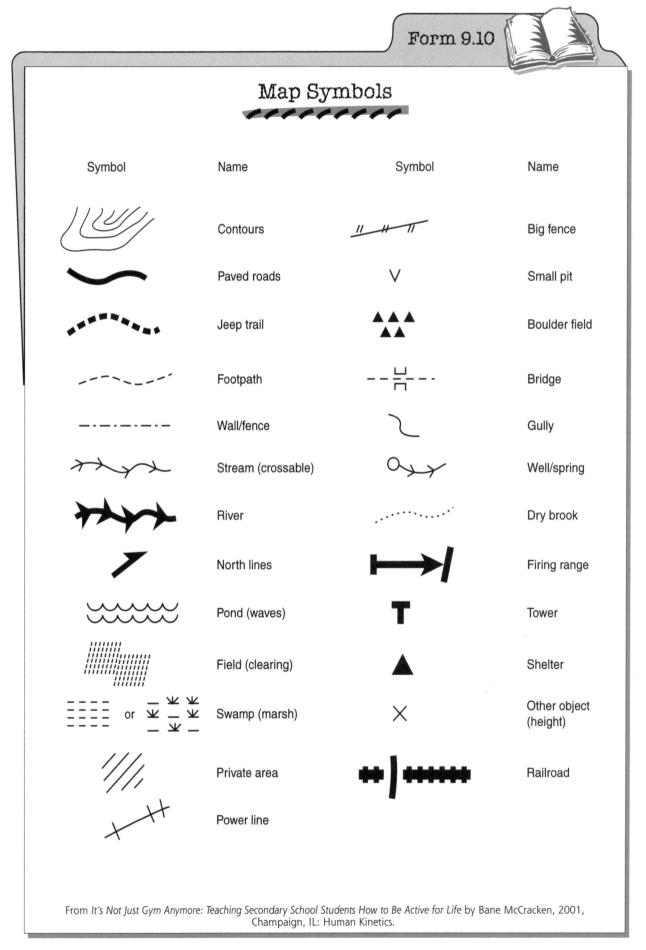

Map Symbols

Symbol	Name	Symbol	Name
	Contours		Big fence
	Paved roads		Small pit
	Jeep trail		Boulder field
	Footpath		Bridge
	Wall/fence		Gully
	Stream (crossable)		Well/spring
	River		Dry brook
	North lines		Firing range
	Pond (waves)		Tower
	Field (clearing)		Shelter
	Swamp (marsh)		Other object (height)
	Private area		Railroad
	Power line		

From *It's Not Just Gym Anymore: Teaching Secondary School Students How to Be Active for Life* by Bane McCracken, 2001, Champaign, IL: Human Kinetics.

Compass Challenge Courses 1 Through 4

Name: _____   *Date:* _____

Part I

Course 1 starts at cone 1	Course 2 starts at cone 2	Course 3 starts at cone 3	Course 4 starts at cone 4
First reading: 20 degrees	First reading: 248 degrees	First reading: 292 degrees	First reading: 270 degrees
Second reading: 270 degrees	Second reading: 315 degrees	Second reading: 135 degrees	Second reading: 112 degrees
Third reading: 180 degrees	Third reading: 67 degrees	Third reading: 0 degrees	Third reading: 292 degrees
Fourth reading: 338 degrees	Fourth reading: 270 degrees	Fourth reading: 248 degrees	Fourth reading: 135 degrees
Fifth reading: 90 degrees	Fifth reading: 212 degrees	Fifth reading: 45 degrees	Fifth reading: 270 degrees
Sixth reading: 290 degrees	Sixth reading: 45 degrees	Sixth reading: 202 degrees	Sixth reading: 22 degrees
Seventh reading: 135 degrees	Seventh reading: 135 degrees	Seventh reading: 90 degrees	Seventh reading: 225 degrees
Eighth reading: 248 degrees	Eighth reading: 225 degrees	Eighth reading: 248 degrees	Eighth reading: 135 degrees

Part II

	Course 1	Course 2	Course 3	Course 4
First reading	Point _____	Point _____	Point _____	Point _____
Second reading	Point _____	Point _____	Point _____	Point _____
Third reading	Point _____	Point _____	Point _____	Point _____
Fourth reading	Point _____	Point _____	Point _____	Point _____
Fifth reading	Point _____	Point _____	Point _____	Point _____
Sixth reading	Point _____	Point _____	Point _____	Point _____
Seventh reading	Point _____	Point _____	Point _____	Point _____
Eighth reading	Point _____	Point _____	Point _____	Point _____

From *It's Not Just Gym Anymore: Teaching Secondary School Students How to Be Active for Life* by Bane McCracken, 2001, Champaign, IL: Human Kinetics.

Compass Challenge Courses 5 Through 8

Name: _____   Date: _____

Part I

Course 5 starts at cone 5	Course 6 starts at cone 6	Course 7 starts at cone 7	Course 8 starts at cone 8
First reading: 235 degrees	First reading: 135 degrees	First reading: 90 degrees	First reading: 0 degrees
Second reading: 112 degrees	Second reading: 338 degrees	Second reading: 338 degrees	Second reading: 90 degrees
Third reading: 270 degrees	Third reading: 135 degrees	Third reading: 270 degrees	Third reading: 248 degrees
Fourth reading: 0 degrees	Fourth reading: 338 degrees	Fourth reading: 135 degrees	Fourth reading: 90 degrees
Fifth reading: 112 degrees	Fifth reading: 270 degrees	Fifth reading: 0 degrees	Fifth reading: 270 degrees
Sixth reading: 338 degrees	Sixth reading: 202 degrees	Sixth reading: 225 degrees	Sixth reading: 45 degrees
Seventh reading: 270 degrees	Seventh reading: 112 degrees	Seventh reading: 22 degrees	Seventh reading: 112 degrees
Eighth reading: 157 degrees	Eighth reading: 248 degrees	Eighth reading: 180 degrees	Eighth reading: 202 degrees

Part II

	Course 5	Course 6	Course 7	Course 8
First reading	Point _____	Point _____	Point _____	Point _____
Second reading	Point _____	Point _____	Point _____	Point _____
Third reading	Point _____	Point _____	Point _____	Point _____
Fourth reading	Point _____	Point _____	Point _____	Point _____
Fifth reading	Point _____	Point _____	Point _____	Point _____
Sixth reading	Point _____	Point _____	Point _____	Point _____
Seventh reading	Point _____	Point _____	Point _____	Point _____
Eighth reading	Point _____	Point _____	Point _____	Point _____

From *It's Not Just Gym Anymore: Teaching Secondary School Students How to Be Active for Life* by Bane McCracken, 2001, Champaign, IL: Human Kinetics.

Compass Challenge Courses 8A Through 5A

Name: _____   Date: _____

Part I

Course 8A starts at cone 8	Course 7A starts at cone 7	Course 6A starts at cone 6	Course 5A starts at cone 5
First reading: 90 degrees	First reading: 67 degrees	First reading: 135 degrees	First reading: 135 degrees
Second reading: 248 degrees	Second reading: 180 degrees	Second reading: 0 degrees	Second reading: 292 degrees
Third reading: 22 degrees	Third reading: 22 degrees	Third reading: 248 degrees	Third reading: 135 degrees
Fourth reading: 270 degrees	Fourth reading: 270 degrees	Fourth reading: 69 degrees	Fourth reading: 22 degrees
Fifth reading: 180 degrees	Fifth reading: 45 degrees	Fifth reading: 270 degrees	Fifth reading: 180 degrees
Sixth reading: 22 degrees	Sixth reading: 248 degrees	Sixth reading: 202 degrees	Sixth reading: 67 degrees
Seventh reading: 138 degrees	Seventh reading: 180 degrees	Seventh reading: 112 degrees	Seventh reading: 112 degrees
Eighth reading: 225 degrees	Eighth reading: 112 degrees	Eighth reading: 248 degrees	Eighth reading: 202 degrees

Part II

	Course 8A	Course 7A	Course 6A	Course 5A
First reading	Point _____	Point _____	Point _____	Point _____
Second reading	Point _____	Point _____	Point _____	Point _____
Third reading	Point _____	Point _____	Point _____	Point _____
Fourth reading	Point _____	Point _____	Point _____	Point _____
Fifth reading	Point _____	Point _____	Point _____	Point _____
Sixth reading	Point _____	Point _____	Point _____	Point _____
Seventh reading	Point _____	Point _____	Point _____	Point _____
Eighth reading	Point _____	Point _____	Point _____	Point _____

Compass Challenge Courses 4A Through 1A

Name: _____   Date: _____

Part I

Course 4A starts at cone 4	Course 3A starts at cone 3	Course 2A starts at cone 2	Course 1A starts at cone 1
First reading: 248 degrees	First reading: 202 degrees	First reading: 22 degrees	First reading: 67 degrees
Second reading: 45 degrees	Second reading: 180 degrees	Second reading: 315 degrees	Second reading: 315 degrees
Third reading: 112 degrees	Third reading: 22 degrees	Third reading: 225 degrees	Third reading: 112 degrees
Fourth reading: 180 degrees	Fourth reading: 225 degrees	Fourth reading: 22 degrees	Fourth reading: 270 degrees
Fifth reading: 112 degrees	Fifth reading: 67 degrees	Fifth reading: 90 degrees	Fifth reading: 45 degrees
Sixth reading: 158 degrees	Sixth reading: 180 degrees	Sixth reading: 258 degrees	Sixth reading: 258 degrees
Seventh reading: 67 degrees	Seventh reading: 315 degrees	Seventh reading: 112 degrees	Seventh reading: 90 degrees
Eighth reading: 225 degrees	Eighth reading: 158 degrees	Eighth reading: 258 degrees	Eighth reading: 212 degrees

Part II

	Course 4A	Course 3A	Course 2A	Course 1A
First reading	Point _____	Point _____	Point _____	Point _____
Second reading	Point _____	Point _____	Point _____	Point _____
Third reading	Point _____	Point _____	Point _____	Point _____
Fourth reading	Point _____	Point _____	Point _____	Point _____
Fifth reading	Point _____	Point _____	Point _____	Point _____
Sixth reading	Point _____	Point _____	Point _____	Point _____
Seventh reading	Point _____	Point _____	Point _____	Point _____
Eighth reading	Point _____	Point _____	Point _____	Point _____

Course Key

1	2	3	4	5	6	7	8	8a	7a	6a	5a	4a	3a	2a	1a
4	1	6	6	7	2	3	6	2	4	2	3	7	2	3	2
6	7	2	3	2	5	4	4	1	2	4	5	8	5	6
5	4	4	6	8	3	6	7	4	3	7	2	4	5	7	3
7	6	7	2	6	4	2	3	6	7	4	3	6	7	6	7
3	7	5	8	3	6	4	7	8	5	6	7	7	4	4	5
6	5	8	5	4	7	8	5	5	6	7	4	8	2	7	6
2	3	2	7	6	2	5	4	3	8	2	8	3	6	2	4
1	1	1	1	1	1	1	1	1	1	1	1	1	1	1	1

Compass Challenge Course

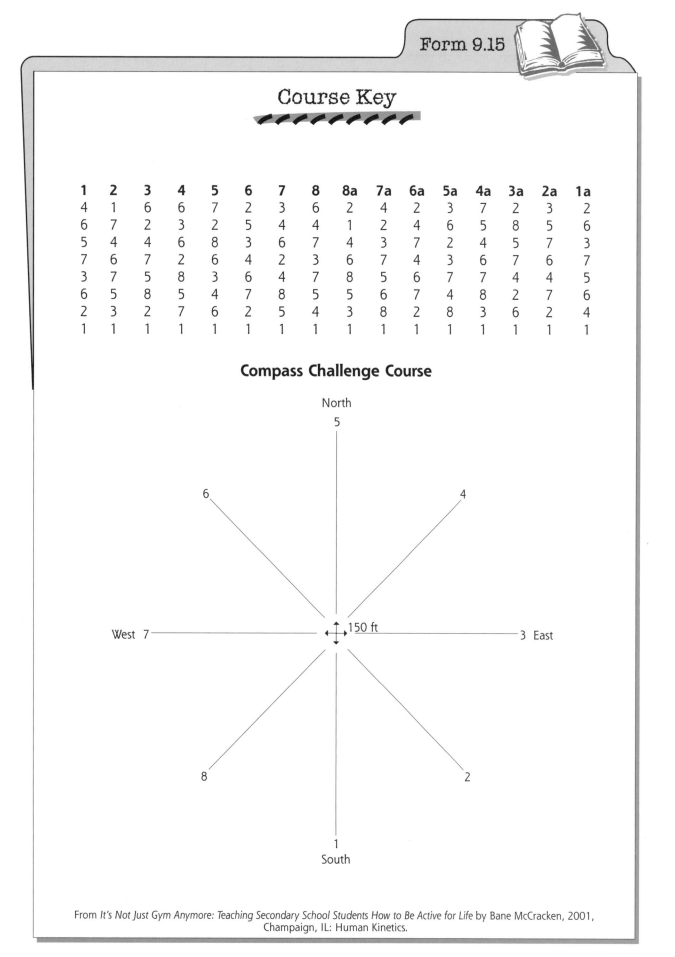

Survival Quiz

Name: _____   Date: _____

Can you survive in the wilderness? How well you can answer the following questions may be an indication.

Rate yourself on a scale of one to five on your ability to answer the following questions. How well you know the answers may save your life.

1. Do you know what a topographical map is?
2. Can you use a compass?
3. Can you identify poison ivy, poison oak, and poison sumac?
4. Can you build a lean-to?
5. Do you know what to do when you fall out of a white-water raft in the middle of a rapid?
6. Can you run two miles without stopping?
7. Can you define foot entrapment?
8. Do you know how to treat a poisonous snakebite?
9. Do you know the simplest way to purify water to drink?
10. Do you know the symptoms of giardia?
11. If confronted with a difficult challenge, can you relax and keep your sense of humor?
12. Can you list ten essential items you should carry in a daypack?
13. Can you list the seven survival priorities?
14. Can you start a fire with just one match?
15. Do you know the symptoms of heat exhaustion?
16. Do you know the symptoms of heat stroke?
17. Do you know how to treat a victim of heat stroke or heat exhaustion?
18. Can you define hypothermia?
19. Can you identify all the poisonous snakes in your area?
20. If you got lost in the wilderness would you know what to do?

Rating

95 to 100 You're a real survivor!

90 to 95 You're able to meet most challenges.

80 to 90 Make more preparations.

Below 80 Don't take any chances.

From *It's Not Just Gym Anymore: Teaching Secondary School Students How to Be Active for Life* by Bane McCracken, 2001, Champaign, IL: Human Kinetics.

Take a Walk on the Wild Side

Procedure

Take a leisurely walk to a quiet, natural setting. Sit quietly for at least five minutes and observe an object of nature. Pay close attention to how the object is moving.

Parts of Speech

Adverbs—words or phrases that modify verbs and explain how, when, where, to what extent, how often.

List adverbs related to how the object is moving.

Adjectives—words that describe nouns (nouns are names of people, places, things, and ideas) and tell which one, what kind, how many, what color, what size, and whose.

Describe the object.

From *It's Not Just Gym Anymore: Teaching Secondary School Students How to Be Active for Life* by Bane McCracken, 2001, Champaign, IL: Human Kinetics.

Dimensions of Hiking

Name: _____ Date: _____

1. What do you need to know to hike the Appalachian Trail? List at least five items in their order of importance.

2. What other activities have you done that are similar to hiking the Appalachian Trail? List five.

3. Choose one of the activities listed above and tell how it is similar to hiking the Appalachian Trail.

4. Let's go hike the trail. Where would you start, when would you go, who would go with you, and how would you get ready?

5. Now that you have studied the Appalachian Trail, what did you learn?

From *It's Not Just Gym Anymore: Teaching Secondary School Students How to Be Active for Life* by Bane McCracken, 2001, Champaign, IL: Human Kinetics.

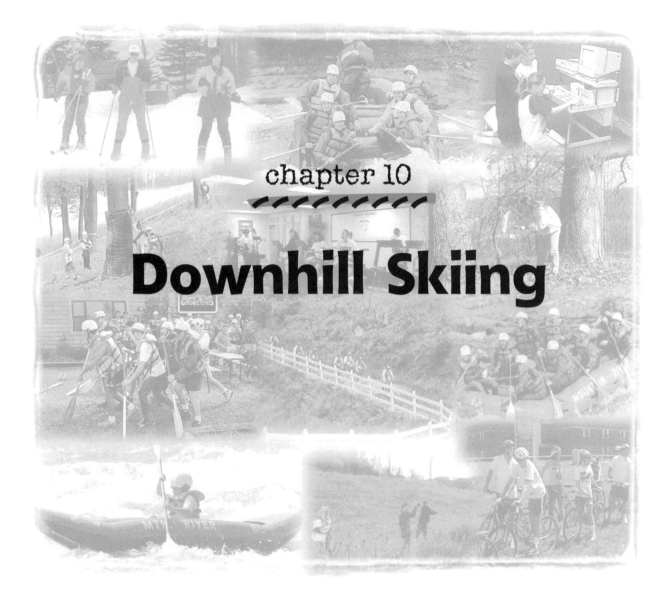

chapter 10

Downhill Skiing

Some schools may have great facilities, but few if any have their own ski slopes. While we can't teach our students how to ski, we can teach them what they need to know to be able to ski successfully. Students can learn how to prepare physically for the upcoming ski season, how to dress, what equipment is necessary, how to plan a trip, and what costs are involved. At the conclusion of a skiing unit, an optional ski trip to a local resort can be offered at the students' expense. Lessons are available at the resort, or students can learn on their own.

Many students have had their first ski experiences as a result of the ski unit and field trips offered at Cabell Midland High School. Almost all have a great time, and many return often and continue to ski as adults. The most important aspect of the downhill ski unit is that students realize that fitter students can ski longer without getting tired and therefore have more fun. This provides a great incentive for the less fit students to get in shape for the next ski trip or the next ski season. Many have taken additional physical education courses or joined fitness or health clubs.

The objectives of a ski unit are to teach students to

- recognize the fitness benefits of skiing,
- analyze the fitness requirements of skiing,
- learn to use a variety of fitness equipment and training methods to develop a personal fitness plan that will help encourage participation in skiing and reduce the risk of injury,
- recognize proper technique and methods of improving skill so they know what they need to do to get ready to ski,
- locate and compare local facilities to those in other locations, and
- identify sources of equipment and supplies and make cost comparisons.

Lesson 1

Invitation to Skiing

1. Show videos of past ski trips. Discuss skiing and ski trips.
2. Announce dates for the ski trips and pass out forms for participation (see figure 5.3).
3. Show videos from past trips of a variety of skiers of different skill levels in different situations.
4. Distribute student portfolios.
5. Have students analyze the fitness requirements of skiing by imitating ski actions.
   a. Distribute pulse monitors.
   b. Demonstrate simulated ski activities and have students practice. Ski actions include the slide trainer, side-to-side rope jump, and jumping off and on step aerobic boxes. Each jump represents a turn in a different direction.
   c. Record pulse levels for each activity.
6. Have students use anatomical charts to help identify the muscles used in skiing.
7. Discuss the fitness requirements of skiing using the fitness rubric (form 6.4).
8. Closure: stretches for skiing and review. Areas to emphasize when stretching for skiing are the calves, thighs, feet, and ankles. A good resource for skiing stretches and all stretching is *Stretching* by Bob Anderson (see resources on p. 238).

Lesson 2

Muscular Strength for Skiing

This lesson should be conducted in a weight room.

1. Review the fitness requirements of skiing and the muscles used.
2. Discuss resistance training for skiing.
3. Demonstrate exercises in the downhill skiing workout (form 10.1) and identify the muscles used in each.
4. Have students complete one set of the downhill skiing workout.
5. Closure: review and stretch for skiing.

Lesson 3

Exercise Machines for Skiing

This lesson should be conducted in a wellness center.

1. Remind students of the date for the ski trip and forms.
2. Demonstrate the use of each machine: treadmill, StairMaster, Life-cycle, NordicTrack, Concept II rower, Airdyne.
3. Distribute pulse monitors.
4. Instruct students to use machines to elevate their pulse to their exercise zone and hold at that level for 10 minutes. After 10 minutes have students rotate to another machine.

5. Closure: discuss the difference between pulse levels achieved on the machines and pulse levels achieved while doing the simulated ski activities of lesson 1. Stretch for skiing.

Lesson 4

Balance Training and Where to Go

1. Hand out portfolios and a state or local skiing magazine.
2. Discuss places to ski in your area.
3. Divide the class into two groups and set up the following stations:
   a. Group 1: Students use magazines and road maps to locate ski resorts and identify them on blank county maps.
   b. Group 2: Balance plyometrics (form 10.2)

   Note: I developed balance plyometric activities while coaching wrestling to improve balance. Plyometrics are great for helping to develop balance for any activity.
4. Closure: review.

Lesson 5

Cyber Ski

This lesson should be conducted in a computer lab.

1. Pass out portfolios and go to the computer lab.
2. Have students use form 10.3 to make a comparison of a local ski resort to a ski resort in another part of the country or the world.

Lesson 6

Muscular Strength for Skiing

This lesson should be conducted in a weight room.

1. Review the fitness requirements of skiing and the muscles used.

2. Discuss resistance training for skiing.
3. Have students complete two sets of the downhill skiing workout (form 10.1).
4. Closure: review and stretch for skiing.

Lesson 7

Exercise Machines for Skiing

This lesson should be conducted in a wellness center.

1. Remind students of the date of the ski trip and forms.
2. Review the use of machines: treadmill, StairMaster, Life-cycle, NordicTrack, Concept II rower, Airdyne.
3. Distribute pulse monitors.
4. Have students use machines to elevate their pulse to their exercise zone and hold at that level for 10 minutes. After 10 minutes they rotate to another machine. Have them record their results on form 10.4.
5. Closure: discuss the difference between the pulse levels achieved on the machines and those achieved while doing the simulated ski activities of lesson 1. Stretch for skiing.

Lesson 8

Balance Training and Dressing for Skiing

1. Discuss proper dress for extreme conditions and skiing. Bring personal clothing samples if possible.
2. Distribute clothing and equipment catalogs (LL Bean, REI, and others will gladly send enough catalogs for the entire class).
3. Divide the class into two groups and set up the following stations:
   a. Group 1: Use catalogs to make a clothing checklist for the ski trip. Follow instructions in portfolios.
   b. Group 2: Balance plyometrics (form 10.2)
4. Closure: review.

Lesson 9

Final Preparations for Ski Trip

1. Check for all fees and forms of students taking the ski trip.
2. Review procedures, the trip itinerary, and rules of conduct.
3. Have students complete the assignments in their portfolios.

Lesson 10

Take a Ski Trip

1. Check in students using a checklist.
2. Review the itinerary and rules. Place a copy of each in plain view.
3. Upon arrival:

   a. Secure lift tickets and distribute rental forms and lesson tickets to students.

   b. Help students with equipment and lockers.

   c. Videotape as much action as possible.
4. Have fun skiing with the students.
5. As the departure time nears, remind students of the time.
6. Help with the return of equipment.
7. Check in students for return.

Lesson 11

Video Review

1. Watch the video of the ski trip (kids love this).
2. Discuss the problems and the successes of the trip. Share stories with students. Skill evaluation is not a significant part of the evaluation. If students were physically active and had a good time, that is all the skill they need.
3. Discuss and have students complete "Dimensions of Skiing" (form 10.5).

Downhill Skiing Workout Record

Name: _____

Date	Bench press wt/reps	T row wt/reps	Military wt/reps	Lat pull-down wt/reps	Squat wt/reps	Leg curl wt/reps	Leg extend wt/reps	Side lunge wt/reps	Other wt/reps

From *It's Not Just Gym Anymore: Teaching Secondary School Students How to Be Active for Life* by Bane McCracken, 2001, Champaign, IL: Human Kinetics.

Balance Plyometrics

Part I

1. 5-min warm-up walk/jog, etc.
2. Group stretch: hold each position for a 5 count, increase pressure for 3 sets (no talking while stretching).
   a. Seated legs spread (right, left, middle)
   b. Seated legs together
   c. Pretzels
   d. Cross-chest
   e. Behind head
   f. Quads and calves against wall
3. Tae Bo kick-boxing for 5 to 10 min

Part II

Go to the wrestling mat, take off your shoes, and practice landing and maintaining balance.

1. Two-foot stand and lean (forward, back, side)
2. One-foot stand and squat, change feet
3. "Stick the landing"
   a. Two-foot jump (forward and back)
   b. One-foot jump (forward and back)

Part III

Divide into four groups of equal size.

Group 1: Alternating-leg lateral box jumps
"Stick the landing." Four to six boxes. Complete 3 sets. Stretch quads and calves.

Group 2: Physio-ball workout
While lying face up on the giant balls, students do the following:

a. 25 crunches
b. 25 oblique crunches (each side)
c. 25 side crunches (each side)
d. 25 "Hammock" (with feet flat on the floor and shoulders supported by the physio ball, rock back and forth like a swing hammock)
e. 10 rolls from face up to face down.
f. 10 hand-stands (while lying face down on the ball, raise legs to a hand/head stand position, lower legs, and repeat

Group 3: Balance "toys"
Take turns using the following:

a. Tilt walker
b. Imitation snowboard/ski trainer
c. Tilt board

Group 4: Slide workout

Part IV

Stretch alone and then with a partner.

From *It's Not Just Gym Anymore: Teaching Secondary School Students How to Be Active for Life* by Bane McCracken, 2001, Champaign, IL: Human Kinetics.

Cyber Ski

Name: _____   Date: _____

To compare two ski resorts, go to their Web sites and answer the questions below.

Nearby ski resort: _____   Ski resort in another part of the country or world: _____

1. How do I get there?

2. How much does it cost?
   Lift tickets:

   Rentals:

   Other:

3. Number of slopes/lifts

4. Conditions

5. Phone numbers

6. Area accommodations (hotels)

7. Special attractions

8. Can you snowboard?

9. Hours

From *It's Not Just Gym Anymore: Teaching Secondary School Students How to Be Active for Life* by Bane McCracken, 2001, Champaign, IL: Human Kinetics.

Wellness Center Workout Record

Name: _____

Date	Machine used	Time	Pace/distance/units	Pulse/pace

Dimensions of Skiing

Name: _____   Date: _____

1. What do you need to know to go skiing? List at least five items in their order of importance.

2. What other activities have you done that are similar to skiing? List five.

3. Choose one of the activities you listed above and tell how it is similar to skiing.

4. Let's go! Make a plan to go skiing (who, when, where, how).

5. Now that you have finished the unit, what did you learn?

From *It's Not Just Gym Anymore: Teaching Secondary School Students How to Be Active for Life* by Bane McCracken, 2001, Champaign, IL: Human Kinetics.

chapter 11

Mountain Biking

When other physical education teachers discover that I teach mountain biking, they have two questions: what about liability and where did I get the bikes? The liability issue is no greater for teaching mountain biking than it is for any other vigorous activity as long as proper procedures are followed. Make sure to use recommended safety equipment, check for the condition of equipment, provide a safe environment, monitor student activity closely, and follow step-by-step developmentally appropriate teaching procedures.

Cycling is one of the best ways to develop and maintain fitness. Professional cyclists are among the fittest of all athletes. Cycling is a lifetime individual activity that does not require team members and is still practiced by many people long after other forms of physical activity are no longer practical. Unlike many other sports, cycling is very low impact; it's great for people who cannot tolerate high-impact activities such as running, which is stressful on the knees and feet.

Because I have been an avid cyclist for over 40 years and have built and maintained my bicycles and participated in numerous races, I feel confident in my ability and my knowledge of cycling. If you need to develop skill before beginning a mountain-biking unit, visit your local cycle shop. Ask about local clubs and organizations that may be willing to help. Several national organizations with local affiliation have programs in place. The League of American Wheelmen offers several courses in effective cycling and certification for instructors. Try cycling—you'll love it.

I began teaching mountain biking by bringing two bikes from home. Students took turns while participating in other activities. When our county built our new school, the state provided funds for the purchase of new equipment. The beginning of our fleet of mountain bikes came from these funds. The owner of a local bike shop contacted representatives from bike manufacturers and obtained special prices, then assembled the bikes for free. Small grants, fund-raisers, and private donations allowed us to acquire a fleet of 30 bikes.

The biggest problem with teaching mountain biking has been maintenance, especially flat tires. If your school is going to purchase bikes, you should decide who will be responsible for repairs—you, a talented student, or a local bike shop. In any case, your budget should include the inevitable cost of parts and repair. Much of the repair cost can be avoided by regularly including maintenance days in your lesson plans. On maintenance days, students clean, lubricate, and learn to inspect and make minor adjustments and repairs. The maintenance days help reduce the cost of repairs and teach the students to be responsible for their equipment.

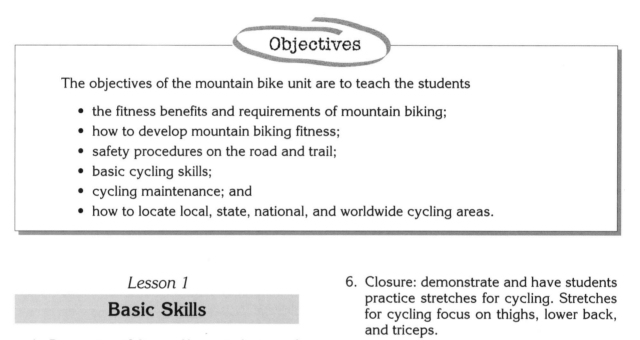

Objectives

The objectives of the mountain bike unit are to teach the students

- the fitness benefits and requirements of mountain biking;
- how to develop mountain biking fitness;
- safety procedures on the road and trail;
- basic cycling skills;
- cycling maintenance; and
- how to locate local, state, national, and worldwide cycling areas.

Lesson 1

Basic Skills

1. Pass out portfolios and have students read and discuss class rules (forms 11.1–11.3).
2. Use the diagram of a mountain bike (form 11.4) to teach terms and parts.
3. Demonstrate the preride inspection (check inflation, brakes and brake alignment, seat adjustment, and wheel locks).
4. Demonstrate bike setup (adjust seat height, angle, and front-to-back alignment).
5. Demonstrate and have students practice mounting, dismounting, starting, stopping, and using the rear brake versus the front brake.
6. Closure: demonstrate and have students practice stretches for cycling. Stretches for cycling focus on thighs, lower back, and triceps.

Lesson 2

Basic Skills

Videotape students performing most of these activities for later use.

1. Review inspection, setup, and class rules.
2. Conduct preride inspections.
3. Review and have students practice start and stop drills.

4. Demonstrate the slalom technique, inside pedal up.

5. Ride bike slalom using the inside-pedal-up technique. Place a series of 6 to 10 cones in a straight line 10 feet apart. Students ride in between the cones.

6. Conduct a short fitness ride (10 minutes) around the school parking lots.

7. Closure: review, stretch, and have students work on "Reflections on Biking Rules of the Road/Trail" (form 11.5).

Lesson 3

Pedal Techniques and Warming Up

1. Demonstrate proper pedal technique on a training stand. Focus on making circles and "spinning."

2. Make sure all students have shifted to the lowest gear (granny gear) and have conducted preride inspections.

3. Have students warm up using very low gears and practicing "spinning."

4. Identify and instruct a ride captain. Take a granny-gear ride around the school; maintain a good pace, and stop at predetermined spots. Instruct the student ride captain to set a pace in front and follow in the rear for observational purposes.

5. Closure: review, stretch, and have students continue to work on "Reflections on Biking Rules of the Road/Trail" (form 11.5).

Lesson 4

Bike-Handling Drills

1. Review videos of previous classes performing bike-handling skill drills.

2. Conduct preride inspections.

3. Demonstrate and have students practice the following while you videotape them in action:

   a. Bike right, hips left

   b. Bike left, hips right

   c. Slalom

   d. Track stand drills

4. Take a short fitness ride (15 minutes) around the school parking lots.

5. Closure: review, stretch, and have students continue to work on "Reflections on Biking Rules of the Road/Trail" (form 11.5).

Lesson 5

Maintenance Day

This lesson is good for a rainy day.

1. Discuss and have students complete the fitness rubric (form 6.4) and self-evaluation (form 11.6).

2. Demonstrate gear changing on a trainer and have students practice on the trainer.

3. Have students wash, adjust, lubricate, and repair all bikes and check for problems.

4. Have students use a computer to complete a cyber bike ride (form 11.7). Students can complete this task while waiting their turns to use maintenance equipment or after they have completed work on their bikes.

5. Closure: check students' progress on portfolio entries.

Lesson 6

Changing Gears

1. Review changing gears and demonstrate on a trainer.

2. Conduct preride inspections.

3. Working in small groups, have students circle while you observe them changing gears on command. As students progress, advanced students may help observe slower students.

4. Take a ride around the school parking lots changing gears on command.

   Note: once students have developed basic skills, fitness rides may be taken around the school. The procedure for any bike ride for the class is as follows:

   a. Select a student leader.

   b. Describe the ride directions to the student leader. This includes where to ride, how fast to go, and where to stop and regroup.

c. Ride with the students. I have found it best to remain near the back in order to better observe the students.

5. Practice progressive drills.

6. Closure: review and stretch.

Lesson 7

Riding Down Hills and on Rough Surfaces

1. Demonstrate on a trainer and use videos from previous classes to show riding positions for rough surfaces and going down hills.

2. Conduct preride inspections.

3. Lead progressive bike-handling drills and warm-up in granny gear.

4. Go to a grassy area with a small downhill.

   a. Demonstrate downhill position: standing on pedals, feet parallel to the ground, knees and arms bent, weight back.

   b. Have students practice downhill techniques.

   c. Videotape students practicing downhill techniques.

5. Take a 10-minute fitness ride.

6. Closure: review and stretch.

Lesson 8

Downhill Braking/Stopping

1. Review downhill techniques using the video from the previous day.

2. Have students evaluate their downhill technique while watching the video.

3. Conduct preride inspections.

4. Lead progressive bike-handling drills and warm-up in granny gear.

5. Go to a grassy area with a small downhill.

   a. Review downhill position: standing on pedals, feet parallel to the ground, knees and arms bent, weight back.

b. Have students practice downhill techniques.

c. Demonstrate downhill braking and stopping techniques and have students practice.

d. Videotape students practicing downhill braking and stopping technique.

6. Closure: review and stretch.

Lesson 9

Slow-Speed Turns

1. Review the video of downhill braking and stopping from the previous day and have students self-evaluate.

2. Show videos from previous classes and demonstrate the slow-speed turning technique.

3. Conduct preride inspections.

4. Divide the class into groups of three and have groups practice tiny turns around cones, that is, turn the wheel and keep the bike vertical—don't lean. Videotape the students.

5. Take a 15-minute fitness ride around the school.

6. Closure: stretch and review.

Lesson 10

Turns on Dry Pavement

1. Review videos of tiny turns from the previous day and have students self-evaluate.

2. Show videos from previous classes and demonstrate techniques for turning on dry pavement.

3. Conduct preride inspections.

4. Lead progressive bike-handling drills and warm-up in granny gear.

5. Review and practice tiny turns.

6. Demonstrate and have students practice turning technique on dry pavement (inside pedal up, lean bike, lean body, inside knee out, inside elbow over knee). Conduct this activity in the parking lot. Place cones so students ride in an oval and make turns at a relatively high speed.

After making several turns in one direction, have them change so that they practice turns in both directions. Videotape this activity.

7. Closure: review and stretch.

Lesson 11

Turns on Soft Surfaces

1. Review the video of turns on dry pavement from the previous day and have students self-evaluate (form 11.6).
2. Show videos from previous classes and demonstrate turns for soft surfaces.
3. Conduct preride inspections.
4. Lead progressive bike-handling drills and warm-up in granny gear.
5. Review and practice tiny turns and turns on dry pavement.
6. Demonstrate and have students practice turning techniques for soft surfaces (bike over, lift on outside handle, push down on inside handle, outside pedal down, weight over outside pedal, body out). Conduct this activity in a large field such as a practice football field. Videotape the students practicing.
7. Closure: stretch and review.

Lesson 12

Turns on Loose Surfaces

1. Review the video of turns on soft surfaces from the previous day and have students self-evaluate (form 11.6).
2. Show videos from previous classes and demonstrate turns for loose surfaces.
3. Conduct preride inspections.
4. Lead progressive bike-handling drills and warm-up in granny gear.
5. Review and practice tiny turns and turns on dry pavement.
6. Demonstrate and have students practice turning techniques for soft surfaces. The technique for loose surfaces is the same as that for dry pavement except that the inside foot is off the pedal and dragging lightly on the surface. This activity is best

conducted on a gravel or sandy surface. Videotape the students practicing.

7. Closure: stretch and review.

Lesson 13

Maintenance Day

1. Review the videos of all of the turning techniques.
2. Distribute magazines or other publications that have information or descriptions of mountain bike trails or rides.
3. Discuss places to ride in your state or area. Use a state road map and state trail map to locate these places and identify them on a blank county map.
4. Have students complete the PMI graph (form 11.8).
5. Have students wash, adjust, lubricate, and repair all bikes and check for problems.
6. Have students use a computer to help find places to ride and to locate and identify biking clubs and organizations. Students can complete this task while waiting their turn to use maintenance equipment or after they have completed work on their bikes.
7. Closure: check students' progress on portfolio entries.

Lesson 14

Riding Over Obstacles

1. Show videos from previous classes and demonstrate the technique for riding over obstacles (knees bent, weight back, lift handlebars and apply pedal pressure as the front wheel comes in contact with an object, shift weight quickly forward so weight is over the front wheel when the rear wheel comes in contact with the object).
2. Conduct preride inspections.
3. Lead progressive bike-handling drills and warm-up in granny gear.
4. Demonstrate and have students practice riding over obstacles such as small logs.
5. Demonstrate and have students practice "bunny hop" technique (approach an obstacle standing on pedals with feet

parallel to the surface, knees and arms flexed. Just before making contact with the object, spring up, and "hop" the bike over the object). This skill is performed at higher speeds and should be done by students only after mastering the first technique and when they feel confident. This activity is best conducted on a grassy surface. Videotape students practicing the technique.

6. Take a fitness ride around the school.
7. Closure: stretch and review.

Lesson 15

Single-Track Technique

Single track is unique to mountain biking. It is a term use to describe areas on a trail that are only wide enough to accommodate one cyclist at a time and that usually have many obstacles such as rocks and logs along the path. This lesson can be repeated to develop skills.

1. Review videos from previous lessons: turning, riding up and down hills, riding over obstacles.
2. Explain the single-track technique combining all previous skills.
3. Show videos of previous classes riding single track.
4. Conduct preride inspections.
5. Lead progressive bike-handling drills and warm-up in granny gear.
6. Review and practice previous skills.
7. Take a single-track ride. The cross country course at Cabell Midland High School is an excellent single-track course. If a similar facility is not available, you can make one with cones, logs, and mounds of dirt. Making a single-track course is like making an obstacle course and takes a little imagination. Cones or building columns can be used to represent trees; dirt and sand piles left from construction can offer climbs and jumps; and railroad ties or logs can be used to provide additional obstacles. Mark the course with spray paint. Have the students try to ride the course without touching a foot to the ground.
8. Closure: review and stretch.

Lesson 16

Weight Training for Cycling

1. Discuss the fitness requirements for cycling (see the fitness rubric in form 6.4).
2. Go to the weight room and demonstrate weight-training techniques for cycling (form 11.9).
3. Have students lift weights for cycling.
4. Closure: review the benefits of weight training and stretch.

Lesson 17

Climbing Technique

1. Show videos of previous classes and demonstrate the technique for climbing hills (weight forward, elbows in, smooth pedal strokes, change one gear at a time, maintain momentum).
2. Conduct preride inspections.
3. Lead progressive bike-handling drills and warm-up in granny gear.
4. Demonstrate and have students practice the climbing technique. Conduct this activity on a steep hill 400 meters long that is part of the cross country course. Videotape students practicing the technique.
5. Take a cool-down ride in easy gears.
6. Closure: review and stretch.

Lesson 18

Fitness and Pulse Monitoring

1. Review the video from the previous lesson (hill climbing) and have students self-evaluate.
2. Distribute pulse monitors.
3. Discuss pulse levels and cycling. Use the fitness rubric (form 6.4).
4. Conduct preride inspections.
5. Lead progressive bike-handling drills and warm-up in granny gear.
6. Take a fun/fitness ride. Incorporate as many skills and elements as possible.

Stop periodically and have students record their pulses.

7. Closure: discuss pulse levels and cycling, stretch.

Lesson 19

Racing

1. Show a video of previous classes racing.
2. Discuss racing: organizations, safety, techniques, rewards.
3. Explain the procedure for tomorrow's race:
   a. Students get their bikes and perform preride inspections.
   b. Students warm up using granny gear on the road next to the school.
   c. Students report to the starting line for race instruction (how many laps and course description).
   d. Students self-seed the start (faster riders in front).
   e. Race begins.
4. Conduct preride inspections.
5. Warm-up in granny gear
6. Take a tour of the race course. Locate problem areas and demonstrate techniques best suited for each situation.
7. Closure: review and discuss racing strategy, stretch.

Lesson 20

Race Day

1. Review race procedures.
2. Conduct preride inspections.
3. Warm up in granny gear.
4. Get it on!!!
5. Post-race cool-down ride
6. Closure: race review and stretch

Lesson 21

Conclusion

1. Review with a "grand finale video" combining the best moments of the class.
2. Discuss and have students complete "Mountain Biker Attribute Web" (form 11.10). An attribute web is a form of graphic organizer. Students fill in the web with the attributes of mountain biking.
3. Discuss and have students complete "Dimensions of Mountain Biking" (form 11.11).
4. Inspect each bike with individual students and make lists of needed parts and repairs.
5. Have students work on completing portfolios.
6. Collect all student work.

Rules and Procedures for Class Bicycle Rides

1. Always inspect and adjust your bike before riding.

2. Always use safety equipment (helmet).

3. Always obey all traffic laws.

4. Always follow prescribed class ride procedures.

5. Always cooperate with the road captain.

6. Always ride within your ability level.

7. Always dismount and walk in situations you do not feel you can handle.

The road captain will always

1. be selected by the teacher,

2. discuss and make sure riders fully understand the day's assignment and procedures,

3. review the ride location, directions, special concerns, and instructions with the teacher prior to departure,

4. set a pace compatible with the slowest rider, and

5. identify predetermined stopping points and be in charge of arranging other students in proper stopping formation.

From *It's Not Just Gym Anymore: Teaching Secondary School Students How to Be Active for Life* by Bane McCracken, 2001, Champaign, IL: Human Kinetics.

Rules of the Road

It is important that every cyclist abide by the rules and regulations of safe bicycle riding. You should take the time to review the following information and understand its importance before you begin to ride. And remember, always wear a helmet!

Cyclists have the same rights and obligations when traveling the roadways as do motorists, so they, too, are subject to fines for disobeying the law. Traffic summonses may be issued to cyclists for running stop signs and red lights or riding on the wrong side of the road. All cyclists are obligated by law to obey all traffic signals. Cyclists have as much right to the roadways as motor vehicles and therefore must abide by the same rules and regulations. The rules are as follows:

- Stop at all marked intersections. At all intersections yell, "car left" or "car right" to warn other cyclists that cars are approaching from either of those directions.

- Ride single file, especially in high-traffic areas and on narrow roads. During cycling tours, stay to the right and ride single file.

- Before making a left turn, first check traffic to see if any cars are coming, then fully extend your left arm and point in that direction. Signal well in advance of the actual turn, and then position your bike so that traffic can move around you.

- When making a right turn, fully extend your right arm and point in the intended direction. Signal well in advance of the actual turn, and then use both hands to steer through the turn.

- If there is debris or a hazard in the road, fully extend your arm and point to the hazard. Sometimes moving your arm while pointing draws more attention to the debris. Potholes, branches, glass, sand, storm drains, and so on, should all be called out verbally as a courtesy to riders in the rear.

- When slowing or stopping, fully extend your arm down and out with the palm of your hand facing those who might be behind you. Call out, "slowing" or "stopping" while displaying your hand signal to warn riders behind you.

- When passing, call to the rider or pedestrian you are passing and announce, "on your left." Check that you are not cutting off another rider and only pass on the left. If you are being passed, continue straight; do not turn and look back.

- When a car is approaching from behind, call out to the riders ahead of you, "car back." This warning should be passed along by each rider to the front of the group until there is no one left to warn.

- When a car is approaching from ahead, call out to the riders behind you, "car up." This warning should be passed along by each rider to the back of the group until there is no one left to warn. On hearing this warning, move to the right and ride single file.

From *It's Not Just Gym Anymore: Teaching Secondary School Students How to Be Active for Life* by Bane McCracken, 2001, Champaign, IL: Human Kinetics.

Rules of the Trail

- Ride on open trails only. Respect trail and road closures and avoid trespassing on private land. Stay on existing trails and do not create new ones.

- Leave no trace of your presence. Be sensitive to the trails you ride. Do not leave evidence of your passing.

- Control your bike. Obey all bicycle speed regulations and recommendations. Space out on grades to allow riders use of the full width of the trail and to select the best line of approach.

- When encountering hikers head on, stop and pull over. If approaching from the rear, greet them, or sound a bell, then pass. Be friendly to land managers, hikers, and equestrians. When encountering equestrians from the front, stop, get off your bike, and move well off the trail until they pass. When approaching from the rear, ask permission to pass and ask for advice as to the best way to pass.

- Never spook animals. Animals are startled by unannounced approaches. Give animals extra room and time to adjust to you. Disturbing wildlife is a serious offense. Leave gates as you found them, or as marked.

- Plan ahead. Know your equipment, your ability, and the area in which you are riding. Be self-sufficient at all times and keep your equipment in good repair. Carry necessary supplies for changes in weather or other conditions. Always wear a helmet!

- Get involved with trail maintenance by using your spare time to clean up and repair the trails you ride.

From *It's Not Just Gym Anymore: Teaching Secondary School Students How to Be Active for Life* by Bane McCracken, 2001, Champaign, IL: Human Kinetics.

A Fully Equipped Mountain Bike

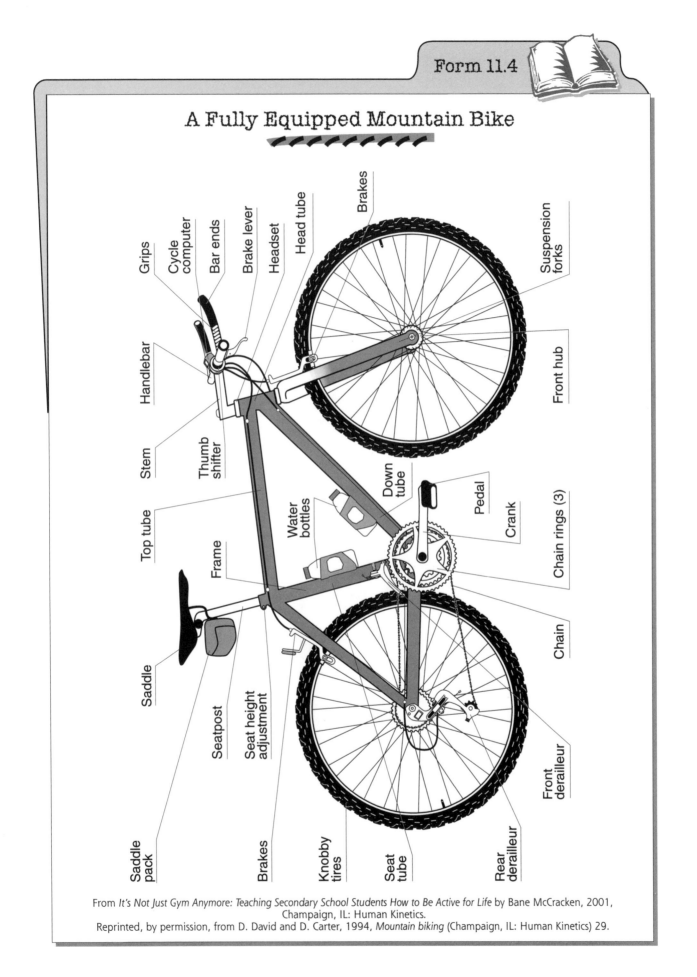

From *It's Not Just Gym Anymore: Teaching Secondary School Students How to Be Active for Life* by Bane McCracken, 2001, Champaign, IL: Human Kinetics.
Reprinted, by permission, from D. David and D. Carter, 1994, *Mountain biking* (Champaign, IL: Human Kinetics) 29.

Reflections on Biking Rules
of the Road/Trail

Name: _____   Date: _____

1. What are three key ideas?

2. What other questions do you have? List two.

3. What changes should you make in the way you ride your bike? List three.

4. How does bicycling relate to another class you now have in school?

From *It's Not Just Gym Anymore: Teaching Secondary School Students How to Be Active for Life* by Bane McCracken, 2001, Champaign, IL: Human Kinetics.

Mountain Biking Self-Evaluation

Name: _____   Date: _____

| **O** = not yet | **X** = getting better | **+** = proper technique |

1st week   *3rd week*   *End of class*

1. _____ _____ _____ Preride inspection and adjustments

2. _____ _____ _____ Fixing a flat tire

3. _____ _____ _____ Always wearing a helmet

4. _____ _____ _____ Following rules of the road

5. _____ _____ _____ Mounting, dismounting, starting, stopping

6. _____ _____ _____ Pedaling smoothly and steadily

7. _____ _____ _____ Maintaining proper following distance

8. _____ _____ _____ Can fix almost any damage

9. _____ _____ _____ Always taking proper care of bike

10. _____ _____ _____ Physical condition

11. _____ _____ _____ Using proper shifting technique

12. _____ _____ _____ Displaying proper respect for the trail

13. _____ _____ _____ Riding over obstacles

14. _____ _____ _____ Maintaining proper riding position

15. _____ _____ _____ Tricks (e.g., "bunny hop" technique)

From *It's Not Just Gym Anymore: Teaching Secondary School Students How to Be Active for Life* by Bane McCracken, 2001, Champaign, IL: Human Kinetics.

Cyber Biking

Name: _____   Date: _____

The Web addresses used in this form were accurate at the time of publication. If the site is no longer active, search **www.yahoo.com** or a similar search engine to find the answers.

1. Go to this site: **www.adventuresports.com**.
a. Make a list of things to bring on a bike trip.

b. What does the site tell you to do with talcum powder?

2. Go to this site and list some tips for beginning riders: **www.greatoutdoors.com**

3. This site has some great tips on doing tricks: **www.mtbonline.net**
a. How many of these tricks can you do?

b. Explain how to pop a wheelie.

4. Are you ready to race? Go to this site to search for mountain biking races near you: **www.mountainbike.com**. What is the closest race to your high school?

5. Are you ready to hit the mountain bike trail? Go to **www.bikezone.com** to find mountain biking trails near you. Write the trail directions here.

From *It's Not Just Gym Anymore: Teaching Secondary School Students How to Be Active for Life* by Bane McCracken, 2001, Champaign, IL: Human Kinetics.

PMI Graph for Mountain Biking

Name: _____   Date: _____

Brief Description of the Ride/Location

Positive Features

Negative Features

Interesting Features

From *It's Not Just Gym Anymore: Teaching Secondary School Students How to Be Active for Life* by Bane McCracken, 2001, Champaign, IL: Human Kinetics.

Weight Training for Mountain Biking

Exercise	Sets	Reps	Weight (First set)	Weight (Second set)
Squat	2	15		
Leg curl	2	15		
Leg extension	2	15		
Calf raise	2	15		
Box step-ups	2	15		
Bench press	2	15		
Tricep push-down	2	15		
T row	2	15		
Curl	2	15		
Dumbbell row	2	15		
Crunches	2	15		

From *It's Not Just Gym Anymore: Teaching Secondary School Students How to Be Active for Life* by Bane McCracken, 2001, Champaign, IL: Human Kinetics.

Mountain Biker Attribute Web

Name: _____   Date: _____

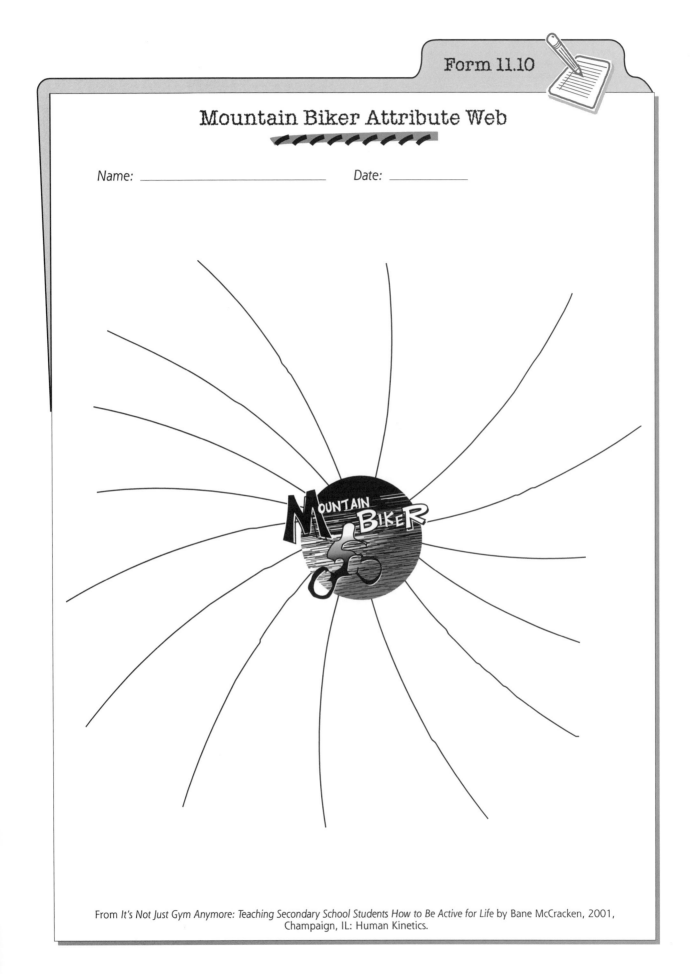

Dimensions of Mountain Biking

Name: _____   Date: _____

1. What do you need to know to go mountain biking? List at least five items in their order of importance.

2. What other activities have you done that are similar to mountain biking? List five.

3. Choose one of the activities you listed above and tell how it is similar to mountain biking.

4. Let's go! Make a plan to go mountain biking (who, when, where, how).

5. Now that you have finished the unit, what did you learn?

From *It's Not Just Gym Anymore: Teaching Secondary School Students How to Be Active for Life* by Bane McCracken, 2001, Champaign, IL: Human Kinetics.

chapter 12

Bow Hunting and Fly-Fishing

Bow hunting and fly-fishing are excellent activities for physical education. Bow hunting is extremely popular in many rural areas. Hunters make elaborate plans, scouting the best places, looking for signs of activity, and practicing their skills while eagerly looking forward to the first day of hunting season. Fishing from a boat or a riverbank does not require much physical activity, but fly-fishing can be quite demanding. Standing knee-deep in a fast-flowing river requires muscular exertion. Interest in fly-fishing has greatly increased since the release of the movie *A River Runs Through It*. Both activities are well justified as course offerings for physical education—they offer good fitness benefits, can be continued as lifetime activities, and are popular among adults. The Centers for Disease Control and Prevention list hunting and fishing among the top 10 activities of fit Americans.

Combining bow hunting and fly-fishing into one unit works well. Limits on equipment availability make it difficult to have all students shooting archery at once, and five students casting fly lines at once is about as many as is feasible. Teaching the two activities at the same time allows for better use of equipment. Some students can be shooting bows while others practice hitting a target with a fly rod.

Numerous resources are available for the teacher not familiar with hunting and fishing practices. Out-fitters such as Cabela's (**www.cabelas.com**), which specialize in outdoor equipment, offer a large selection of books and instructional videos on both fly-fishing and bow hunting. Numerous magazines are available, and Internet resources seem endless.

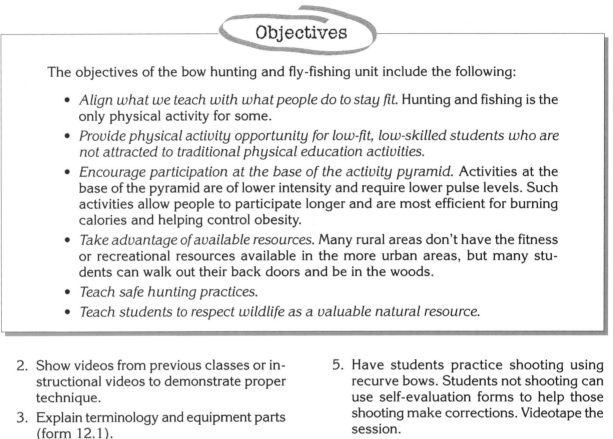

Objectives

The objectives of the bow hunting and fly-fishing unit include the following:

- *Align what we teach with what people do to stay fit.* Hunting and fishing is the only physical activity for some.
- *Provide physical activity opportunity for low-fit, low-skilled students who are not attracted to traditional physical education activities.*
- *Encourage participation at the base of the activity pyramid.* Activities at the base of the pyramid are of lower intensity and require lower pulse levels. Such activities allow people to participate longer and are most efficient for burning calories and helping control obesity.
- *Take advantage of available resources.* Many rural areas don't have the fitness or recreational resources available in the more urban areas, but many students can walk out their back doors and be in the woods.
- *Teach safe hunting practices.*
- *Teach students to respect wildlife as a valuable natural resource.*

2. Show videos from previous classes or instructional videos to demonstrate proper technique.
3. Explain terminology and equipment parts (form 12.1).
4. Explain safety procedures (form 12.2).
5. Demonstrate the 10 basic steps to shooting and have students practice (form 12.3).
6. Set up targets and have students practice shooting using recurve bows.
7. Closure: review.

Lesson 2

Shooting Technique

1. Review safety procedures and archery rules (form 12.2).
2. Review and practice the 10 steps to shooting (form 12.3).
3. Explain shooting self-evaluation (form 12.4).
4. Go to the shooting range and review procedures.

5. Have students practice shooting using recurve bows. Students not shooting can use self-evaluation forms to help those shooting make corrections. Videotape the session.
6. Closure: review

Lesson 3

Scoring

1. Show the video of students shooting from the previous lesson.
2. Discuss tips for improving shooting (form 12.5).
3. Explain scoring and rules for target archery (form 12.6).
4. Go to the shooting range and review procedures.
5. Have students practice shooting using recurve bows and keep score. Students not shooting can use self-evaluation forms to help those shooting make corrections. Videotape the session.
6. Closure: review.

Lesson 4

Compound Bows

1. Show the video from the previous lesson and have students self-evaluate (form 12.4).
2. Introduce the compound bow, discuss its benefits and advantages, and compare it to the recurve bow. (The compound bow uses concentric wheels that act as pulleys to reduce the effort needed to draw the bow to the shooting position. The amount of resistance may be changed to accommodate a wider range of students. Although more expensive than the recurve bow, the extra expenditure is well advised.)
3. Go to the shooting range and review procedures.
4. Have students practice shooting using compound bows and keep score. Students not shooting can use self-evaluation forms to help those shooting make corrections. Videotape the session.
5. Closure: review.

Lesson 5

Cyber Shopping

This lesson should be held in the computer lab.

1. Discuss the equipment necessary for bow hunting: bow, quiver, arrows, sight, release, peep site, and arrow rest.
2. Research the prices of a complete bow hunting outfit using form 12.7. Use the Internet and catalogs and compare the prices to those at local retail outlets. Outfitters will gladly supply catalogs for use in classes.

Lesson 6

Introduction to Fly-Fishing

1. Show an instructional fly-fishing video to demonstrate technique.
2. Discuss fly-fishing and compare it to traditional fishing.
3. Demonstrate the knots used for fly-fishing (form 12.8).

4. Have students work in small groups and practice tying knots.
5. Demonstrate how to set up a fly reel.
6. Divide the class into groups of five to six students. Have each group of students set up a fly reel: backing, fly line, leader, and tippet.
7. Closure: review.

Lesson 7

Fly-Casting

1. Show a video of fly-casting technique.
2. Demonstrate fly-casting technique and have students practice.
3. Videotape students' casting techniques.
4. Closure: use video to analyze students' techniques.

Lesson 8

Guest Speaker From the Department of Natural Resources

1. Discuss wildlife and fish stocking programs in the state or area.
2. Explain hunting and fishing regulations and fees.
3. Discuss ethical hunting and fishing practices.
4. Discuss special fly-fishing areas or streams.

Lesson 9

Cyber Fishing

This lesson should be held in the computer lab.

1. Review the topics of the guest speaker.
2. Have students visit the state Department of Natural Resources Web page.
3. Have students identify special fly-fishing streams and label them on state maps.
4. Have students search for fly-tying Web pages (there are hundreds with complete instructions).
5. Have students copy instructions for tying a fly.

Lesson 10

Fly-Tying

1. Show an instructional video of fly-tying technique.

2. Discuss fly-tying and explain equipment and procedure.

3. Divide the class into four groups. Set up an archery range and fly-casting practice area just outside the gym door to allow for supervision of both inside and outside activities.

    a. Group 1: Fly-tying (use an instructional video, or students may use instructions from the Internet)

    b. Group 2: Portfolio work at the computer

    c. Group 3: Archery

    d. Group 4: Fly-casting (videotape students)

4. Closure: review.

Lesson 11

Self-Evaluation .

Repeat this lesson until all students have had a chance to complete the assignments.

1. Review the videos of students fly-casting and have students self-evaluate (form 12.9).

2. Divide the class into four groups. Set up an archery range and fly-casting practice area just outside the gym door to allow for supervision of both inside and outside activities.

    a. Group 1: Fly-tying (use an instructional video, or students may use instructions from the Internet)

    b. Group 2: Portfolio work at the computer

    c. Group 3: Archery

    d. Group 4: Fly-casting (videotape students)

3. Closure: review. Discuss and have students complete "Dimensions of Fly-Fishing" (form 12.10).

Archery Terminology

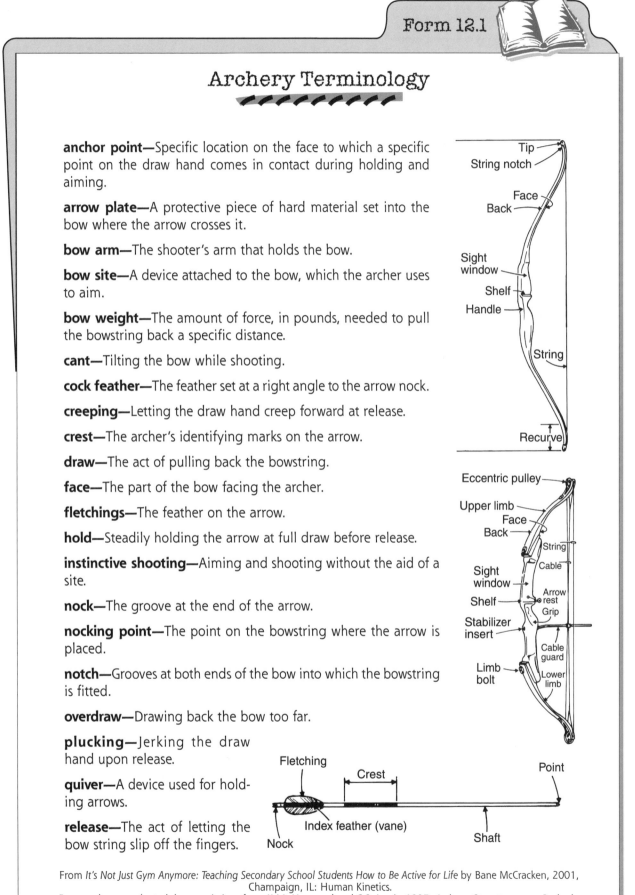

anchor point—Specific location on the face to which a specific point on the draw hand comes in contact during holding and aiming.

arrow plate—A protective piece of hard material set into the bow where the arrow crosses it.

bow arm—The shooter's arm that holds the bow.

bow site—A device attached to the bow, which the archer uses to aim.

bow weight—The amount of force, in pounds, needed to pull the bowstring back a specific distance.

cant—Tilting the bow while shooting.

cock feather—The feather set at a right angle to the arrow nock.

creeping—Letting the draw hand creep forward at release.

crest—The archer's identifying marks on the arrow.

draw—The act of pulling back the bowstring.

face—The part of the bow facing the archer.

fletchings—The feather on the arrow.

hold—Steadily holding the arrow at full draw before release.

instinctive shooting—Aiming and shooting without the aid of a site.

nock—The groove at the end of the arrow.

nocking point—The point on the bowstring where the arrow is placed.

notch—Grooves at both ends of the bow into which the bowstring is fitted.

overdraw—Drawing back the bow too far.

plucking—Jerking the draw hand upon release.

quiver—A device used for holding arrows.

release—The act of letting the bow string slip off the fingers.

From *It's Not Just Gym Anymore: Teaching Secondary School Students How to Be Active for Life* by Bane McCracken, 2001, Champaign, IL: Human Kinetics.
Bows and arrow adapted, by permission, from K.M. Haywood and C.S. Lewis, 1997, *Archery: Steps to success*, 2nd ed., (Champaign, IL: Human Kinetics), 11–13.

Safety Procedures for Target Archery

1. Check bow string before shooting.

2. Shoot only at target.

3. Do not draw bow when anyone is between you and the target.

4. Do not retrieve arrows until command is given.

5. Never shoot into the air or in any direction where damage may be done.

6. Always be sure area in back of target is clear or has proper backdrop.

7. Do not overdraw bow.

8. Do not release a fully drawn bow without an arrow.

9. No horseplay!!!

10. Always carry arrows with pile ends pointed toward ground.

11. When finished shooting, stand behind other archers until all shooting is completed.

From *It's Not Just Gym Anymore: Teaching Secondary School Students How to Be Active for Life* by Bane McCracken, 2001, Champaign, IL: Human Kinetics.

Ten Basic Steps to Shooting

1. Establish proper stance.

2. Nock the arrow.

3. Set the hook.

4. Establish bow hold.

5. Raise the head.

6. Raise the unit.

7. Draw and anchor.

8. Aim and hold.

9. Release.

10. Follow through.

From *It's Not Just Gym Anymore: Teaching Secondary School Students How to Be Active for Life* by Bane McCracken, 2001, Champaign, IL: Human Kinetics.

Shooting Self-Evaluation

Name: _____

Place the appropriate symbol in the space provided.

O = not yet	**X** = getting better	**+** = proper technique

Date: _____   _____   _____   _____

1. _____   _____   _____   _____ Stance

2. _____   _____   _____   _____ Bow grip

3. _____   _____   _____   _____ Nocking

4. _____   _____   _____   _____ Hook

5. _____   _____   _____   _____ Head position

6. _____   _____   _____   _____ Unit position

7. _____   _____   _____   _____ Draw

8. _____   _____   _____   _____ Draw arm

9. _____   _____   _____   _____ Bow arm

10. _____   _____   _____   _____ Wrist

11. _____   _____   _____   _____ Hold

12. _____   _____   _____   _____ Anchor

13. _____   _____   _____   _____ Aim

14. _____   _____   _____   _____ Release

15. _____   _____   _____   _____ Follow-through

From *It's Not Just Gym Anymore: Teaching Secondary School Students How to Be Active for Life* by Bane McCracken, 2001, Champaign, IL: Human Kinetics.

Tips for Better Shooting

1. Inconsistency

   a. Check anchor point. Make sure to use the same anchor point consistently.

   b. Take time to hold and aim.

   c. Check basic technique. Make sure bow arm is solid.

2. High arrow flights

   a. Keep focused on target after release.

   b. Check grip. Make sure to hold grip between thumb and first finger.

   c. Check stance. Keep weight balanced between front and back foot.

   d. Check for overdraw.

3. Low arrow flights

   a. Check for creeping.

   b. Make sure you are not holding too long.

   c. If string is hitting the arm, check bow-arm position and grip.

   d. Check posture. Stand erect.

4. Left arrow flights

   a. Keep back of draw hand flat.

   b. Move anchor point to the right.

   c. Check alignment of bow, body, and string.

5. Arrows falling off arrow rest

   a. Keep draw hand flat.

   b. Pinch arrow nock with fingers.

   c. Use release.

From *It's Not Just Gym Anymore: Teaching Secondary School Students How to Be Active for Life* by Bane McCracken, 2001, Champaign, IL: Human Kinetics.

Archery Scoring Record

Name: _____

| | **Score of best** |
| **Date:** | **round for the day** |

1. _____   _____ pts
2. _____   _____ pts
3. _____   _____ pts
4. _____   _____ pts
5. _____   _____ pts
6. _____   _____ pts

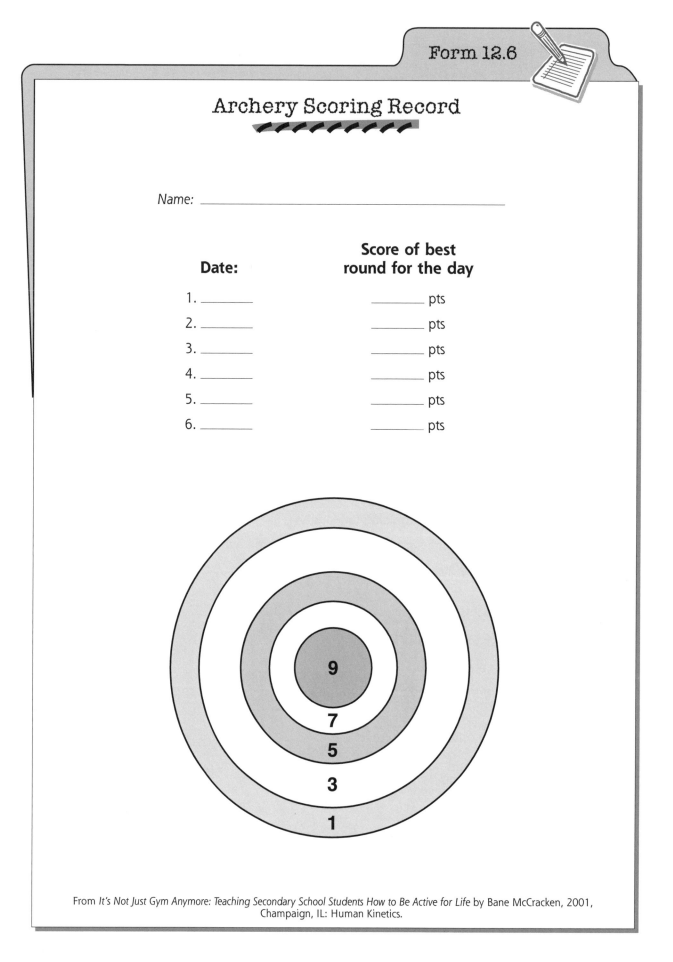

Cyber Shopping

Bow-hunting equipment is expensive. Comparing prices can save money. Check the prices for a complete bow-hunting outfit on Web sites on the Internet, in catalogs, and in local retail outlets. List the prices for each item in the spaces below.

Equipment	Internet price	Catalog price	Local retailer price

From It's Not Just Gym Anymore: Teaching Secondary School Students How to Be Active for Life by Bane McCracken, 2001, Champaign, IL: Human Kinetics.

Fly-Tying Knots

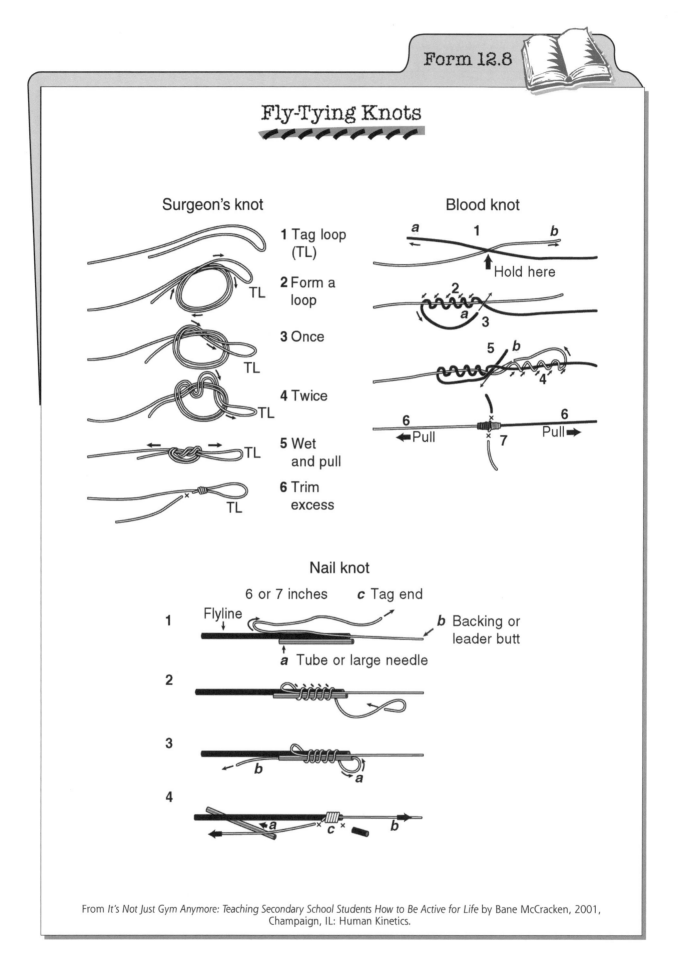

Surgeon's knot

1 Tag loop (TL)

2 Form a loop

3 Once

4 Twice

5 Wet and pull

6 Trim excess

TL

Blood knot

1 Hold here

2
3
a

5 b
4

6 ←Pull 6 Pull→
7

Nail knot

6 or 7 inches   *c* Tag end

1 Flyline

b Backing or leader butt

a Tube or large needle

2

3 *b* *a*

4 *a* *c* *b*

From *It's Not Just Gym Anymore: Teaching Secondary School Students How to Be Active for Life* by Bane McCracken, 2001, Champaign, IL: Human Kinetics.

Fly-Casting Self-Evaluation

Name: _____   Date: _____

Place the appropriate symbol in the space provided.

O = not yet	**X** = getting better	**+** = proper technique

	1st day	2nd day	Final evaluation	
1.	_____	_____	_____	Grip
2.	_____	_____	_____	Hand position
3.	_____	_____	_____	Arm position
4.	_____	_____	_____	Back cast
5.	_____	_____	_____	Fore cast
6.	_____	_____	_____	Rhythm
7.	_____	_____	_____	Hitting targets

Casting techniques

8.	_____	_____	_____	Shooting line
9.	_____	_____	_____	Roll cast
10.	_____	_____	_____	Single haul
11.	_____	_____	_____	Double haul

From *It's Not Just Gym Anymore: Teaching Secondary School Students How to Be Active for Life* by Bane McCracken, 2001, Champaign, IL: Human Kinetics.

Dimensions of Fly-Fishing

Name: _____   Date: _____

1. What do you need to know to go fly-fishing? List at least five items in their order of importance.

2. What other activities have you done that are similar to fly-fishing? List five.

3. Choose one of the activities you listed above and tell how it is similar to fly-fishing.

4. Let's go! Make a plan to go fly-fishing (who, when, where, how).

5. Now that you have completed the fly-fishing unit, what did you learn?

From *It's Not Just Gym Anymore: Teaching Secondary School Students How to Be Active for Life* by Bane McCracken, 2001, Champaign, IL: Human Kinetics.

chapter 13

Personal Fitness

Kenneth Cooper's (1968) book *Aerobics* and Frank Shorter's 1972 Olympic marathon victory helped spark a national interest in running and fitness. As the nation began to join health clubs and read about fitness, some leading physical education programs began to offer personal fitness classes for their students. Personal fitness should be a part of any physical education unit and is the focus of all units presented in this book. However, there is a strong rationale for personal fitness to be a unit in and of itself, and it can certainly be offered as a separate class. Students need to know the principles of fitness and understand that fitness is a skill that needs to be developed in the same manner as sport skills. At Cabell Midland High School personal fitness is a unit offered during our required class (Introduction to Physical Education) and is offered as an elective class as well.

Our school's physical education facilities include a wellness center complete with the following exercise machines: 2 Lifecycles, 2 treadmills, 3 Concept II Rowers, 2 NordicTracks, 2 StairMasters, 2 Airdynes, 6 step machines, and 1 Cross Aerobics.

The personal fitness classes I teach are designed to take advantage of this unique facility. The resources available to you may change the way you introduce and organize lessons.

The objectives of the personal fitness unit are to teach students the following:

- The importance of maintaining a high level of personal fitness
- The five components of fitness: muscular strength, muscular endurance, flexibility, cardiovascular fitness, and body composition, and methods of analyzing and improving each
- How to use a variety of equipment for developing muscular strength and endurance: free weights, dumbbells, stretch cords, and resistance machines
- How to use a variety of methods for developing cardiovascular fitness: walking, jogging, running, aerobics, step aerobics, and dance
- How to analyze body composition
- Proper warm-up and cool-down techniques
- The relationship among exercise, diet, and weight control
- Good nutritional practices
- The effects of stress on personal health and methods for reducing stress through physical activity
- How to develop personal fitness plans

Lesson 1

Components of Fitness

1. Discuss the 1996 surgeon general's report on physical activity and health.
2. List and discuss the benefits of physical activity and exercise (form 13.1).
3. Define and discuss the five components of fitness (form 13.1).
4. Demonstrate and practice the use of the exercise machines in the wellness center.
5. Instruct students to begin keeping diet logs of everything eaten each day.
6. Conclusion: stretch and review.

Lesson 2

Pulse Monitoring

1. Explain and discuss pulse levels and exercise intensity.
2. Have students calculate exercise pulse levels (form 13.2).
3. Distribute pulse monitors to students.
4. Have students complete the pacing guide (form 6.1).

5. Check diet logs.
6. Closure: stretch and review.

Lesson 3

Exercise Machines, Step Aerobics, and Pulse Levels

Regardless of how many machines you have at your disposal, class size is never small enough to allow all students to use machines at once.

1. Review the results from pacing guide.
2. Distribute pulse monitors.
3. Divide the class into two groups. Have one group work on machines while another group learns step aerobics. Alternate groups after a designated time period. At the end of each time period, have students record their pulses and times (form 13.3).
4. Compare and discuss the pulse levels from the pacing guide while using machines and doing step aerobics.
5. Closure: review cardiovascular fitness and stretch.

Lesson 4

Muscular Strength and Endurance

1. Define and discuss muscular strength and endurance.
2. In the weight room, demonstrate a basic circuit and have students practice (form 13.4). Students should record weights and reps.
3. Closure: review muscular strength and endurance and stretch.

Lesson 5

Body Composition

1. Define body composition and the methods for calculating percent body fat, ideal body weight, and lean body weight.
2. Use skin calipers and form 6.2 to calculate body composition.
3. Have students spend 15 minutes in their exercise zone while waiting their turn.
4. Review body composition and stretch.

Lesson 6

Let's Dance

1. Discuss and compare exercise and physical activity.
2. Distribute pulse monitors.
3. Demonstrate "The Electric Slide" and "Slapping Leather" and have students practice. For these and other line dances, see **http://hometown.aol.com/cactusstar/home.htm**.
4. Closure: compare pulse levels while dancing to pulse levels during the pacing guide, during step aerobics, and while working on machines. Stretch.

Lesson 7

Dumbbells

1. Explain and discuss resistance-training methods.

2. Distribute pulse monitors.
3. Divide students into two groups and set up the following stations:
   a. Group 1: Have students work on machines and record results using form 13.5.
   b. Group 2: Demonstrate dumbbell workout and have students practice (form 13.6).
4. Check diet logs and remind students to complete logs for next class.
5. Closure: discuss and compare pulse levels achieved while using machines to those achieved lifting dumbbells. Stretch.

Lesson 8

Diet

1. Define *calorie* and discuss caloric intake versus energy output. (Calorie: The amount of energy it takes to raise the temperature of one gram of water one degree centigrade.)
2. Discuss exercise, diet, and weight control.
3. Review body composition.
4. Divide students into three groups and set up the following stations:
   a. Group 1: Students use a computer program to analyze their diets. See resources on p. 238.
   b. Group 2: Students work in their "zones" using machines.
   c. Group 3: Students do step aerobics: basic step, alternating knee, V step, and V step with lunge and punch.
5. Instruct students to bring in food labels the next day.
6. Closure: review and discuss diet analysis. Stretch.

Lesson 9

Reading Labels

1. Explain and discuss the relationship among protein, carbohydrates, and fat in diet.

2. Use food labels to analyze food content. Discuss the importance of a low-fat diet.

3. Discuss ways to lower fat in diet.

4. Discuss carbohydrates and exercise. Refer to "Energy Boosters and Zappers" (form 13.7).

5. Go to the weight room and do a basic circuit (form 13.4).

6. Closure: review and stretch.

Lesson 10
Exercise and Calories

1. Explain and discuss caloric balance.

2. Use the following Web site to calculate calorie output: **www.msnbc.com/modules/ quizzes/caloriecalc.asp**.

3. Divide students into three groups and set up the following stations:

   a. Group 1: Students use a computer program to calculate caloric output.

   b. Group 2: Students work in their "zones" using machines.

   c. Group 3: Students do step aerobics: basic step, alternating knee, V step, and V step with lunge and punch. Add turn step with arms, T step, tap-up, tap-down, going over the top, and lunges to routine.

4. Closure: discuss caloric balance. Stretch.

Lesson 11
Let's Dance

1. Discuss and compare exercise and physical activity.

2. Distribute pulse monitors.

3. Demonstrate swing dance steps and have students practice.

4. Closure: compare pulse levels achieved while dancing to those achieved during the pacing guide, during step aerobics, and while working on machines. Stretch.

Lesson 12
T'ai Chi

1. Discuss the causes of stress, the physical and psychological effects of stress, the effects of stress on learning, and ways of dealing with stress.

2. Discuss physical activity and stress reduction.

3. Demonstrate the "infinite nine" basic movements of t'ai chi and have students practice. The Web site **www.easytaichi.com** provides information and resources.

4. Closure: review and discuss the effects of t'ai chi.

Lesson 13
Stretch Cords

1. Explain and discuss alternative methods of resistance training: body weights, homemade equipment, and stretch cords.

2. Divide students into two groups and set up the following stations, rotating students through both stations:

   a. Group 1: Have students work in their "zones" using machines.

   b. Group 2: Demonstrate stretch cord exercises and have students practice.

3. Closure: t'ai chi, review, and stretch.

Lesson 14
Dimensions of Fitness

1. Introduce and discuss "Dimensions of Fitness" (form 13.8).

2. Have students develop their own three-week fitness plans.

Benefits of Physical Activity and Exercise

- Reduces risk of heart disease

- Decreases hypertension and high blood pressure

- Decreases cholesterol levels

- Helps shed excess pounds

- Slows the aging process

- Reduces risk of osteoporosis

- Improves and maintains mental health

- Improves the quality of the air we breathe

- Prevents and controls diabetes

- Prevents the common cold and flu

- Improves arthritis

- Relieves back pain

Five Components of Fitness

Define each of the following:

1. Muscular strength

2. Muscular endurance

3. Cardiovascular fitness

4. Flexibility

5. Body composition

How to Calculate
Your Exercise Pulse Levels

Name: _____   Date: _____

Your maximum pulse is determined by subtracting your age from 220.

   220

– _____ your age

= _____ maximum heart rate

90% is _____ bpm

80% is _____ bpm

70% is _____ bpm

60% is _____ bpm

50% is _____ bpm

Pulse Log

Name: _____

Date	Activity	Time	Pulse rate

From *It's Not Just Gym Anymore: Teaching Secondary School Students How to Be Active for Life* by Bane McCracken, 2001, Champaign, IL: Human Kinetics.

Basic Circuit Workout

Name: _____

Date	Bench press wt/reps	T row wt/reps	Military press wt/reps	Lat pulldown wt/reps	Squat wt/reps	Leg curl wt/reps	Leg extend wt/reps

From *It's Not Just Gym Anymore: Teaching Secondary School Students How to Be Active for Life* by Bane McCracken, 2001, Champaign, IL: Human Kinetics.

Wellness Center Workout Record

Name: _____

Date	Machine used	Time	Pace/distance/units	Pulse/pace

From *It's Not Just Gym Anymore: Teaching Secondary School Students How to Be Active for Life* by Bane McCracken, 2001, Champaign, IL: Human Kinetics.

Dumbbell Workout

First set: 10 to 12 reps—light weight

Second set: 15 to 25 reps—medium weight

Third set: 8 to 10 reps—light weight

1. Alternate-arm overhead press

2. Standing fly

3. Alternate-arm standing front raise

4. Alternate-arm prone press

5. Prone fly

6. Alternate-arm standing row

7. Alternate-arm bent row

8. Bent fly

9. Curl

10. Half squat

11. Parallel squat

12. Toe raise

From *It's Not Just Gym Anymore: Teaching Secondary School Students How to Be Active for Life* by Bane McCracken, 2001, Champaign, IL: Human Kinetics.

Energy Boosters and Zappers

Energy Boosters

The following foods have been found to give increased energy and are good to eat before exercise, competition, or practice.

1. Sports bars such as Power Bars, low-fat granola bars, etc.

2. Breakfast cereals: Make sure to use low-sugar cereal and skim or low-fat milk.

3. High carbohydrate power foods: baked potato, pasta, rice

4. Nonfat yogurt mixed with fruit

5. Fruits: banana, melons, etc. (best of all are dried figs)

6. Extra-lean meat (fish and skinless poultry)

7. Nonfat milk

8. Power snack foods: dried fruit, rice cakes, whole grain breads

9. Crunchy veggies

Energy Zappers

The following foods have been found to slow digestion and metabolism and therefore should be avoided before exercise, competition, or practice.

1. Chips: high in fat

2. Sugary foods

3. Anything fried

4. Candy bars (don't believe the Snickers commercials)

5. Whole milk and high-fat cheeses

6. Spreads and dressings

7. High-fat meals

8. Deli meats

9. Ice cream

10. Fruit drinks (not to be confused with fruit juices)

From *It's Not Just Gym Anymore: Teaching Secondary School Students How to Be Active for Life* by Bane McCracken, 2001, Champaign, IL: Human Kinetics.

Dimensions of Fitness

Name: _____ Date: _____

1. What do you need to know to stay fit? List at least five items in their order of importance.

2. What activities can you do to help you stay fit? List five in order of their fitness benefits.

3. Choose two of the activities you listed above and compare the fitness benefits of each. How are they similar?

4. Let's work out. Make a plan for a daily workout (who, when, where, how).

5. Now that you have finished this unit, what did you learn?

chapter 14

Conditioning and Weight Training

Football coaches began to recognize the benefits of weight training in the 1960s. Players' performances improved and injury rates declined as a result of weight-training programs. Other sports not considered to be strength sports also began to see improved results from strength training. While the public was keeping records of Michael Jordan on the court, Michael was keeping his personal records in the weight room, and while the fans were counting Mark McGwire's home runs, Mark was counting exercise repetitions. It is now recognized that regular strength training should be a part of everyone's fitness program.

Some form of strength training in a fitness program is highly recommended for both men and women and should be continued throughout one's adult life, especially as maturity sets in. Adults past the age of 25 begin to lose muscle mass. As muscle mass continues to decline, their ability to burn calories declines as well, and the middle-age spread becomes evident. Women in particular benefit from participating in strength-training programs. Studies have shown that women who are strong are slimmer and have less incidence of osteoporosis.

Conditioning and weight training has always been one the most popular units in the CMHS required physical education classes, and the conditioning and weight-training class is the most popular of our electives. Each class is one credit and lasts one semester on a 90-minute block schedule. The weight room at our school sits adjacent to the track and is used by the students during their training programs. The class is taught in three units: basic circuit training, bodybuilding and toning, and sport-specific training.

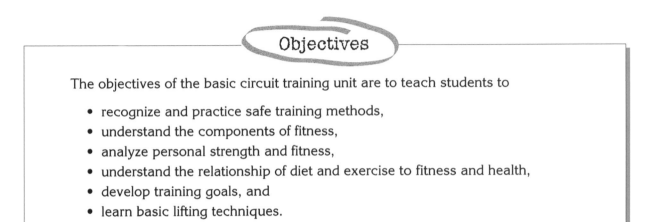

Objectives

The objectives of the basic circuit training unit are to teach students to

- recognize and practice safe training methods,
- understand the components of fitness,
- analyze personal strength and fitness,
- understand the relationship of diet and exercise to fitness and health,
- develop training goals, and
- learn basic lifting techniques.

BASIC CIRCUIT TRAINING

Basic circuit training is the first six-week unit. The training program starts easy and focuses on large muscles. Students are encouraged to use lighter weights at first and very gradually increase intensity. The theme for each day is to not get hurt and to prepare their muscles for the more intense training programs that follow.

Lesson 1

Introduction

1. Discuss procedures, expectations, and weightlifting terms.
2. Explain warm-up procedures (students jog half a mile to the weight room each day as part of their warm-up).
3. Discuss weight room expectations and rules of conduct (form 14.1).
4. Demonstrate the lifting, spotting, and teamwork required for basic upper- and lower-body circuits (forms 14.2 and 14.3).
5. Divide the class into two groups of three-person teams. Have one group do an upper-body workout while the other group does a lower-body workout. Within each team, one student lifts while another spots and helps as the third student gets ready. Students perform one set of 12 repetitions for each exercise and record results in portfolios. After each set of lifts, students rotate positions.

6. Closure: review and stretch.

Lesson 2

Introduction

1. Repeat lesson 1 and make sure all students have completed all exercises at least once. Students change workouts. Those that did upper body in Lesson 1 do lower body today.
2. Check for proper technique and procedures.

Lesson 3

Pacing Guide

This lesson will take more than one day.

1. Distribute pulse monitors to students.

2. Explain pulse rates and calculate exercise pulse levels (see form 13.2).
3. Complete the pacing guide (form 6.1).

Lesson 4
Body Composition

This lesson will take more than one day.

1. Discuss the relationship of body composition to fitness, performance, and health.
2. Explain the methods of calculating body composition.
3. Lead warm-up jog to the weight room
4. Divide the class into two groups and have one group do an upper-body workout while the other does a lower-body workout. Rotate groups each day.
5. Take skinfold measurement of students while they are completing assignments. Have students use form 6.2 to calculate body composition.
6. Closure: review and discuss body composition. Check students' calculations and stretch.

Lesson 5
Impedance

This lesson will take more than one day.

1. Review the relationship of body composition to fitness, performance, and health.
2. Explain the impedance method of calculating body composition (this is explained on p.15).
3. Lead warm-up jog to the weight room
4. Divide the class into two groups. Have group 1 complete the weight room workout while group 2 uses the impedance computer to calculate body composition. Group 2 must not work out until after they have had their body fat calculated. These students may complete assignments in their portfolios while waiting. Change groups each day.
5. Closure: compare methods of body composition analysis using students' results. Stretch.

Lesson 6
Diet Analysis

1. Define calories and discuss the relationship of diet and exercise to caloric requirements.
2. Have students calculate daily caloric requirements using form 14.4.
3. Lead warm-up jog to the weight room
4. Have student groups do assigned exercise program (either upper- or lower-body workout).
5. Have small groups of students use a computer software program to analyze their diets. (A variety of software programs that count calories are available. See resources on p. 238.)
6. Closure: discuss caloric balance and weight gain or loss. Stretch.

Lesson 7
Muscular Strength and Endurance Testing

1. Define and discuss muscular strength and endurance.
2. Lead warm-up jog to the weight room
3. Have students do the assigned exercise program (either upper- or lower-body workout).
4. Have students test muscular strength and endurance on the bench press using form 14.5.
5. Closure: discuss results of test, stretch.

Lesson 8
Weightlifting Anatomy

1. Review previous lessons.
2. Explain antagonistic muscle pairing. Identify muscle groups using front and back muscle charts.
3. Lead warm-up jog to the weight room
4. Place muscle charts at various locations throughout the weight room so students can identify muscles used for each lift while lifting.

5. Have students do the assigned lifting circuit and identify muscles used for each exercise using form 14.6, part I.

6. Closure: review muscle anatomy and stretch.

Lesson 9

Antagonistic Pairings and Balanced Workouts

1. Review muscle anatomy and muscles used for each exercise.

2. Explain and identify antagonistic muscle pairings.

3. Discuss the importance of developing a balanced training program and the relationship of antagonistic muscles to balancing a program.

4. Have students identify antagonistic exercises using form 14.6, part II, while doing the basic circuit.

5. Closure: review and stretch.

Lesson 10

Cyber Iron

This lesson should be conducted in a computer lab.

1. Have students complete form 14.7.

Lesson 11

Reflections

1. Discuss fitness test results and fitness goals.

2. Lead warm-up jog to the weight room

3. Have students complete the assigned basic circuit.

4. Have students complete "Reflections on Fitness" (form 14.8).

5. Closure: review, stretch.

Weight Room Expectations and Rules of Conduct

- Take pride in your weight room.

- Keep weights off the floor.

- Pick up litter and trash.

- Use a spotter.

- Use proper language.

- Play acceptable music.

- Keep horseplay outside.

- Refrain from tobacco and all tobacco products.

From *It's Not Just Gym Anymore: Teaching Secondary School Students How to Be Active for Life* by Bane McCracken, 2001, Champaign, IL: Human Kinetics.

Upper-Body Basic Circuit Workout

Name: _____

Date	Bench press wt/reps	T row wt/reps	Military wt/reps	Lat pull-down wt/reps	Curl wt/reps	Triceps push-down wt/reps	Other wt/reps

From *It's Not Just Gym Anymore: Teaching Secondary School Students How to Be Active for Life* by Bane McCracken, 2001, Champaign, IL: Human Kinetics.

Lower-Body Basic Circuit Workout

Name: _____

Date	Squat wt/reps	Leg extend wt/reps	Leg curl wt/reps	Box lunge wt/reps	Calf raise wt/reps	Crunch wt/reps	Other wt/reps

Daily Caloric Requirements

Name: _____

1. Body weight _____ divided by 2.2

   equals your weight in kilograms _____

2. Body weight in kilograms _____ × 24

   equals _____ daily calories needed

3. Activity factor: multiply daily calories needed by one of the following:
   Light activity: 1.3
   Moderate activity: 1.4
   Heavy activity: 1.5

   _____ daily calores × _____ activity factor

   equals total daily calorie requirements _____

Keep track of everything you eat for one day in the space below, then count your calories for the day and compare the results to your daily requirements calculated above.

From *It's Not Just Gym Anymore: Teaching Secondary School Students How to Be Active for Life* by Bane McCracken, 2001, Champaign, IL: Human Kinetics.

Muscular Strength and Endurance Test

16-year-old males	
Bench press lean body weight until failure.	
Superior:	15+ reps
Excellent:	12 reps
Good:	9 reps
Fair:	7 reps
Poor:	5 reps
16-year-old females	
Bench press 75% of lean body weight until failure.	
Superior:	15+ reps
Excellent:	12 reps
Good:	9 reps
Fair:	7 reps
Poor:	5 reps

From *It's Not Just Gym Anymore: Teaching Secondary School Students How to Be Active for Life* by Bane McCracken, 2001, Champaign, IL: Human Kinetics.

Muscle Matching

Name: _____   *Date:* _____

Part I

List the muscles used for each of the following exercises:

Bench press	Biceps curl	Leg curl
T row	Triceps pushdown	Lunge
Military press	Squat	Calf raise
Lat pulldown	Leg extension	Crunch

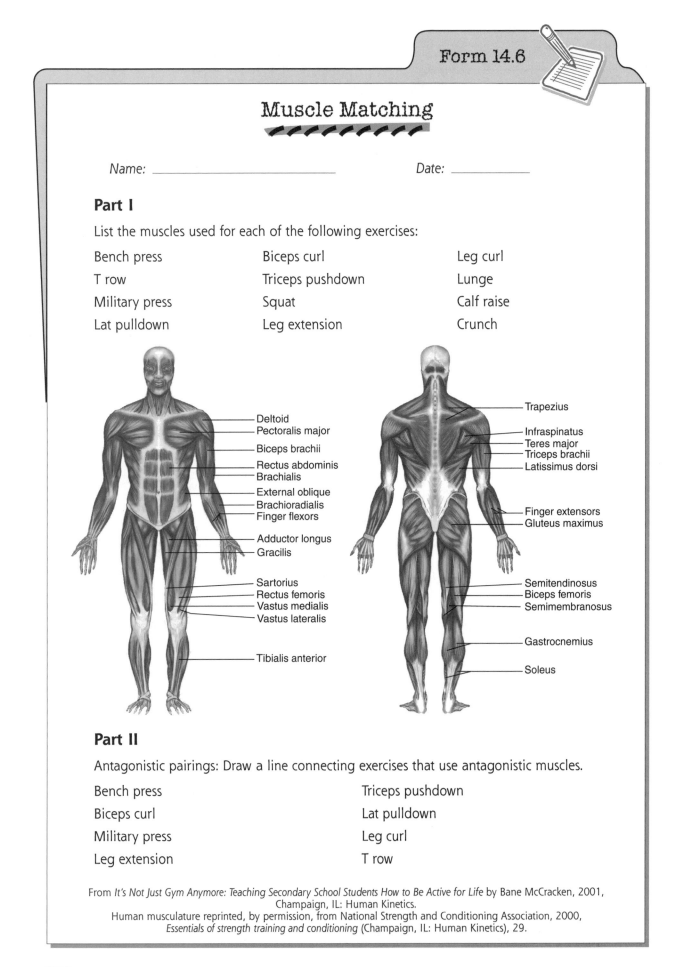

Deltoid
Pectoralis major
Biceps brachii
Rectus abdominis
Brachialis
External oblique
Brachioradialis
Finger flexors
Adductor longus
Gracilis
Sartorius
Rectus femoris
Vastus medialis
Vastus lateralis
Tibialis anterior

Trapezius
Infraspinatus
Teres major
Triceps brachii
Latissimus dorsi
Finger extensors
Gluteus maximus
Semitendinosus
Biceps femoris
Semimembranosus
Gastrocnemius
Soleus

Part II

Antagonistic pairings: Draw a line connecting exercises that use antagonistic muscles.

Bench press	Triceps pushdown
Biceps curl	Lat pulldown
Military press	Leg curl
Leg extension	T row

From *It's Not Just Gym Anymore: Teaching Secondary School Students How to Be Active for Life* by Bane McCracken, 2001, Champaign, IL: Human Kinetics.
Human musculature reprinted, by permission, from National Strength and Conditioning Association, 2000, *Essentials of strength training and conditioning* (Champaign, IL: Human Kinetics), 29.

Cyber Iron

Name: _____   Date: _____

Note: The Web addresses used in this form were accurate at the time of publication. If the site is no longer active, search **www.yahoo.com** or a similar search engine to find the answers.

1. These sites provide good advice about maintaining fitness: **www.justmove.org** and **www.fitnessonline.com.** What did you find interesting?

2. Surf the Web to find a workout for your sport. Describe the workout you found most interesting.

3. Go to this site: **www.fitnesslink.org** to find out how to create a home gym. Describe what you'd need to do to create a home gym. Is a home gym right for you?

4. Surf this site: **www.healthclubs.com** to find a health club near you.
   a. Where is the club located?

   b. How much does it cost to become a member?

   c. What is the phone number?

   d. What kinds of services and facilities does it have?

   e. How do you choose the right club for you?

5. Here is a good site to find other places: **http://k2.kirtland.cc.mi.us/~balbachl/fitness.htm**

List some of the sites you found interesting and tell why.

From *It's Not Just Gym Anymore: Teaching Secondary School Students How to Be Active for Life* by Bane McCracken, 2001, Champaign, IL: Human Kinetics.

Reflections on Fitness

Name: _____

1. What do you think of your fitness test results?

2. What are your personal workout goals?

3. What changes do you need to make?

4. How does fitness relate to any other subject you now have in school?

From *It's Not Just Gym Anymore: Teaching Secondary School Students How to Be Active for Life* by Bane McCracken, 2001, Champaign, IL: Human Kinetics.

The objectives of the bodybuilding and toning unit are to teach students to

- recognize techniques for developing individual muscles and muscle groups,
- develop personalized training goals based on personal goals,
- recognize and compare simple and complex exercises and the proper use of each in training,
- determine personal dietary needs and supplements,
- develop good consumer practices by learning to recognize exaggerated product advertising claims,
- understand advanced techniques for increasing muscle size and performance, and
- understand advanced techniques for improving body composition.

BODYBUILDING AND TONING

Bodybuilding and toning is phase two of the weight-training program. In this unit students are introduced to very intense strength development programs in which they are encouraged to lift to failure on alternating days. Students learn techniques that increase muscle size and strength as well as methods of reducing fat and leaning out.

Lesson 1

Introduction and Exercises for the Chest and Back

1. Explain the purpose of and procedures for a body parts strength-training program (form 14.9).
2. Demonstrate exercises for the chest and back and have students practice (forms 14.10 and 14.11).
3. Closure: review and stretch.

Lesson 2

Exercises for the Shoulders and Arms

1. Review the procedure for and purpose of a body parts program.
2. Demonstrate exercises for the shoulders and arms and have students practice (forms 14.12 and 14.13).

3. Closure: review and stretch.

Lesson 3

Exercises for the Legs and Abdominal Muscles

1. Review the procedures for and purpose of a body parts program.
2. Demonstrate exercises for the legs and abdominal muscles and have students practice (forms 14.14 and 14.15).
3. Closure: review and stretch.

Lesson 4

Designing Individual Programs

1. Help students use form 14.9 to develop a three-week training schedule.
2. Have students complete beginning anthropometric measurements (form 14.16).
3. Encourage students to follow three-week training programs.
4. Closure: review and stretch.

Lesson 5

Boosters and Zappers

1. Discuss the relationships among foods, supplements, and ergogenic aids taken before, during, and after exercise (see

form 13.7). Explain how some foods help and others hinder performance.

2. Encourage students to continue three-week training schedules.

3. Closure: discuss good after-exercise foods and rehydration techniques.

Lesson 6

Nutrition Quiz

1. Give students the nutrition quiz (form 14.17).

2. Discuss the results of the nutrition quiz and boosters and zappers (form 13.7).

3. Encourage students to follow three-week training schedules.

4. Closure: discuss nutrition and stretch.

Lesson 7

Reflection on Nutrition

1. Have students complete "Reflections on Nutrition and Exercise" (form 14.18).

2. Students complete three-week training program.

3. Closure: discuss reflections assignment, stretch.

Lesson 8

Rest, Recovery, Rehydration, Resupply

1. Discuss and explain proper rest, recovery, rehydration, and resupply and the relationship between these and successful training.

2. Students complete three-week workout program.

3. Closure: review principals of rest, recovery, rehydration, and resupply; stretch.

Lesson 9

Advertising Claims

1. Copy and play television commercials for nutritional supplements and exercise equipment. Distribute magazine articles and advertisements for exercise supplements and equipment.

2. Discuss and evaluate the claims of the advertisers.

3. Have students continue their three-week training programs to maintain fitness.

4. Closure: review advertising claims and ask students to create a fictitious product of their own and think of ways they could make exaggerated claims for their products. Stretch.

Lesson 10

Placebo-Genics, "Before" Pictures

1. Review and discuss advertising claims.

2. Have students share their fictitious products and help students having trouble, e.g., "Mike's Miracle Salve" or "Paul's Powerful Protein Powder."

3. Take "before" pictures of selected students. These are taken with students standing in front of many bright lights that allow for no shadows and hide all muscle definition. Instruct students to slouch, push out their bellies, and not to flex their muscles. This creates a picture of an unfit, weak individual before using the training aid.

4. Students continue three-week training programs.

5. Closure: remind students to refine their fictitious product and develop exaggerated claims. Stretch.

Lesson 11

Placebo-Genics, "After" Pictures

1. Review and discuss students' fictitious advertising claims.

2. Students continue three-week training programs.

3. Take "after" pictures of selected students. Use special lighting from above the subject, which creates shadows that heighten definition and make muscles appear to be larger and more defined. Also, take

pictures after or during exercise so muscles are "pumped," and have students stand erect and flex their muscles. This creates the picture of an individual after using the product.

4. Closure: discuss the procedure for the computer-lab lesson for the next session.

Lesson 12
Microsoft® PowerPoint® Presentations

This lesson will require at least two days in a computer lab for all students to complete their assignments.

1. Instruct students on how to use PowerPoint® or another presentation program to make an advertisement for their fictitious product. Students are limited to three slides. Slide 1 describes the product and makes the exaggerated claims. Slide 2 shows the "before" picture and describes the poor state of the subject.

Slide 3 shows the "after" picture and provides a testimonial of the product's success.

2. Upon completion of the assignments, have the students print their advertisements for evaluation.

Lesson 13
Conclusion

1. Review and discuss advertising and gimmicks.
2. Select volunteers to share their portfolio presentations with the class.
3. Have students continue their three-week training programs.
4. Have students complete second anthropometric measurements and compare to the first anthropometric measurements.
5. Collect and evaluate portfolios and return.
6. Closure: review and discuss training results.

Body Parts Strength Training Program

Instructions
Attempt to work out two body parts per day with two different lifts for each body part. Each workout sheet is for a different body part. Do not work a body part a second time until lifts for all other body parts have been completed.

Sets and reps

(4 to 5 sets for each station)

Heavy days
Set 1: Warm up with 10 to 15 reps (very light weight)

Set 2: Highest weight—8 reps (min) to 12 reps (max)—to fatigue

Set 3: 20% less weight than set 2 to fatigue

Set 4: 20% less weight than set 3 to fatigue

Set 5: 20% less weight than set 4 to fatigue

Make sure at least 8 reps can be achieved before fatigue. After reps have increased to 12, increase weight. Don't add too much weight; the increase in weight will most likely be only 5 to 10 lb in most cases.

Light days
Do the same number of reps for each set as on heavy days but use at least 25% less weight.

Day 1: Shoulders/legs—heavy

Day 2: Chest/back—light

Day 3: Arms/abs—heavy

Day 4: Off

Day 5: Shoulders/legs—light

Day 6: Chest/back—heavy

Day 7: Arms/abs—light

Shoulders: Behind-back military and standing flys

Legs: Squats, leg extensions, leg curls, seated calf raises

Chest: Bench or incline and prone flys

Back: T row, lat pulldown and bent flys

Arms: Preacher curls and dumbbell curls, cable pushdowns and brain busters

Abs: Abs of steel or another good abs video

From *It's Not Just Gym Anymore: Teaching Secondary School Students How to Be Active for Life* by Bane McCracken, 2001, Champaign, IL: Human Kinetics.

Chest Workout

Name: _____

Date	Bench press wt/reps	Incline bench wt/reps	Dumbbell fly wt/reps	Pec deck wt/reps	Dip wt/reps	Dumbbell press wt/reps	Other wt/reps

From *It's Not Just Gym Anymore: Teaching Secondary School Students How to Be Active for Life* by Bane McCracken, 2001, Champaign, IL: Human Kinetics.

Back Workout

Name: _____

Date	T row wt/reps	Bent DB row wt/reps	Bent fly wt/reps	Standing row wt/reps	Lat pull-down wt/reps	Other wt/reps

From *It's Not Just Gym Anymore: Teaching Secondary School Students How to Be Active for Life* by Bane McCracken, 2001, Champaign, IL: Human Kinetics.

Shoulder Workout

Name: _____

Date	Military press wt/reps	Standing fly wt/reps	Front raise wt/reps	Shrug wt/reps	Dumbbell press wt/reps	Other wt/reps

Arm Workout

Name: _____

Date	Curl wt/reps	Hammer wt/reps	Cable push-down wt/reps	Concen-tration curls wt/reps	Brain busters wt/reps	Other wt/reps

From *It's Not Just Gym Anymore: Teaching Secondary School Students How to Be Active for Life* by Bane McCracken, 2001, Champaign, IL: Human Kinetics.

Leg Workout

Name: _____

Date	Squats wt/reps	Leg extension wt/reps	Leg curl wt/reps	Calf raise wt/reps	Box lunges wt/reps	Other wt/reps

From *It's Not Just Gym Anymore: Teaching Secondary School Students How to Be Active for Life* by Bane McCracken, 2001, Champaign, IL: Human Kinetics.

Ab Workout

Name: _____

Date	Crunch	Oblique crunch	Side crunch	Roll-up	Leg raise	Other

From *It's Not Just Gym Anymore: Teaching Secondary School Students How to Be Active for Life* by Bane McCracken, 2001, Champaign, IL: Human Kinetics.

Anthropometric Measurements

Name: _____

	Before	**Three weeks later**
Neck	_____	_____
Chest	_____	_____
Chest expanded	_____	_____
Waist	_____	_____
Biceps	_____	_____
Forearms	_____	_____
Thigh	_____	_____
Calf	_____	_____

From *It's Not Just Gym Anymore: Teaching Secondary School Students How to Be Active for Life* by Bane McCracken, 2001, Champaign, IL: Human Kinetics.

Compute Your Nutrition Condition

Do you:	Rarely	Sometimes	Often
Participate in regular physical activity?	1	3	5
Choose foods from the milk group?	1	3	5
Eat breakfast?	1	3	5
Drink carbonated beverages?	5	3	1
Eat raw fruits and vegetables?	1	3	5
Use foot power instead of horsepower?	1	3	5
Eat candy?	5	3	1
Salt your food?	5	3	1
Choose whole grain cereal or bread?	1	3	5
Maintain ideal weight?	1	3	5
Eat fried foods?	5	3	1
Skip meals?	5	3	1
Try new sports?	1	3	5
Binge/overeat?	5	3	1
Avoid unfamiliar foods?	5	3	1
Drink water?	1	3	5
Eat processed snack foods?	5	3	1
Try fad diets?	5	3	1
Eat a variety of protein foods?	1	3	5
Get adequate sleep?	1	3	5

Score: 80 or above .... you're a winner
        70 to 80 .... you're in the running
        below 70 .... try harder

From *It's Not Just Gym Anymore: Teaching Secondary School Students How to Be Active for Life* by Bane McCracken, 2001, Champaign, IL: Human Kinetics.
Adapted, by permission, from the American Dietetic Association, *Compute your nutrition condition* (Chicago: author).

Reflections on Nutrition and Exercise

Name: _____   Date: _____

1. List three good things about your diet.

2. List three changes you need to make in your diet.

3. What supplements do you think would help your program?

4. How does this unit relate to any other subject you now have in school?

From *It's Not Just Gym Anymore: Teaching Secondary School Students How to Be Active for Life* by Bane McCracken, 2001, Champaign, IL: Human Kinetics.

The objectives for the sport- and activity-specific training unit are to teach students to

- understand and use various modes of training: over-speed, continuous, interval, progressive-resistance, and circuit;
- understand and compare activities using slow-twitch and fast-twitch muscle fibers and training techniques for each;
- understand and use balance-training techniques;
- understand energy sources for exercise: ATP, CP, and aerobic metabolism; and
- understand and compare aerobic and anaerobic activities and training techniques for each.

SPORT- AND ACTIVITY-SPECIFIC TRAINING

Sport-specific training is the final section of the weight-training class. In this unit students learn to design programs that improve performance, maintain or improve conditioning, and help promote continued participation in a variety of activities.

Lesson 1
Principles of Training

1. Explain and discuss the principles of training: over-speed, continuous, interval, progressive-resistance, and circuit.
2. Have students do the "Super 600 Total Fitness Workout" (form 14.19).
3. Conclusion: review and stretch. Have students evaluate the program using form 14.20.

Lessons 2 and 3
Fast-Twitch and Slow-Twitch Muscle Fibers

1. Define, explain, and discuss fast- and slow-twitch muscle fibers.
2. Demonstrate a workout for improving the 40-yard dash and have students complete it (form 14.21). (It is not necessary to complete all five days of the 40-yard-dash

program. Select any two that are distinctly different. Students should be able to understand the principle of over-speed training from two lessons.)
3. Closure: stretch and review fast- and slow-twitch muscle fibers. Review and discuss over-speed training principles. Have students evaluate the program using form 14.20.

Lesson 4
Plyometrics

Plyometric training programs should be done only once a week.

1. Define, explain, and discuss plyometric training techniques.
2. Demonstrate a plyometric workout and have students complete it (form 14.22).
3. Closure: stretch and review plyometric training concepts and techniques. Have students evaluate the program using form 14.20.

Lessons 5 and 6
Training for Basketball

1. Analyze and discuss the fitness requirements of basketball.
2. Divide the class into two groups and demonstrate the two-part training program for basketball in form 14.23. Have

one group complete the strength-training section of the program while the other group does the aerobic and agility training section. Change groups on the second day.

3. Review and discuss how each part of the workout program helps meet the fitness requirements of basketball. Have students evaluate the program using form 14.20.

4. Closure: stretch.

Lessons 7 and 8
Training for Baseball/Softball

1. Analyze and discuss the fitness requirements of baseball/softball.

2. Divide the class into two groups and demonstrate the two-part training program for baseball/softball in form 14.24. Have one group do the strength training while the other group does the agility and conditioning drills. Change groups on the second day.

3. Review and discuss how each part of the workout program helps meet the fitness requirements of baseball/softball. Have students evaluate the program using form 14.20.

4. Closure: stretch.

Lessons 9 and 10
Training for Football

1. Analyze and discuss the fitness requirements of football.

2. Divide the class into two groups and demonstrate the two-part training program for football in form 14.25. Have one group do strength training while the other group does the aerobic, speed, and agility training. Change groups on the second day.

3. Review and discuss how each part of the workout program helps meet the fitness requirements of football. Have students evaluate the program using form 14.20.

4. Closure: stretch.

Lessons 11 and 12
Training for Hiking

1. Analyze and discuss the fitness requirements of hiking.

2. Divide the class into two groups and demonstrate the two-part training program for hiking in form 14.26. Have one group do strength training while the other group does the aerobic training. Change groups on the second day.

3. Review and discuss how each part of the workout program helps meet the fitness requirements of hiking. Have students evaluate the program using form 14.20.

4. Closure: stretch.

Lesson 13
Training for Mountain Biking

1. Analyze and discuss the fitness requirements of mountain biking.

2. Demonstrate the training program for mountain biking and have students complete it (form 14.27).

3. Review and discuss how each part of the workout program helps meet the fitness requirements of mountain biking. Have students evaluate the program using form 14.20.

4. Closure: stretch.

Lesson 14
Training for Distance Running and Soccer

1. Analyze and discuss the fitness requirements of distance running and soccer.

2. Demonstrate the training program for distance running and soccer and have students complete it (form 14.28).

3. Review and discuss how each part of the workout program helps meet the fitness requirements of distance running and soccer. Have students evaluate the program using form 14.20.

4. Closure: stretch.

Lessons 15 and 16

Training for Tennis

1. Analyze and discuss the fitness requirements of tennis.
2. Divide the class into two groups and demonstrate the two-part training program for tennis in form 14.29. Have one group do the strength training while the other group does the aerobic and agility training. Change groups on the second day.
3. Review and discuss how each part of the workout program helps meet the fitness requirements of tennis. Have students evaluate the program using form 14.20.
4. Closure: stretch.

Lessons 17 and 18

Training for Wrestling

1. Analyze and discuss the fitness requirements of wrestling.
2. Divide the class into two groups and demonstrate the two-part training program for wrestling in form 14.30. Have one group do the strength training while the other group does the aerobic training. Change groups on the second day.
3. Review and discuss how each part of the workout program helps meet the fitness requirements of wrestling. Have students evaluate the program using form 14.20.
4. Closure: stretch.

Lessons 19 and 20

Training for Volleyball

1. Analyze and discuss the fitness requirements of volleyball.
2. Divide the class into two groups and demonstrate the two-part training program for volleyball in form 14.31. Have one group do the strength training while the other group does the aerobic and agility training. Change groups on the second day.
3. Review and discuss how each part of the workout program helps meet the fitness requirements of volleyball. Have students evaluate the program using form 14.20.
4. Closure: stretch.

Lesson 21

Balance Training

1. Discuss the importance of balance in relationship to performance.
2. Explain the factors that influence balance: posture, position, fatigue, and training.
3. Discuss the strengthening muscles involved in balance.
4. Demonstrate the balance plyometrics workout and have students complete it (form 10.2).
5. Review and discuss how balance can be improved through training.
6. Have students evaluate the program using form 14.20.
7. Closure: stretch.

Super 600 Total Fitness Workout

Jog 1 to 2 miles

Stretch

Abdominals (125)

50 crunches

50 side crunches

25 hip raises

Chest (100)

25 flys

50 alternate-arm dumbbell presses

25 bench presses

Back (125)

25 bent or T rows

50 alternate-arm dumbbell presses

25 prone flys

25 lat pulldowns

Shoulders (150)

25 military presses

50 alternate-arm dumbbell presses

25 standing flys

25 shrugs

25 standing rows

Legs (100)

25 squats

25 calf raises

25 leg extensions

25 leg curls

From *It's Not Just Gym Anymore: Teaching Secondary School Students How to Be Active for Life* by Bane McCracken, 2001, Champaign, IL: Human Kinetics.

Conditioning and Weight Training
Program Evaluation

1. Were you able to complete the workout as directed?

2. What part of this workout gave you the most problems?

3. Identify one part of the program that uses each of the modes of training. If none were used, write *none*.
   a. Overspeed

   b. Continuous

   c. Interval

   d. Progressive resistance

   e. Circuit

4. What did you learn while doing this workout? (If you didn't learn anything, you failed!)

Workout to Improve 40-yd Dash Time

Monday

Jog 5 min, stretch.

20-yd fast feet (5×)

20-yd high knees (5×)

20-yd kick butt (5×)

400 yd—Jog 200 yd then acceler-ate to full speed at end. (2×)

40-yd downhill sprints (4×) (Add 2 per week for 4 weeks.)

Tuesday

Jog 5 min, stretch.

400-yd long strides (2×)

100-yd strides (4×)

20-yd fast feet (5×)

20-yd high knees (5×)

20-yd kick butt (5×)

Jog/walk, stretch

Do embedded circuit in weight room (see form 14.28).

Wednesday

Jog 5 min, stretch.

20-yd fast feet (5×)

20-yd high knees (5×)

20-yd kick butt (5×)

10-yd starts (5×)

Hammers

40-yd bounds (5×)

40-yd skips (5×)

One-leg box jumps (10× each way)

Jog 5 min, stretch.

Thursday

Jog 5 min, stretch.

20-yd fast feet (5×)

20-yd high knees (5×)

20-yd kick butt (5×)

100-yd strides with 20-yd downhill finish (5–10×)

Do embedded circuit in weight room.

Friday

Jog 5 min, stretch.

20-yd fast feet (5×)

20-yd high knees (5×)

20-yd kick butt (5×)

Hammers

40-yd bounds (5×)

40-yd skips (5×)

One-leg box jumps (10× each way)

Hammers

40-yd dash downhill (4×)

Jog/walk to cool down, stretch.

From *It's Not Just Gym Anymore: Teaching Secondary School Students How to Be Active for Life* by Bane McCracken, 2001, Champaign, IL: Human Kinetics.

Plyometric Circuit

Part I

Assemble equipment in gym area

1. 5-min warm-up walk or jog, etc.
2. Group stretch: Hold each position for a 5 count, increase pressure for 3 sets (no talking while stretching).
   a. Seated legs spread (right, left, middle)
   b. Seated legs together
   c. Pretzels
   d. Cross-chest
   e. Behind head
   f. Quads and calves against wall
3. Feet drills: fast feet, high knees, kick butt
4. 20-yd high-knee skips (4×)
5. 40-yd strides (4×)
6. Stretch: hammers and quads

Part II

Working in pairs or threes, place equipment in proper areas and take places in one of the 15 stations. Begin exercises at a signal from the instructor and follow directions for each station. Continue at each station for 3 to 4 min and change stations on instructor's command, moving from station to station in designated order.

Stations

1. Increasing rope jump: One student holds one end of a rope at chest height. The other end is secured at floor level. The second student begins jumping over the rope at lowest level and continues toward higher end until failure. Rotate positions.
2. Stretch quads and calves against wall.
3. Descending box jumps: Step up and fall off boxes, leaning forward.
4. Stretch calves and quads.
5. Body bag: Do five punches with each hand. Make sure to use gloves.
6. Upper-body stretch
7. Alternate-leg box jumps
8. Stretch: Hammers with a partner
9. Medicine ball chest pass
10. Upper-body partner stretch
11. Kneeling overhead medicine ball pass
12. Pretzel stretch
13. Around-the-body medicine ball pass
14. Seated split-leg stretch
15. 10-yd starts

Part III

Cool down with a jog or walk and stretch as a group.

From *It's Not Just Gym Anymore: Teaching Secondary School Students How to Be Active for Life* by Bane McCracken, 2001, Champaign, IL: Human Kinetics.

Training Program for Basketball

Strength Training

Lower body
Squats: 5 sets of 3 to 8 reps

Lunges: 3 sets of 8 to 12 reps

or

Step-ups: 3 sets of 8 to 12 reps

Abdominal muscles
25 back raises

50 crunches

25 cross crunches (each side)

Upper body
Incline bench presses: 5 sets of 3 to 8 reps

Shoulder presses with dumbbells: 3 sets of 8 to 12 reps

Lat pulldowns: 3 sets of 8 to 12 reps

Aerobic and Agility Training

30-min jog or walk in exercise zone

Sprints: 30-sec rest between each set

10 yd (1×)

20 yd (1×)

40 yd (1×)

100 yd (1×)

Jumps: 60-sec rest between each set

5 rim jumps (5×)

5 box jumps (5×)

2 sets hot dots or skip rope for 5 min

From *It's Not Just Gym Anymore: Teaching Secondary School Students How to Be Active for Life* by Bane McCracken, 2001, Champaign, IL: Human Kinetics.

Training Program for Baseball/Softball

Strength Training

Legs (3 sets of 8–12 reps)
Squats

Leeper

Calf raises

Abdominal muscles
10 back raises

50 crunches

25 cross crunches (each side)

100 bicycles

Upper body (3 sets of 8–12 reps)
Bench presses

T row

Alternate-arm overhead dumbbell press

Stretch cord throw

Agility and Conditioning Drills

10-min warm-up jog

3- to 5-min short warm-up tosses with
partner

5 maximum throws with weighted ball

4 maximum throws with regulation ball

1 min rest

4 maximum throws

1 min rest

4 maximum throws

1 min rest

5 maximum throws with Wiffle ball

Aerobic conditioning and speed
2- to 5-min jog

40-yd sprints (4×)

10-yd sprints (4×)

Run bases (3×)

Cool-down walk and stretch

From *It's Not Just Gym Anymore: Teaching Secondary School Students How to Be Active for Life* by Bane McCracken, 2001, Champaign, IL: Human Kinetics.

Training Program for Football

Strength Training

T row: 3 sets of 8 to 12 reps

Bench presses: 3 sets of 3 to 8 reps

Power cleans: 3 sets of 5 to 10 reps

Incline bench presses: 3 sets of 8 to 12 reps

Squats: 5 sets of 3 to 8 reps

Aerobics, Speed, and Agility

Jog: 12 to 15 min in exercise zone

Stretch

5 × 20 fast feet

high knees

kick butt

10-yd starts (5×)

Hammer stretches

40-yd bounds (5×)

40-yd skips (5×)

10 one-leg box jumps (each way)

5-min jog and stretch

Training Program for Hiking

Strength Training

Lower body
Squats: 2 sets of 15 reps

Leg curls: 2 sets of 15 reps

Step-ups with dumbbells: 2 sets of 15 reps

Abdominal
50 crunches

25 side crunches

25 hyperextensions

Upper body
Bench press: 2 sets of 8 to 10 reps

T row: 2 sets of 8 to 10 reps

Overhead dumbbell presses: 8 to 12 reps

Lat pulldowns: 2 sets of 8 to 12 reps

Aerobic Training

30 to 40 min of fast-pace walking

5 to 8 sets of stadium stairs with 40-lb backpack

From *It's Not Just Gym Anymore: Teaching Secondary School Students How to Be Active for Life* by Bane McCracken, 2001, Champaign, IL: Human Kinetics.

Training Program for Mountain Biking

Exercise	Sets	Reps	Set 1 Weight	Set 2 Weight
Squats	2	15		
Leg curls	2	15		
Leg extensions	2	15		
Calf raises	2	15		
Box step-ups	2	15		
Bench presses	2	15		
Triceps push-downs	2	15		
T row	2	15		
Curls	2	15		
Dumbbell rows	2	15		
Crunches	2	15		

From *It's Not Just Gym Anymore: Teaching Secondary School Students How to Be Active for Life* by Bane McCracken, 2001, Champaign, IL: Human Kinetics.

Training Program for Distance Running and Soccer

Embedded Circuit Workout

Instructions
Do 8 to 12 reps with lower body.

Do 12 to 15 reps with upper body.

Jog or jump rope for 30 sec between each station.

Do all exercises in order.

Warm-up
1- to 2-mile jog

Exercises
1. Bench press
2. Prone dumbbell fly
3. Lat. pulldown
4. One-arm row
5. Leg extension
6. Lunge
7. Leg curl
8. Standing dumbbell press (alternate-arm)
9. Dumbbell fly (standing)
10. Shrug
11. Upright row
12. Triceps pushdown
13. Dumbbell curl (alternate-arm)

Cool-down
1-mile walk or jog.

From *It's Not Just Gym Anymore: Teaching Secondary School Students How to Be Active for Life* by Bane McCracken, 2001, Champaign, IL: Human Kinetics.

Training Program for Tennis

Strength Training

Bench presses using alternate-arm dumbbells: 2 sets of 15 to 25 reps

One-arm row: 2 sets of 15 to 25 reps

Standing flys: 2 sets of 15 to 20 reps

Lunges with dumbbells: 2 sets of 12 to 15 reps

Triceps pushdown: 2 sets of 12 to 15 reps

Squats: 2 sets of 8 to 12 reps

Aerobic and Agility Training

Jog 20 min in exercise zone.

20-yd sprints (5×, no rest)

Box drill: 3 sets of 4 with 60-sec rest between sets

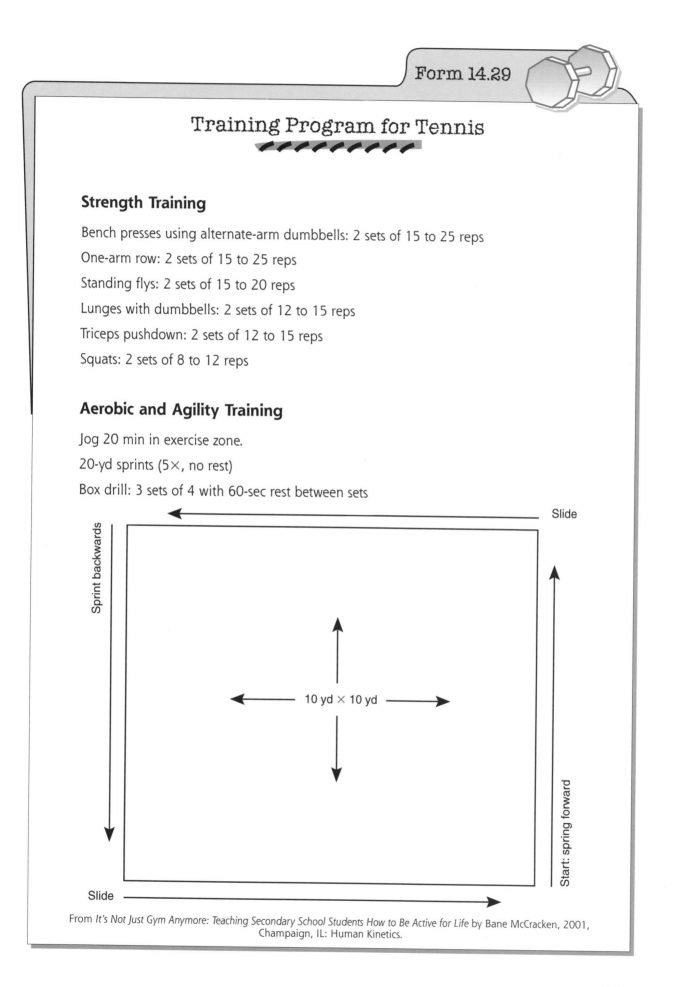

From *It's Not Just Gym Anymore: Teaching Secondary School Students How to Be Active for Life* by Bane McCracken, 2001, Champaign, IL: Human Kinetics.

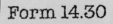

Training Program for Wrestling

Strength Training

Bench presses: 3 sets of 12 to 15 reps

T rows: 3 sets of 12 to 15 reps

One-arm row: 1 set of 15 to 20 reps (each arm)

Lat pulldowns with towel: 2 sets of 12 to 15 reps

Dips: 2 sets of 25+ reps

Squats: 2 sets of 15 to 25 reps

Single-leg dips with dumbbells: 1 set of 15 to 20 reps (each leg)

Lunges with dumbbells: 1 set of 25 reps

Standing rows: 2 sets of 8 to 12 reps

Aerobic Training

30-min jog in exercise zone

3 sets of 3 stadium stairs with 30-sec rest between sets

Jump rope for 10 to 15 min

From *It's Not Just Gym Anymore: Teaching Secondary School Students How to Be Active for Life* by Bane McCracken, 2001, Champaign, IL: Human Kinetics.

Training Program for Volleyball

Strength Training

Lower body
Squats: 2 sets of 8 to 12 reps

Calf Raises: 2 sets of 15 to 20 reps

Leg Curls: 2 sets of 8 to 12 reps

Leg Extensions: 2 sets of 8 to 12 reps

Abdominal muscles
50 crunches

25 oblique crunches

25 hyperextensions

Upper body
Bench presses: 2 sets of 8 to 12 reps

T rows: 2 sets of 8 to 12 reps

Overhead dumbbell presses: 2 sets of 8 to 12 reps

Aerobic and Agility

Walk/jog 12 min in exercise zone

Jump rope 10 to 12 min

Five sets of ten 30-in. high box jumps

10 overhead medicine ball tosses with partner

From *It's Not Just Gym Anymore: Teaching Secondary School Students How to Be Active for Life* by Bane McCracken, 2001, Champaign, IL: Human Kinetics.

Resources

Chapter 9
Video: *How to Hike the Appalachian Trail*
Contact: Lynne Whelden, 1025 Shaw Place, Williamsport, PA 17701
http://members.tripod.com/lwgear

Chapter 10
Stretching book:
A good resource for skiing stretches and all stretching is *Stretching* by Bob Anderson (Bolinas, CA: Shelter, 1980).

Plyometric Equipment:
Contact: Sportime International, One Sportime Way, Atlanta, GA 30340
800-283-5700
www.sportime.com

Chapter 11
League of American Bicyclists offers several courses in effective cycling and certification for instructors.
Contact: League of American Bicyclists, 1612 K Street NW, Ste. 401, Washington, DC 20006-2082
Phone: 202-822-1333; Fax: 202-822-1334
E-mail: **bikeleague@bikeleague.org**
www.bikeleague.org

Chapter 12
Fly-fishing video:
Fly-Fishing Made Easy
Contact: Scientific Anglers, 3M Center Building, St. Paul, MN 55144-1000
www.3m.com/market/consumer/scianglers

Chapter 13
Line dancing video:

Christy Lane's Complete Guide to Line Dancing Video
Contact in the United States: Human Kinetics, P.O. Box 5076, Champaign, IL 61825-5076, 800-747-4457
Contact in Canada: Human Kinetics, 475 Devonshire Rd., Unit 100, Windsor, ON N8Y 2L5, 800-465-7301
www.humankinetics.com

T'ai Chi Video:
T'ai Chi for Busy People
Contact: **www.easytaichi.com/video.htm**

Chapters 13 and 14
Software programs:
Health First "Tri Fit" Version 4.0 offers complete wellness technology.
Contact: HealthFirst Corporation, 6811 Academy Parkway East, Albuquerque, NM 87109
Phone: 800-841-8333; Fax 505-344-1200
www.healthfirstusa.com

FITNESSGRAM® 6.0 Test Kit, 1999, Champaign, IL: Human Kinetics.
Contact in the United States: Human Kinetics, P.O. Box 5076, Champaign, IL 61825-5076, 800-747-4457
Contact in Canada: Human Kinetics, 475 Devonshire Rd., Unit 100, Windsor, ON N8Y 2L5, 800-465-7301
www.humankinetics.com

Bioanalogics Diet Systems Inc. has a very simple diet program.
Contact: 9000 S.W. Gemini, Beaverton, OR 97005

Form Answers

Form 7.3

1. James Naismith
2. peach basket
3. YMCA and playgrounds and schools
4. Springfield, Massachusetts
5. True
6. False
7. True
8. True
9. False
10. 2, 1, 4, 3, 5

Form 8.10

1. a
2. c
3. h
4. d
5. k
6. j
7. l
8. o
9. m
10. n
11. g
12. f
13. e
14. i
15. b

References

Centers for Disease Control and Prevention, Aug. 27, 1993. *CDC surveillances summaries.*

Cooper, Kenneth H., 1968. *Aerobics.* New York: Evans; distributed in association with Lippincott, Philadelphia.

Dennison, Paul, and Gail Dennison, 1986. *Brain gym: Simple activities for whole brain learning.* Ventura, CA: Edu-Kinesthetics.

Jensen, Eric, 1998. *Teaching with the brain in mind.* Alexandria, VA: Association for Supervision and Curriculum Development.

Marzano, Robert, 1992. *A different kind of classroom: Teaching with dimensions of learning.* Alexandria, VA: Association for Supervision and Curriculum Development.

Sammann, Patricia, 1998. *Active youth: Ideas for implementing CDC physical activity promotion guidelines.* Champaign, IL: Human Kinetics.

U.S. Department of Health and Human Services. 1996. *Physical activity and health: A report of the Surgeon General.* Atlanta: United States Government Printing Office.

Wechler, Howell, 1999. *Making the case: Why schools should promote physical activity and healthy eating and prevent tobacco use.* Atlanta: U.S. Department of Health and Human Services, Centers for Disease Control and Prevention, National Center for Chronic Disease Prevention and Health Promotion.

Index

About the Author

Bane McCracken, a physical education teacher at Huntington High School in Huntington, West Virginia, has nearly three decades of teaching and coaching experience. He chaired the department of physical education at Cabell Midland High School in Ona, West Virginia, when the Centers for Disease Control and Prevention recognized the program for its exemplary promotion of physical activity. In 1997 he was named the National Association for Sport and Physical Education's Secondary Physical Education Teacher of the Year in recognition of the success of his lifetime fitness approach to physical education.

McCracken, who received his MS in educational administration from Marshall University, has received numerous other honors and distinctions, including the 1996 Midwest District Association for Health, Physical Education, Recreation and Dance (AHPERD) Teacher of the Year award; West Virginia Association for Health, Physical Education, Recreation and Dance (WVAHPERD) presidential citations in 1995 and 1996; the 1995 WVAHPERD Secondary Physical Education Teacher of the Year award; and the 1995 Regional Wrestling Coach of the Year award.

An active presenter and workshop leader, McCracken is chair and former vice president of the physical education division of the Midwest District AHPERD, and he is a member of its ad hoc committee on networking. He is also the WVAHPERD section chair and a member of the resident assembly, as well as a member of the West Virginia Coalition for Physical Activity Executive Committee, the Governor's Council on School Health, the West Virginia Physical Education Curriculum Team, and the West Virginia Physical Education State Conference Planning Committee.

McCracken practices what he preaches by leading a physically active life. He has completed more than 20 marathons and numerous triathlons and duathlons. He also races bikes, lifts weights avidly, and is a keen outdoor enthusiast. In 1994 McCracken was the Mountain State Road Series Champion in the age 50 and over category. He lives in Ona, West Virginia, with his wife, Joyce.